BASICS OF GENEALOGY REFERENCE

A Librarian's Guide

Jack Simpson

A Member of the Greenwood Publishing Group

Westport, Connecticut • London

Library of Congress Cataloging-in-Publication Data

Simpson, Jack, 1970-
  Basics of genealogy reference : a librarian's guide / Jack Simpson.
    p. cm.
  Includes bibliographical references and index.
  ISBN 978-1-59158-514-5 (alk. paper)
  1. Reference services (Libraries)—United States. 2. Genealogy. 3. United States—Genealogy. I. Title.
  Z711.6.G46S56 2008
  929'.1072073—dc22   2008010596

British Library Cataloguing in Publication Data is available.

Library of Congress Catalog Card Number: 2008010596
ISBN: 978-1-59158-514-5

First published in 2008

Libraries Unlimited, 88 Post Road West, Westport, CT 06881
A Member of the Greenwood Publishing Group, Inc.
www.lu.com

Printed in the United States of America

The paper used in this book complies with the Permanent Paper Standard issued by the National Information Standards Organization (Z39.48–1984).

10 9 8 7 6 5 4 3 2 1

Contents

Acknowledgments

I would like to thank the staff at libraries where I did research, particularly the National Archives and the Family History Library. Thanks also to my editors at Libraries Unlimited, particularly Sue Easun and Sue Stewart. My colleagues at the Newberry Library made this book possible, especially the members (and alumni) of the Local and Family History Department: Grace Dumelle, Ginger Frere, Sharon Gissy, Teresa Sromek, Rhonda Frevert, John Brady, Katie McMahon, and Susan Fagan. Special thanks are due to Matt Rutherford, who assisted with the research and preparation of the book. I owe Megan Bowen for sharing her family history and helping with my research. Thanks to all my friends and family. Most of all, I would like to thank my wife, Celia, for everything.

Introduction

At the Everytown Public Library, it is a busy morning. You have just opened the reference desk, and already you have:

- a new resident on the phone asking about recreational sports leagues
- a regular at the desk looking for the new Elmore Leonard novel
- a computer freezing up

Into this scene strides a patron with a pile of disorganized papers in his hand and a confused expression on his face. He begins to speak, tentatively at first but with increasing fervor as he warms to his subject:

Um ... Hi ... I'm trying to get started on my family history, and I was told you have good resources here at the public library. I guess I'm mostly English and Scottish but maybe also German. The German was my Mom's side I think, and then the Irish was her dad's side. But I'm interested in my great-grandfather on my Dad's side because my Grandpa never really talked about him. There's some mystery there. He had the same name as me. He was a mine manager in Pennsylvania but also in West Virginia, but that side of the family is also supposed to be from Ohio, so I guess he moved around. He died when my Grandpa was young. Then, my Grandpa married my Grandma, who was also from Ohio, and her family had a general store

This is when panic sets in. You are unsure of how to help this patron, and if you do not do something, the stream-of-consciousness recital of the family epic might go on for hours.

The goal of this book is to replace your panic with a basic strategy for helping genealogy researchers.

Genealogy has long been an extremely popular subject for research, but the role of public libraries has changed a great deal in the last 10 years. Before the Internet, many public libraries had fairly sparse genealogy holdings: basic guides, reference books, and genealogy materials on the local community. Researchers who wanted to do in-depth genealogical research had to travel to specialized institutions.

With the creation of free resources on the Internet (such as the Ellis Island database) and subscription services (such as HeritageQuest Online), a great deal of genealogical information is available at the public library. It is as if each public library has added a new wing devoted to genealogy research, including every U.S. census, volumes of passenger arrival records, and thousands of other resources. For public librarians, navigating these new resources can be overwhelming.

This book is designed to help in two ways. In the first section of the book, I will outline a very basic starting strategy for genealogy research. I will use four case studies to illustrate the techniques and sources I discuss, but I also encourage readers to test the strategy using their own research. Empathy is an extremely important quality in a reference librarian, and trying out these basic steps will help you see through the eyes of your patrons.

In the final chapters, I will talk more specifically about genealogical librarianship: how to conduct a reference interview, how to continue to learn about the profession, and some basic resources for your collection.

In the appendices, I describe my four case studies with more detailed narratives.

Family history is a very personal and meaningful topic for many of your patrons. Although some pursue it as a light-hearted hobby and become addicted to the detective work, other patrons are researching traumatic events in their family history that have shaped their lives. Some patrons may be researching their family medical history or may need family data to apply for a scholarship. Librarians have an obligation to help all of these varied patrons, and I hope this book will help you get started. Although genealogy reference is challenging, it is also very rewarding, once you have learned the basics.

FOUR CASE STUDIES

To help explain some of the challenges and rewards of genealogy research, I will be using four case studies throughout this work. Here are short summaries of the case studies.

John Simpson

My grandfather was named John William Simpson. His father, also named John William Simpson, was a mine manager in Uniontown, Pennsylvania. I knew relatively little about my grandfather's ancestors when I began doing genealogy research. This case study shows how I traced them backwards for several generations.

Jeanette Winter

A friend of mine asked me to research her grandmother, Jeanette Winter. Jeanette's father was a muralist named Ezra Winter and her mother was an artist's model, born Vera Beaudette. This case study follows the Beaudette line backwards through divorces, name changes, and war.

Coleman Young

Coleman Young was the first African-American mayor of my hometown, Detroit. He was born in Alabama, and this case study traces his African-American ancestors back to Alabama in the 1860s.

Stanley Kubrick

I chose to follow Stanley Kubrick's ancestry because I wanted to include a case study of central European ancestry. Kubrick's grandfather was a Jewish immigrant from the Austrian empire. The case study demonstrates some of the difficulties of researching Central and Eastern Europeans, including surname changes and shifting national borders.

1

First Steps in Genealogy Research

I prioritize four starting steps in genealogy research: getting organized, talking to family members, searching the U.S. census, and searching for vital records. Not every researcher will start with these steps; some may start with a wealth of information from other sources, whereas others will not be able to complete each of these steps. However, for the typical researcher, starting with these four basic steps makes the research process easier. This chapter describes the first two steps: getting organized and talking to family. The following chapters describe the third and fourth steps.

Four Basic Steps

1. Get organized
2. Interview relatives
3. Research in the U.S. Census
4. Research in vital records

STEP ONE: GETTING ORGANIZED

Consider the verbose patron depicted in the introduction. His question is vexing because it presents a large amount of information in a disorganized way. However, his recitation reflects how most people carry around their family history: as a disjointed collection of half-remembered anecdotes.

You have two parents, four grandparents, eight great-grandparents, and sixteen-great-great grandparents. Over our lives, most of us have heard something about the lives of our parents and grandparents at family gatherings or casual conversation, but many of us were not listening that carefully. We were understandably more interested in hanging out with our friends than in listening to Grandma's stories of life in central Ohio. This leaves us with a messy, error-filled story of the lives of our numerous ancestors. Rather than try to research in this morass, the first step is to organize the facts that we are fairly certain about in a simple way; then, we can build upon this basic framework.

One basic principle of genealogy research is to start with yourself and move backwards, generation by generation. This way, you are moving carefully from the known towards the unknown, from your own life towards your distant ancestors' lives. This strategy is reflected in the basic organizational tool for genealogists: the family tree chart.

The Family Tree Chart

Figure 1.1 shows a basic family tree chart, also known as a pedigree chart.

For a beginner, the chart starts with the researcher (1), the researcher's father (2), the researcher's mother (3), and so on. Researchers often accompany the family tree chart with a family group sheet (figure 1.2) for each family.

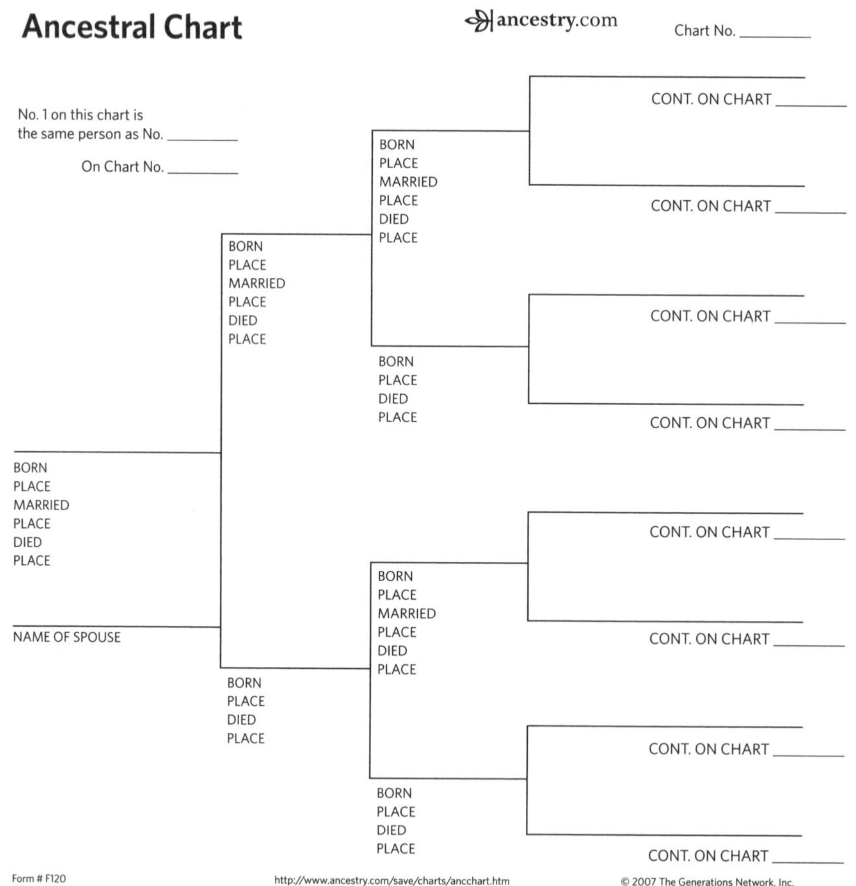

Ancestral Chart

ancestry.com

Chart No. ________

No. 1 on this chart is the same person as No. ________

On Chart No. ________

BORN
PLACE
MARRIED
PLACE
DIED
PLACE

NAME OF SPOUSE

BORN
PLACE
MARRIED
PLACE
DIED
PLACE

BORN
PLACE
DIED
PLACE

BORN
PLACE
MARRIED
PLACE
DIED
PLACE

BORN
PLACE
DIED
PLACE

BORN
PLACE
MARRIED
PLACE
DIED
PLACE

BORN
PLACE
DIED
PLACE

CONT. ON CHART ________

CONT. ON CHART ________

CONT. ON CHART ________

CONT. ON CHART ________

CONT. ON CHART ________

CONT. ON CHART ________

CONT. ON CHART ________

CONT. ON CHART ________

Form # F120

http://www.ancestry.com/save/charts/ancchart.htm

© 2007 The Generations Network, Inc.

Figure 1.1. Basic pedigree chart.

Family Group Record ancestry.com

Prepared By ____ Relationship to Preparer ____

Address ____ Date ____ Ancestral Chart # ____ Family Unit # ____

Husband	Date—Day, Month, Year	Occupation(s) City	County	State or Country	Religion
Born					
Christened					Name of Church
Married					Name of Church
Died					Cause of Death
Buried		Cem/Place			Date Will Written/Proved
Father		Other Wives			
Mother					

Wife maiden name		Occupation(s)			Religion
Born					
Christened					Name of Church
Died					Cause of Death
Buried		Cem/Place			Date Will Written/Proved
Father		Other Husbands			
Mother					

•	Sex MF	Children Given Names	Birth Day Month Year	Birthplace City	County	St./Ctry.	Date of first marriage/Place Name of Spouse	Date of Death/Cause City County State/Country	Computer I.D. #
		1							
		2							
		3							
		4							
		5							
		6							
		7							
		8							
		9							
		10							
		11							
		12							

NOTE=Direct Ancestor Form # F106 http://www.ancestry.com/save/charts/familysheet.htm © 2007 The Generations Network, Inc.

Figure 1.2. Family group sheet.

Filling out a family tree chart helps visualize what is known and unknown, thereby identifying areas for research. For example, let us chart the disorganized reference question above. Now for some disclosure: that garbled story represents what I knew about my own family history when I began researching. Figure 1.3 shows that some of that basic information in chart form. (I have redacted some of the names for privacy reasons.)

Although the researcher's question is still difficult, organizing it in a chart makes it easier to identify where he or she might start researching.

You can download pedigree charts and family group sheets for free from Ancestry.com. To find other paper charts, see the Web sites linked from Cyndi's List (an online genealogy directory), under the category of "Supplies, Charts, Forms" (http://www.cyndislist.com/supplies.htm).

Genealogy Organizing Software

Many genealogists use software for organizing their research. There are a number of different brands of genealogy organizing software; FamilyTreeMaker, Generations Family Tree, and The Master Genealogist are examples of commercial genealogy software. Although each program has unique features, all are essentially databases that record relationships between generations of a family. Most genealogy programs support GEDCOM, a software standard for family tree files. The GEDCOM standard allows any of these programs to open any GEDCOM file: if you use FamilyTreeMaker, and your cousin uses The Master Genealogist, you can still share family tree files.

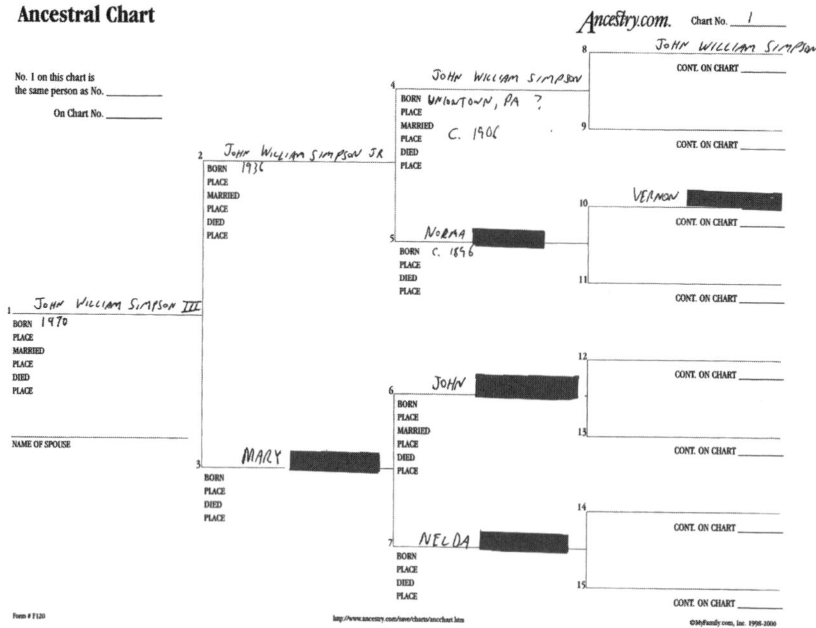
Ancestral Chart

Ancestry.com. Chart No. 1

No. 1 on this chart is the same person as No. ______

On Chart No. ______

1 John William Simpson III
BORN 1970
PLACE
MARRIED
PLACE
DIED
PLACE

NAME OF SPOUSE

2 John William Simpson Jr
BORN 1936
PLACE
MARRIED
PLACE
DIED
PLACE

3 Mary
BORN
PLACE
DIED
PLACE

4 John William Simpson
BORN Uniontown, PA ?
PLACE
MARRIED c. 1906
PLACE
DIED
PLACE

5 Norma
BORN c. 1896
PLACE
DIED
PLACE

6 John
BORN
PLACE
MARRIED
PLACE
DIED
PLACE

7 Nelda
BORN
PLACE
DIED
PLACE

8 John William Simpson
CONT. ON CHART ______

9
CONT. ON CHART ______

10 Vernon
CONT. ON CHART ______

11
CONT. ON CHART ______

12
CONT. ON CHART ______

13
CONT. ON CHART ______

14
CONT. ON CHART ______

15
CONT. ON CHART ______

Form # F120

http://www.ancestry.com/save/charts/ancchart.htm

©MyFamily.com, Inc. 1998-2000

Figure 1.3. Pedigree chart example.

The Family History Library (FHL) of the Church of Latter Day Saints has created its own software, called Personal Ancestral File. The FHL offers this software for free on its Web site, http://www.familysearch.org. Because this software is free, I often recommend it to beginners. If a researcher decides to purchase another kind of software as their research advances, he or she can transfer the GEDCOM files they create with Personal Ancestral File to the new program.

This area of genealogy research is changing rapidly. Since I began writing this book, several new online genealogical storage tools have emerged. The most prominent at the moment is Geni.com, which allows collaborative online work on family pedigrees.

STEP TWO: TALKING TO FAMILY MEMBERS

Some of the most valuable information about a family is not in libraries or archives, but rather in the memories of family members. Talking to family members, especially older relatives, is an important step in genealogy research. Interviewing relatives can help fill in blank spaces in the family tree chart by providing names, birthplaces, and other details. Those details will make the next stages of research easier. Beyond such facts, the memories of family members provide an emotional depth to the family history that is difficult to coax from sources such as the census. What did it feel like to move from Mississippi to Chicago? What kind of person was your great-grandfather? Why did your grandmother become a teacher?

If possible, researchers should interview older relatives and record the conversation, either by taking notes or with an audio recording. Recording oral history is a skill, and genealogists should read a guide such as *Doing Oral History: A Practical Guide* (Ritchie, 2003) before talking to their ancestors. Sharing the family tree chart or family photographs with a relative is a good starting point.

Research Using Documents

Following the steps above will help any researcher start their genealogy research. By gathering family information and organizing it, the researcher has a starting point for research in historical documents. The next chapters will discuss the most basic genealogy documents: the U.S. census and vital records (birth, death, and marriage documents.)

REFERENCES

Ancestry.com. "Genealogy, Family Trees and Family History Records Online," http://ancestry.com/ (accessed August 10, 2007).

Integrated Public Use Microdata Series. "Census Questions," http://usa.ipums.org/usa/voliii/tQuestions.shtml (accessed August 1, 2007).

FamilySearch.org. "Family History and Genealogy Records," http://www.familysearch.org/ (accessed August 1, 2007).

Ritchie, Donald A. *Doing Oral History: A Practical Guide*. Oxford: Oxford University Press, 2003.

2

Census Basics

Once a researcher has queried relatives for information and organized his or her basic information, he or she is ready to begin research using historical documents. The U.S. census is the best starting source for most American genealogy research.

WHY START WITH THE CENSUS?

The U.S. Census is a good starting point for a number of reasons:

- The census attempted to include most Americans and generally did an impressive job. As a result, researchers have a very good chance of finding ancestors listed on the census.
- The census is a rich source of information, so that if researchers find an ancestor listed, they learn significant facts about them
- Censuses record family members as a group, so a census record can connect one generation to another.
- Through subscription databases such as Ancestry.com and HeritageQuest Online, the entire U.S. census is accessible in many public libraries.

As an inclusive, informative, and accessible source for genealogy, the U.S. census is unequaled.

A basic principle of genealogy research is to start with easier, more accessible sources. This might sound self-evident, but many researchers are interested in a particular part of their family history and want to start researching there. For example, some researchers are very interested in ancestors in the American Revolution or want to find employment records for their coal-mining ancestors. Eventually, researchers can find sources for those subjects, but they are difficult investigations to start with. Instead, easier sources such as the census are better to start with because they provide information that will ultimately help locate and interpret the more advanced sources.

One caveat is that although most patrons will find the U.S. census to be useful, researchers whose families were not in the United States or Puerto Rico by 1930 are an exception. Because the 1930 schedule is the most recent year available to the public, more recent immigrants will have to rely on the other sources, such as vital records, to start their research.

WHAT IS THE CENSUS?

The census is a count of the American population that the federal government is constitutionally required to take every ten years. Counting the population is necessary to apportion congressional districts, and the first censuses were essentially simple counts of population. However, as the nation grew, the federal government began to use the census to gather statistics about the population's health, housing, employment, education, and more.

HOW IS THE CENSUS TAKEN?

The Federal government has taken the census every ten years starting in 1790. Historically, to take the census, each county was divided into smaller geographic divisions; starting in 1880, these were called enumeration districts (EDs). In each ED, a census taker walked around the district and recorded who lived in each dwelling and their personal data on a sheet called a *population schedule*. When the census taker was done, he or she sent the population schedule to Washington, DC, where the recorded information was tabulated. Once the statistics were counted, a report of the census statistics was compiled and published. This *statistical report* of the census was released as soon as it was completed, generally a year or so after the counting was done.

Genealogists are more interested in the population schedule than the statistical report because only the former gives information about individuals. For privacy reasons, the population schedules of the U.S. census are closed for 72 years. The 1930 census is the most recent population schedule available for research. In 2012, the 1940 population schedules will be opened to the public.

Two Parts of the Census

1. Population schedule. The list of names that makes up the raw material for census statistics. Closed to the public for seventy-two years. Of great interest to genealogists.
2. Statistical report. The report of the statistics compiled from the raw schedules. Generally released within a year of the completed count. Of great interest to demographers and sociologists, less interesting to genealogists.

WHAT WAS RECORDED ON THE CENSUS?

The questions asked on the census changed over the years. For a full list of the questions asked, visit the Web site of the Integrated Public Use Microdata Series from the University of Minnesota, http://usa.ipums.org/usa/voliii/tQuestions.shtml. Following is a brief overview of the changes in the census over the years.

1790–1840

The census in this period only recorded the head of the household by name, and the approximate ages of other members of the household. Censuses from this period are sparse compared with those from later years.

1850–1860

In 1850, the census began recording the names of every member of a household, including children, making this the first census that clearly links generations. The 1850 census also recorded an individual's place of birth (U.S. state or foreign nation) for the first time. In 1850 and 1860, the census also recorded slaveholders and statistical information about their slaves on separate *slave schedules*. Although these schedules do not record the names of slaves, they can help identify possible connections between slaveholders and slaves.

1870

The 1870 census asked where an individual's parents were born for the first time (U.S state or foreign country). It is also the first postemancipation census, so it is the first census to include all African Americans.

1880

The 1880 census recorded the street and house number for dwellings for the first time, making it possible to see who was living at a particular address.

1890

The 1890 population schedules were almost completely destroyed by fire, so it is rarely of use to genealogists. A separate schedule of Civil War veterans was saved for some states.

1900–1930

Starting in 1900, the census began asking when immigrants arrived in the country and whether they were naturalized, important information for tracking immigrant ancestors.

CENSUS RESEARCH STRATEGY

The census is useful in giving some structure to the disorganized, half-remembered family history. To start, researchers should try to find an ancestor in the U.S. census of 1930 and then use the information found there to track the ancestor or his parents in 1920, then 1910, and so on. Using this strategy, family historians can build a grid of information about ancestors, as they discover where they were living and who was in their household every ten years.

Researching the Census Using Databases

The easiest way to begin research is using commercial databases such as Ancestry.com or HeritageQuest Online. Between the two databases, the entire U.S. census has been indexed. Figure 2.1 is a chart of the censuses and indexes available online at the time of writing, but the chart will probably change as these companies improve their indexes. Note that for most census years going back to 1850, an every-name index is available on one of these services, which means that both adults and children are searchable.

The easiest way to explain census searching is to use an example from our case study of Coleman Young. According to biographical information in Wikipedia, Coleman Young, the future mayor of Detroit, was born in Tuscaloosa, Alabama, in 1918. His father was also named Coleman Young, and his mother's maiden name was Ida Reese Jones. His family moved to Detroit in 1923. Based on this information, we should find him in Detroit in 1930. Because "Coleman Young" is probably a fairly uncommon name, I entered only his name into the search form on http://Ancestry.com and left the other fields blank (fig. 2.2).

Patrons who do not have experience with database searching will often fill out every blank space on these forms, but this should be discouraged. Researchers often fill in too much information, and if one piece of information is entered differently than it is recorded on the census, legitimate results are eliminated. For instance, if we entered all of the information we know about Coleman Young, we would get no results. When we examine the search results, we will see why.

My search for people named "Coleman Young" nationwide in the 1930 census returned 33 results (fig. 2.3). Browsing the list, I saw one Coleman Young in Detroit, born about 1919, in the household of Ida Young and William C. Young. Because this

Year	Ancestry.com	HeritageQuest Online
1790	Head of Household	Head of Household
1800	Head of Household	Head of Household
1810	Head of Household	Head of Household
1820	Head of Household	Head of Household
1830	Head of Household	
1840	Head of Household	
1850	Every Name	
1860	Every Name	Head of Household
1870	Every Name	Head of Household
1880	Every Name	
1890	Every Name (For surviving pages)	Every Name (for surviving pages)
1900	Every Name	Head of Household
1910	Head of Household	Every Name
1920	Every Name	Head of Household
1930	Every Name	Head of Household (for Connecticut, Delaware, Maryland, Texas and Virginia)

Figure 2.1.

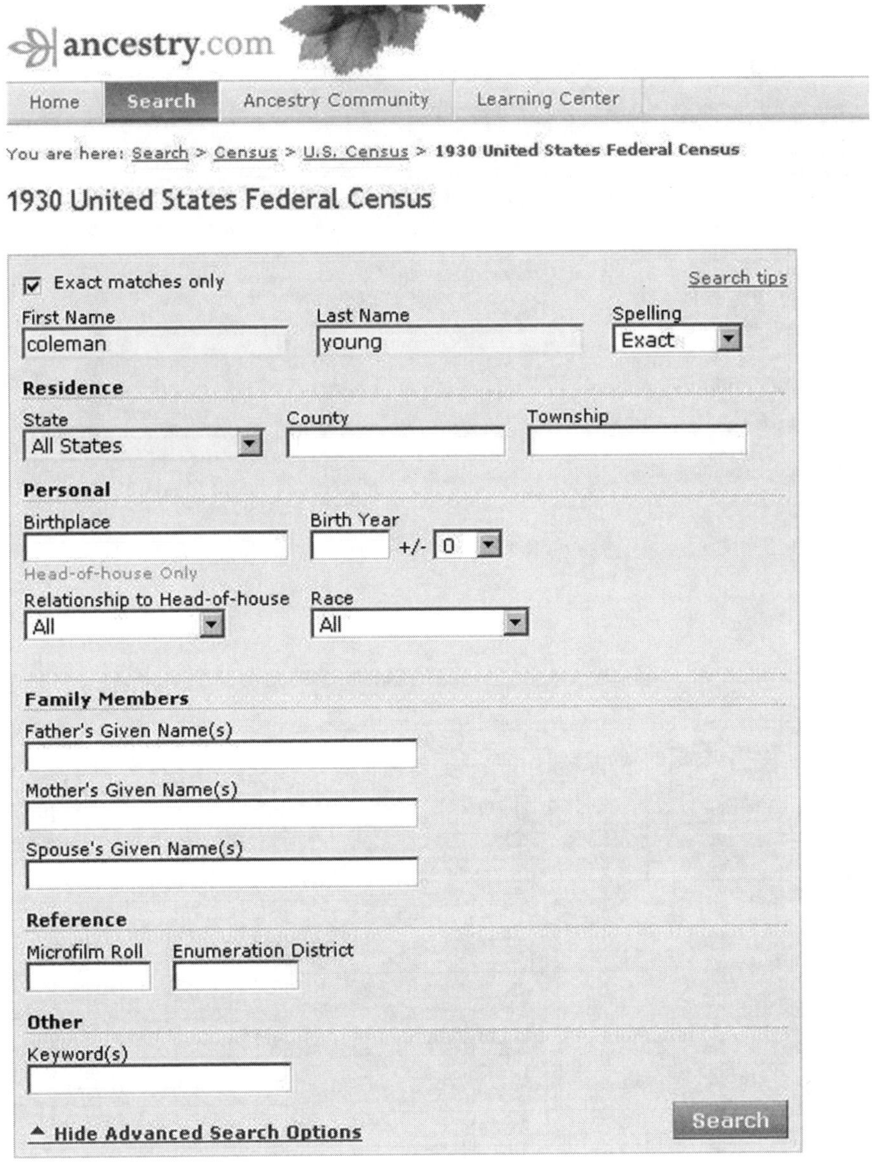

ancestry.com

Home | Search | Ancestry Community | Learning Center

You are here: Search > Census > U.S. Census > 1930 United States Federal Census

1930 United States Federal Census

Exact matches only
Search tips
First Name: coleman
Last Name: young
Spelling: Exact
Residence
State: All States
County
Township
Personal
Birthplace
Birth Year +/- 0
Head-of-house Only
Relationship to Head-of-house: All
Race: All
Family Members
Father's Given Name(s)
Mother's Given Name(s)
Spouse's Given Name(s)
Reference
Microfilm Roll
Enumeration District
Other
Keyword(s)
Hide Advanced Search Options
Search

Figure 2.2. 1930 Census search in Ancestry.com. Courtesy of Ancestry.com.

is a close match, I pulled up the full census record. Note, however, that if I had searched for a Coleman Young with a father named Coleman Young, I would have not found this record because his father is listed as William Young.

We can glean considerable information about the Young family by examining the 1930 census record (fig. 2.4) closely. Figures 2.5 through 2.10 are details of this census page. The Young family lived at 2235 Macomb Street in Detroit, Michigan.

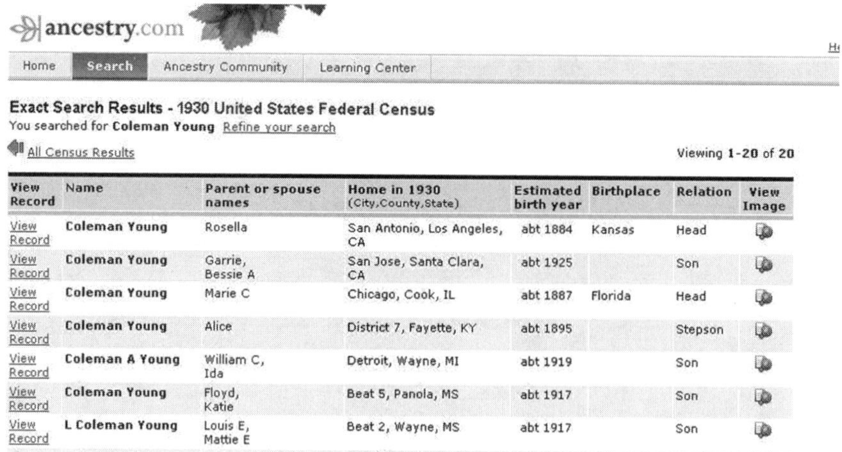

ancestry.com

Home | Search | Ancestry Community | Learning Center

Exact Search Results - 1930 United States Federal Census

You searched for **Coleman Young** Refine your search

All Census Results

Viewing **1-20** of **20**

View Record	Name	Parent or spouse names	Home in 1930 (City,County,State)	Estimated birth year	Birthplace	Relation	View Image
View Record	Coleman Young	Rosella	San Antonio, Los Angeles, CA	abt 1884	Kansas	Head	
View Record	Coleman Young	Garrie, Bessie A	San Jose, Santa Clara, CA	abt 1925		Son	
View Record	Coleman Young	Marie C	Chicago, Cook, IL	abt 1887	Florida	Head	
View Record	Coleman Young	Alice	District 7, Fayette, KY	abt 1895		Stepson	
View Record	Coleman A Young	William C, Ida	Detroit, Wayne, MI	abt 1919		Son	
View Record	Coleman Young	Floyd, Katie	Beat 5, Panola, MS	abt 1917		Son	
View Record	L Coleman Young	Louis E, Mattie E	Beat 2, Wayne, MS	abt 1917		Son	

Figure 2.3. Partial search results, 1930 Census. Courtesy of Ancestry.com.

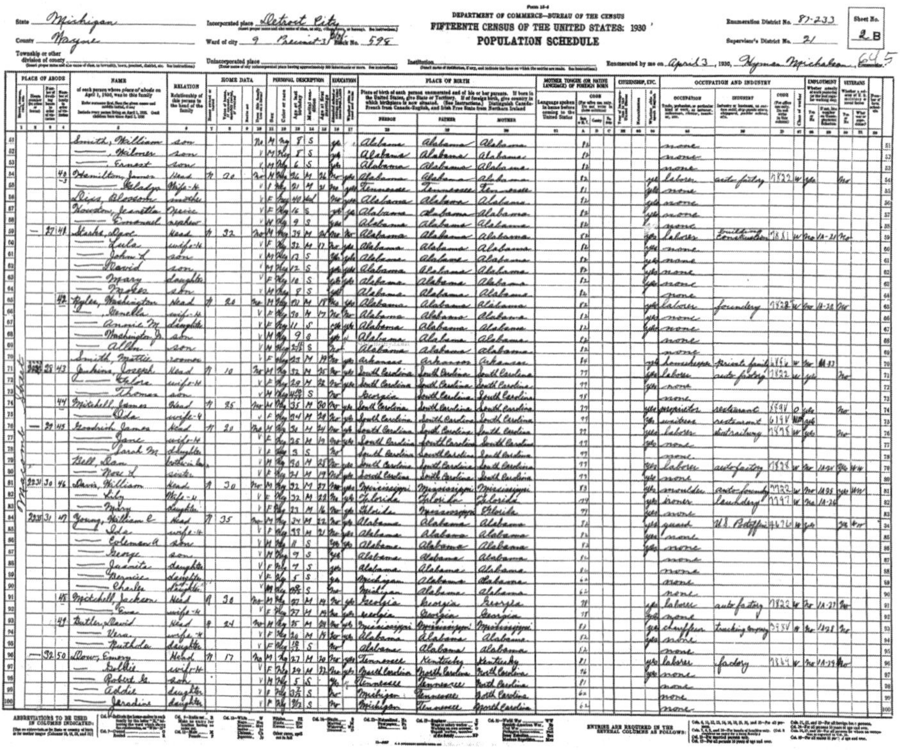

Figure 2.4. Coleman Young and family, 1930 U.S Federal Census, 1930; census place, Detroit, Wayne, Michigan; roll, 1040; page, 2B; enumeration district, 233; Image, 724.0. Courtesy of Ancestry.com.

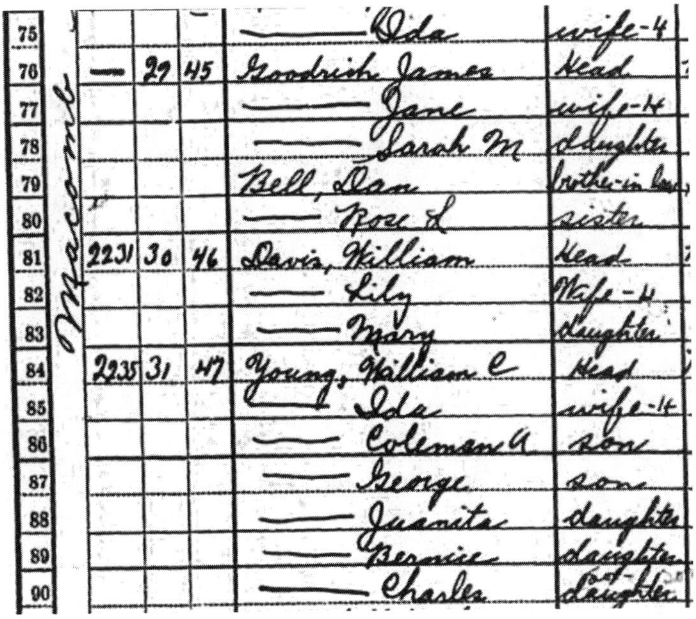

75				——— Ida	wife-H
76	—	29	45	Goodrich, James	Head
77				——— Jane	wife-H
78				——— Sarah M	daughter
79				Bell, Dan	brother-in-law
80				——— Rose L	sister
81	2231	30	46	Davis, William	Head
82				——— Lily	Wife-H
83				——— Mary	daughter
84	2235	31	47	Young, William C	Head
85				——— Ida	wife-H
86				——— Coleman A	son
87				——— George	son
88				——— Juanita	daughter
89				——— Bernice	daughter
90				——— Charles	daughter

Figure 2.5.

Several other families lived at the same address, so the Youngs appear to have lived in a small apartment building or divided house. The seventh column indicates that the Youngs are renting the apartment. The eighth column indicates that they pay $35 a month in rent.

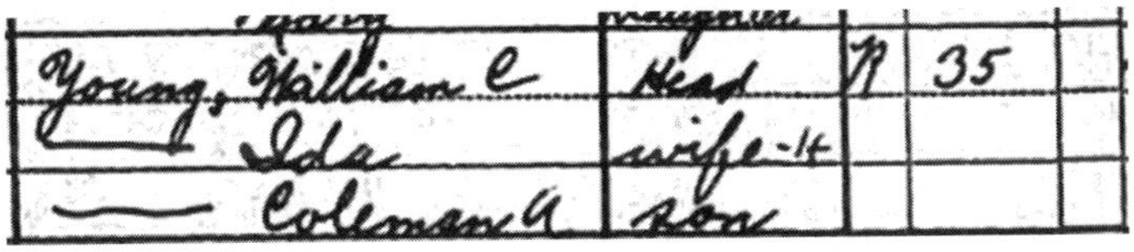

Young, William C	Head	R	35
——— Ida	wife-H		
——— Coleman A	son		

Figure 2.6.

William C. Young was the head of the household. His is listed as Negro, married, and 34 years old. He was first married at 22. He and both of his parents were born in Alabama.

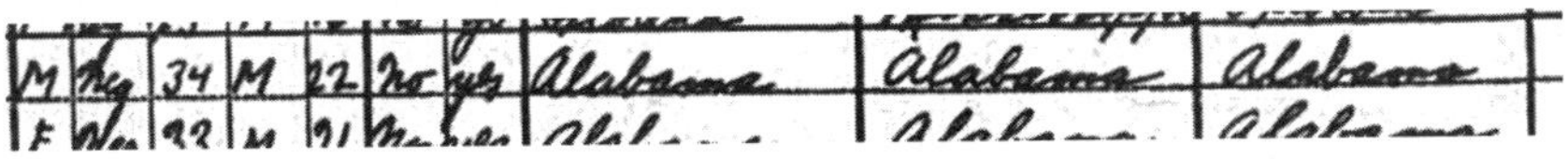

M	Neg	34	M	22	no	yes	Alabama	Alabama	Alabama

Figure 2.7.

He worked as a guard at the post office, and he was a veteran of the First World War.

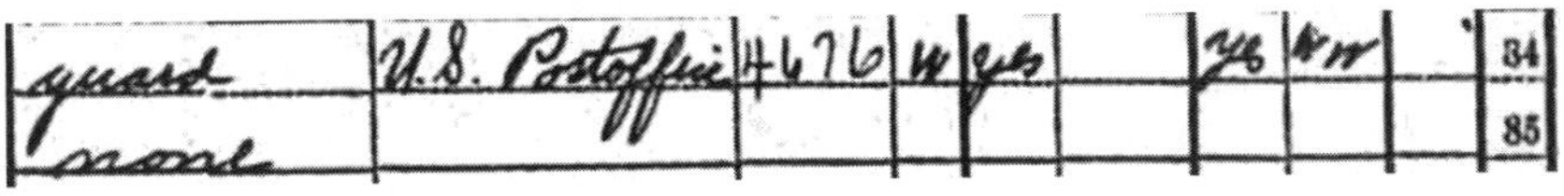

guard	U.S. Postoffice	4676	W	yes	yes	WW		84
none								85

Figure 2.8.

His wife, Ida, is listed as Negro, married, and 33 years old. She was first married at 21. She and both of her parents were born in Alabama.

V	F	Neg	33	M	21	No	yes	Alabama	Alabama	Alabama

Figure 2.9.

The couple had 5 children: Coleman A., 11 years old, born in Alabama; George, 9 years old, born in Alabama; Juanita, 7 years old, born in Alabama; Bernice, 5 years old, born in Michigan; and Charles, 3 years, 9 months, born in Michigan. It looks as if Charles was originally listed as a daughter; then, the correction "son" was penciled in.

— Ida	wife-H	V	F	Neg	33	M	21	No	yes	Alabama
— Coleman A	son	V	M	Neg	11	S		yes	yes	Alabama
— George	son	V	M	Neg	9	S		yes		Alabama
— Juanita	daughter	V	F	Neg	7	S		yes		Alabama
— Bernice	daughter	V	F	Neg	5	S		yes		Michigan
— Charles	son / daughter	V	M	Neg	3 9/12	S		no		Michigan

Figure 2.10.

This census record tells us about the life of the family in 1930 and also suggests where we might find more records. Juanita was born in Alabama seven years earlier, and Bernice was born in Michigan 5 years earlier, so this indicates that they moved from Alabama between 5 and 7 years earlier. Based on this information, we can expect to find William, Ida, and Coleman on the Alabama census of 1920.

We also learned that William and Ida were each first married around 12 years earlier. We do not know for certain that they were first married to each other, but it seems likely. This suggests there might be a marriage record for them in Alabama around 1918. William is listed as a veteran of the First World War, so there might be a military record for him.

Searching 1920, we find William, Ida, and Coleman in Tuscaloosa that year (fig. 2.11)

In 1910, there was not a William Young in the Ancestry.com index who seemed to match. However, there was a Coleman Young whose age of 14 matches the age of "William Young" on the 1920 and 1930 census records (fig. 2.12).

He was living in Demopolis, Alabama, though, not Tuscaloosa. However, his father, Alex Young, was a barber, just as "William C. Young" was in 1920. If he is our "William C. Young," his 1910 record connects him to another generation of the Young family, as he is listed with his father and mother. We will return to the Young family later using other records to try to see whether this is indeed the father of Mayor Coleman Young.

With a fairly quick search, we confirmed some basic facts about Coleman Young: his birth in Alabama, his childhood move to Detroit, and his mother's name. We also learned some new information: that his father was named or went by the name William rather than Coleman, the rough date of his parents' marriage, his siblings' names and ages, and his father's service in World War I. We also may have found earlier generations of Youngs, although we will need to use other kinds of records to confirm their relevance. The clues we found on the records of 1930 and 1920 will help us with further research.

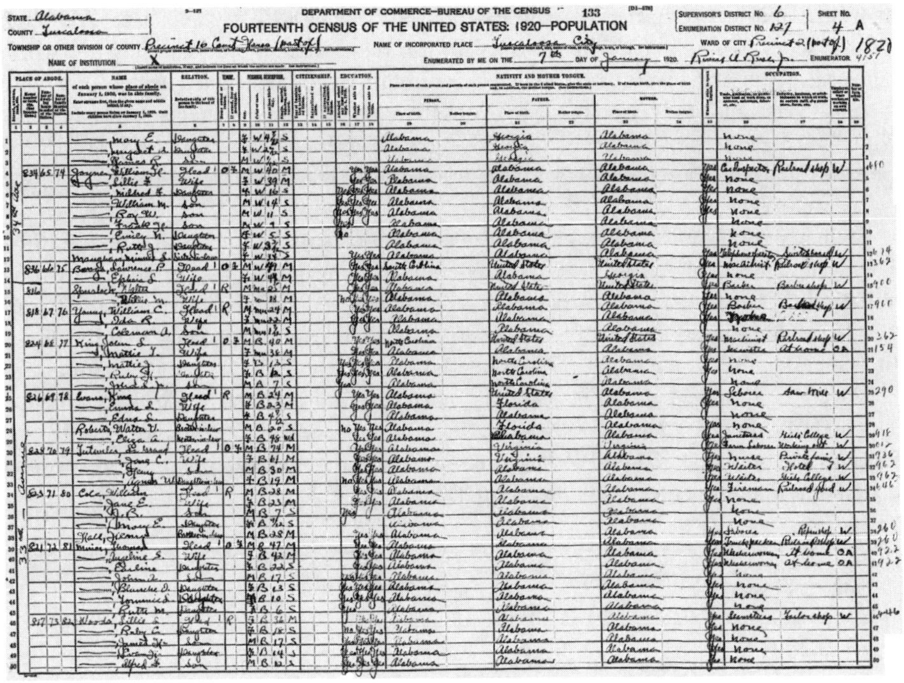

DEPARTMENT OF COMMERCE—BUREAU OF THE CENSUS

FOURTEENTH CENSUS OF THE UNITED STATES: 1920—POPULATION

Figure 2.11. Young family in 1920. U.S Federal Census, 1920; census place, Tuscaloosa, AL; roll, T625_45; page, 4A; enumeration district, 127; image, 843. Courtesy of Ancestry.com.

Researching the Census Using Print Indexes and Microfilm

Before the creation of the electronic indexes to the census, the census population schedules were kept on microfilm and were searched using book indexes or microfilm indexes. Although electronic databases have replaced the older search methods for many researchers, it is still useful to know about the older method of census research.

Print indexes exist for most states for the census years 1790–1860. So, for example, to research Charles Chenoweth in Ohio in 1860, a researcher would look for the Ohio 1860 index and then look alphabetically for Charles Chenoweth. In 1860, there is a printed index by Linda Harshman, which contains one entry for a Charles Chenoweth: *Chenoweth, Charles DKHR 14.*

From the key in the front of the book, we can learn that DKHR 14 means Darke County, Harrison Township, page 14. The researcher would then get the roll of microfilm containing Darke County, scroll forward to Harrison Township and look for page 14. The image on the microfilm is the same as the scanned images on Ancestry.com or HeritageQuest Online.

Microfilm Soundex Indexes

For the years 1880–1920, the U.S. government created microfilm indexes to the census, using a system called Soundex. Before the digitization of the census, these microfilm indexes were the main access point for the 1880–1920 censuses. Although most readers of this book will not need to use the Soundex indexes, they are worth knowing about for several reasons. First, veteran researchers may be familiar with them and ask questions about them; to assist these patrons, it helps to be familiar with their research experiences. Second, they offer an alternate access point to the censuses and are sometimes worth recommending when results are not found in the online indexes.

Soundex is a kind of index based on the sound of a name, rather than its spelling. The system was created to help researchers overcome problems caused by spelling variation. For example, in a strictly alphabetical index, Charles Smyth and Charles Smith would be filed separately, and researchers would need to check two locations. In a Soundex index, the names are grouped together. Here's how Soundex works.

To use a Soundex index, researchers must derive a Soundex code from a name. The code is always a letter followed by three numbers. The letter is always the first letter of the surname. To derive the three numbers, ignore the remaining vowels and code the remaining consonants based on Table 1.

Table 2.1 Soundex Coding

1 = B, P, F, V
2 = C, S, G, J, K, Q, X, Z
3 = D, T
4 = L
5 = M, N
6 = R
Do not code the following letters A, E, I, O, U, Y, H, and W.
Double consonants are coded as a single number.

Let us try Beaudette as an example. We start with the first letter of the surname "B." Then we ignore the vowels as listed in the Soundex coding guide: B~~EAU~~D~~E~~TT~~E~~.

This leaves us with three consonants: "D" and two "Ts." D codes as a 3. Double consonants are only counted once (because they sound the same as a single consonant when spoken), so "TT" codes as a 3 . Because there are only two coded consonants, the third number is a 0; the code for "Beaudette" is B330. This is also the code for Bodette or Beaudet. For those who do not enjoy deriving codes, there is a shortcut on the Internet: the free Web site Rootsweb offers an automatic Soundex converter, http://searches.rootsweb.com/cgi-bin/Genea/soundex.sh.

To search for Adolphus Beaudette of Chicago in the census of 1900, we would need to get the microfilm Soundex index of 1900 for Illinois. Soundex indexes can be found at branches of the National Archives, some major research libraries, and in the Family History Library.

The Soundex is organized by code and then alphabetically by first name. To find Adolphus Beaudette, we would go to code B330 and scroll forward past Abby, Abner, and so on, until we came to Adolphus. Figure 2.13 shows the 1900 Illinois Soundex entry for Adophus Beaudette.

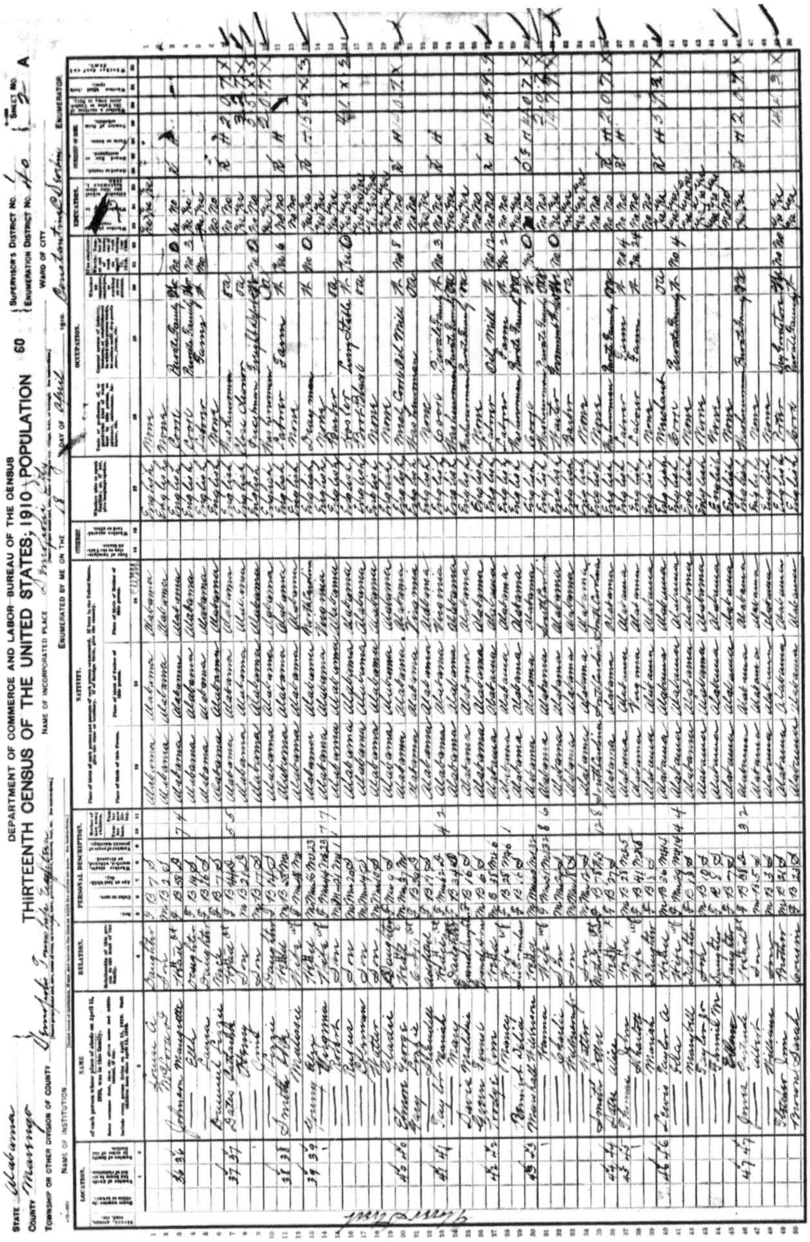

DEPARTMENT OF COMMERCE AND LABOR—BUREAU OF THE CENSUS

THIRTEENTH CENSUS OF THE UNITED STATES: 1910—POPULATION

Figure 2.12. Alex Young and family, 1910. U.S. Federal Census, 1910; census place: Demopolis, Marengo, Alabama; Roll: T624_24; Page: 2A; Enumeration District: 40; Image 869; courtesy of Ancestry.com.

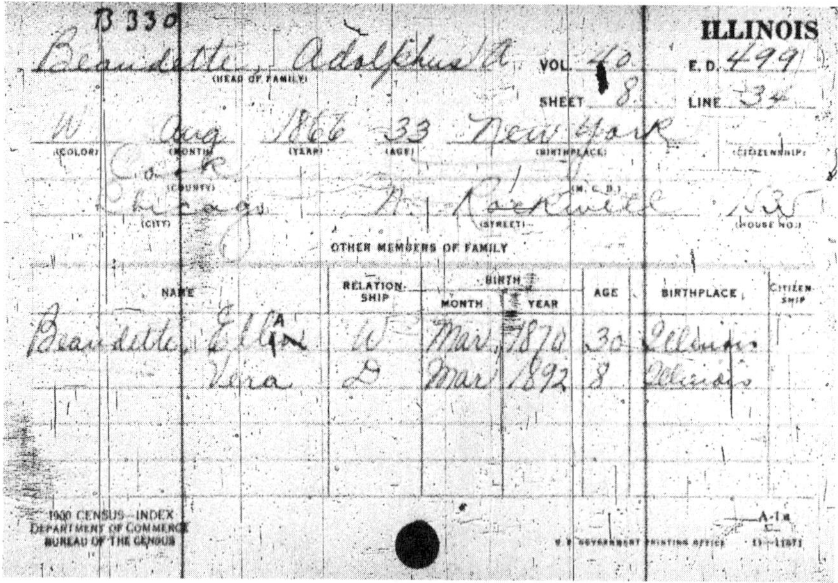
B 330 ILLINOIS

Beaudette, Adolphus A. (HEAD OF FAMILY) VOL. 40 E.D. 499 SHEET 8 LINE 34

W (COLOR) Aug (MONTH) 1866 (YEAR) 33 (AGE) New York (BIRTHPLACE) (CITIZENSHIP)

Cook (COUNTY) (M. C. D.)

Chicago (CITY) N. Rockwell (STREET) 1635 (HOUSE NO.)

OTHER MEMBERS OF FAMILY

NAME	RELATIONSHIP	BIRTH MONTH	BIRTH YEAR	AGE	BIRTHPLACE	CITIZENSHIP
Beaudette, Ella	W	Mar.	1870	30	Illinois	
Vera	D	Mar	1892	8	Illinois	

1900 CENSUS—INDEX
DEPARTMENT OF COMMERCE
BUREAU OF THE CENSUS

Figure 2.13. 1900 Soundex entry, Adolphus Beaudette. *Index (Soundex) to the Population Schedules of the Twelfth Census of the United States, 1900, Illinois.* National Archives microfilm publications, T1043. Washington, DC: National Archives.

A reference in the Soundex microfilm gives us some basic information about an entry in the census and gives us the information necessary for locating the full census record. In the case of Adolphus Beaudette, we know that we have found the correct person, because we can see that he is living with his wife, Ella, and his daughter, Vera. The Soundex gives us some other basic identifying information about Adolphus: his age, birth state, race, and home address. To find the full census record, we would follow the reference in the upper right corner and go to the microfilm containing enumeration district 499, and then scroll forward to sheet 8 and look at line 34 (the volume number in the upper right hand corner refers to the original paper volumes and is not useful for searching microfilm or digital records; researchers can ignore it).

Soundexing is also used in most genealogy databases as a way to broaden surname searching. We will discuss using the digital Soundex option in the next chapter.

Beyond the Basics

In this chapter, we have learned the basics of census research: how to look up a name and find a census record, using both microfilm and digital records. For many researchers, though, these basic steps might fail to provide results, even when their ancestors are recorded in the census. The next chapter will discuss more difficult census research and provide strategies for success.

REFERENCES

Ancestry.com. "Genealogy, Family Trees and Family History Records Online," http://ancestry.com/ (accessed August 10, 2007).

Ancestry.com. "Soundex Conversion Program," http://searches.rootsweb.com/cgi-bin/Genea/soundex.sh (accessed August 10, 2007).

Harshman, Linda Flint, and United States. *Index to the 1860 Federal Population Census of Ohio*. Mineral Ridge, OH: Harshman, 1979.

HeritageQuest Online. "HeritageQuest Online Index," http://heritagequestonline.com/ (accessed August 10, 2007).

Integrated Public Use Microdata Series. "Census Questions," http://usa.ipums.org/usa/voliii/tQuestions.shtml (accessed August 10, 2007).

National Archives (United States). *Index (Soundex) to the population schedules of the twelfth census of the United States, 1900, Illinois*. Washington, DC: National Archives, 1960.

Wikipedia. "Coleman Young: Wikipedia, the Free Encyclopedia," http://en.wikipedia.org/wiki/Coleman_Young (accessed August 10, 2007).

3

Advanced Census Research

"I think my ancestors were involved in some shady business—gunrunning, bootlegging—something like that, because every time the census taker came, they must have hid ..."

This is a comment we often hear from novice researchers at the reference desk. Many beginners pursue the basic census research described in the previous chapter without success: they search indexes, but they do not find their ancestors. This leads them to incorrectly conclude that the census does not contain information about their ancestors. Usually, their ancestors are listed somewhere in the census, but locating them requires the additional research techniques described in this chapter.

In most years, the U.S. census is remarkably complete, and most known residents of the United States can be found in the census. However, the census indexes are like the "telephone game" played by children. In the telephone game, children sit in a circle and pass a message around the circle by whispering in their neighbor's ear. The passage from child to child inevitably garbles the message. Similarly, the information in the census is passed forward several times, with numerous opportunities to become scrambled. First, the researcher's ancestor may have provided his or her name verbally to the census taker in a heavy accent. The census taker may have misheard the name or may have spelled it differently from the ancestor. Next, an indexer reading the census may have had trouble reading the census taker's script or a badly preserved census image and may have transcribed the text incorrectly. The final product is a name in the database of Ancestry.com or HeritageQuest that is considerably different from the name the ancestor used.

Many researchers also start with flawed information. As I mentioned earlier, most people have a hazy understanding of their own family history and may make incorrect assumptions. They might misremember a great-grandmother's name or believe that the family was in San Francisco in 1880, when in fact the family did not move there until 1910. Therefore, it is important for researchers to be flexible and try many approaches to finding ancestors in the census.

COMMON PROBLEMS

There are some major causes of difficulty in census research.

Surname Variation

Census takers did not cross-check people's names against other legal documents, so the name recorded is the census taker's best effort. As a result, mistakes or spelling variations on surnames are common in the census. With Anglophone names, this may mean simply substituting one vowel for another. For instance, my grandmother's surname is alternately spelled Chenowith or Chenoweth in the census. Non-Anglophone names are often more profoundly distorted. In Chicago, we notice this particularly with Polish names.

Ancestors may also have used variations on their names themselves. Many of our ancestors who lived before the 20th century were illiterate or semiliterate agricultural laborers, who existed in a primarily verbal culture. They may have considered their written names as a phonetic transcription of what they were called and may not have valued consistent spelling.

We find the spelling variation problem in many of the names in the case studies. In our case study of Stanley Kubrick, we find that his parents name is spelled Kubrik in 1920. Jeanette Winter's grandfather Otto Tischer is listed as Otto Thischer in the 1880 census.

First Name Variation

As with surnames, census-takers recorded first names as they heard them. That means that the census is full of nicknames, abbreviations, and variations. In the 19th century, it was common for men to go by their initials, and they are often listed that way in the census. Children are often listed by a nickname or diminutive. Immigrants often Americanized their first names after residing in the United States for a number of years.

We see first name variations in many other examples from the case studies: Coleman Young's father was listed as Coleman in 1910, but he went by William in the 1920 census. Ella Palma Beaudette is listed as Palma E. Lovgren in the 1910 census. Stanley Kubrick's father is listed as Jacob in 1910, but he was called Jack in 1920 and 1930. John Simpson is recorded as JW in the 1910 census.

Legal Name Change

In addition to the name variations listed above, many people also legally changed their names. In earlier generations, most women changed their name when they married. Many immigrants officially adopted American or Anglophone names. A child whose mother remarried after a death or divorce also may appear in the census with a new surname. Most of the women in our case studies legally changed their name at least once. In the Jeanette Winter case study, Ella Palma Tischer appears in documents with at least four different surnames throughout her life (Tischer, Beaudette, Lovgren, and Neal). Ella's first husband also changed his first name from Adolphus to Robert.

Indexing Error

We also find many errors in indexing in the census; unusual names or other information often throws off indexers. For example, a close examination of the 1930 census record for Stanley Kubrick shows his family listed as Kubrick, but the indexer has read the name as Kabrick. Adolphus Beaudette is recorded correctly in the 1880 census itself but is indexed as Adolphues Beaudette in Ancestry's index.

SOLUTIONS FOR COMMON PROBLEMS

Most of the problems listed above can be circumnavigated by avoiding a search of the exact name. Below are listed a number of search techniques to try when a basic census index search fails to locate a person.

Soundexing

In the previous chapter, I explained microfilm Soundex indexes, which code words by their sound. Most genealogical databases also allow a Soundex search option, which will automatically convert the search terms into a Soundex search. The Soundex option broadens the search, returns more results, and sometimes solves the problem of spelling variations.

An example from the Stanley Kubrick case study shows the usefulness of Soundex searching. When I search performed an "exact spelling" search for the name "Stanley Kubrick" in Ancestry's 1930 census index, I got no results, so I broadened the search to an "exact spelling" search of just the last name "Kubrick," figuring that baby Stanley might have had a nickname. This search returned 12 names but did not find Stanley Kubrick or his family. Therefore, I broadened the search by choosing the Soundex option for the surname. This proved too broad; the Soundex search for "Kubrick" in New York, returned 1,536 results. Rather than look through that many results, I searched for "Stanley Kubrick" using the Soundex option on the surname. This returned 11 results, including a child named "Stanley Kabrick" with parents named Rose and Jack. He proved to be our Stanley Kubrick.

Other Ways to Broaden Searches

Besides Soundex searching, there are other ways to broaden searches. One method is to search only on the last name. This method might circumvent misspelled or variant first names. However, this technique only makes sense if you are searching for a very unusual name, or if you are searching for a more common name in a limited geographical area. In other words, it is not practical to look through all of the people named "Anderson" in Chicago in 1920; you would have to look through 14,639 results. However, it might make sense to look through all the Andersons in, say, rural Benzie County, Michigan, in 1920; Ancestry only returns 43 Andersons there. Also, it would make sense to search for all the people with an unusual surname such as "Beaudette" in Chicago; Ancestry records only 12 Chicagoans with that name in the 1920 census.

To use an example from the Coleman Young case study, I could not find Coleman Young's great-grandfather Robert Napier in the 1860 census, so I searched for all people named "Napier" in Marengo County, Alabama. There, I found Robert Napier listed as "Robe. Napier."

To consider this strategy more broadly, researchers should consider all of the search options offered by a particular database and focus on the unusual aspects of their search target. When searching for someone with an unusual first name, search on just the first name. When searching for someone with an unusual birthplace, try using that as an element of the search.

Consider the example of Otto Tischer, from the Jeanette Winter case study. I was trying to locate Otto Tischer and his wife, Clara, in Illinois in the 1880 census. I tried searching on each of their names, and both exact searches and Soundex searches failed to locate them. I tried typing in some possible variations or misreadings of the name—Otto Fisher, Otto Tisch—with no results, so I tried to think what was unusual about this couple and examined the search options. The 1880 census form on Family Search.org allows you to include "head of the household" as a search option for a particular individual, so you can search for person "x" in a household headed by person "y." It also allows you to search on first names only, without entering a surname. If Clara and Otto were married and living together, Otto would be listed as the head of the household. I wondered how many households in Illinois headed by an Otto included a Clara, so I entered just Clara's first name and just the first name Otto as "Head of the Household" (fig. 3.1). This search returned 25 results, including a Clara and Otto Thischer. The other family members in the household confirmed that this was the family I was searching for. For some reason, the Soundex system used by FamilySearch did not pick up this name variation in the Soundex search of Tishcher.

The keys to success in searching the census are creativity and persistence. If an initial search is unsuccessful, researchers should try different search criteria, focusing

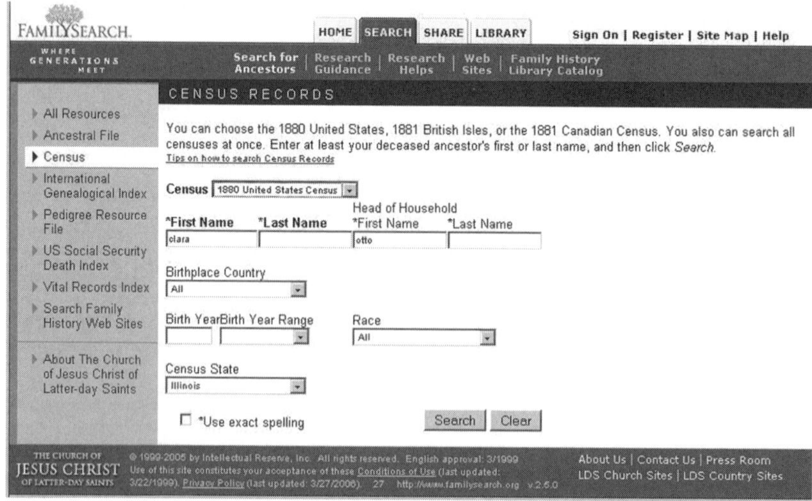

Figure 3.1. Advanced search for Otto and Clara Tischer in the 1880 census index. Family Search.org © 1999–2005 by Intellectual Reserve, Inc. Used by permission.

on the unusual qualities of your search target that might distinguish them from the mass of people in the census.

Enumeration District (ED) or Township Search

Another way to get around name errors in the census is to browse geographically rather than by name. If you are not finding a person in the census index, you might look through the pages of the census that cover the area where you believe the person resided. Before 1880, addresses were not recorded, so this strategy requires paging through a city ward or a rural township looking for the person's name.

Starting with the census of 1880, the U.S. Census Bureau divided counties into small areas called enumeration districts or EDs. The bureau also directed census takers to record addresses in urban areas. As a result, geographic searching is easier in the censuses of 1880 and later.

The first step in geographical research is finding where a person lived. The best source for urban research is a city directory from the census year. The city directory will also indicate where the address was: what major streets it was between. This information is helpful in searching for the ED. For an example of how to use the city directory to discover the location of an address, turn to the example of Otto Tischer in the 1900 Chicago city directory in Chapter Five.

Once a researcher knows what an address was and where that address was located, he or she is ready to figure out which ED included that location. There are a number of ways to do this. For some places, there are ED maps, which makes ED searching easiest. For instance, a genealogist has posted ED maps for Chicago on the Web site, *A Look at Cook* (http://www.alookatcook.com). Other ED maps are available on microfilm at the regional branches of the National Archives.

Returning to example of Otto Tischer, we know he lived at 831 N. Robey (now Damen Ave.) in Chicago, which was north of Wabansia and south of Wilmot. Comparing the ED map of this area with the 1900 street directory, we can see the address would be south of Bloomingdale Avenue and north of North Avenue and that odd numbers would be on the west side of the street. Looking at the map, this places the Tischer address in ED 465 (fig. 3.2).

Once we have the ED number, we can search the microfilm of that district for the address. If you do not have access to the microfilm, the Stephen Morse Web site, http://www.stevemorse.org, allows you to search Ancestry.com's census database for certain years using the ED as a field. Once I found that the Tischer household was in ED 465, I used Morse's tool to search Ancestry.com's index for people with the first name "Otto" in district 465. This turned up an Otto and Clara Fisher in the ED. Pulling up the full record, I found Otto and Clara Tischer listed at 831 N. Robey. Alternately, users can browse through the census pages for a district on Ancestry or HeritageQuest.

Because maps are difficult to come by, Stephen Morse has also created a database of ED boundaries for major cities in the years 1910–1940 that researchers can freely access at his Web site. By entering cross streets, researchers can determine the ED for a particular street intersection.

Researchers looking for ancestors in rural areas might also consider geographic browsing. In rural areas, this searching is less complex than in a large city. Because

Figure 3.2. Portion of 1900 ED map of Chicago, courtesy of *A Look at Cook.*

the population in these areas is less dense, they are less difficult to browse. Therefore, if researchers are aware of the rural town or township an ancestor lived in, they might simply scroll through the entire microfilm or set of digital images containing that area.

ADVANCED CENSUS RESOURCES

Steve Morse Web Site

As mentioned above, Stephen P. Morse's Web site, http://www.stevemorse.org, has some great resources for advanced census searching. Morse is a genealogist who has created a number of "front-ends" to databases that allow more flexible searching. I have already mentioned his tools for locating EDs and census searching. He also offers search tools for making census browsing easier. Although Morse's site is free, some of his tools work only in conjunction with subscription databases.

Census Enumerators' Instructions

Each year, the information recorded on the census changed slightly, and each census schedule has quirks and mysteries. Researchers can resolve many of these mysteries by reading the instructions the Census Bureau issued to its census takers. The enumerators' instructions are available online from the Integrated Public Use Microdata Series (IPUMS) at the University of Minnesota, http://www.usa.ipums.org/usa/voliii/tEnumInstr.shtml.

These instructions help to explain a mysterious notation on Stanley Kubrick's census record for 1930. In the sixth column of the census, his mother Gertrude is listed as "Wife-H." What does this mean? If we look at the enumerator's instructions from 1930, we find the following directive: *132. Home-maker.-Column 6 is to be used also to indicate which member of the family is the "home-maker," that is, which one is responsible for the care of the home and family. After the word "wife," "mother," or other term showing the relationship of such person to the head of the family, add the letter "H," thus: "Wife-H." Only one person in each family should receive this designation.*

For a more extensive example of the enumerators' instructions, see the directions for recording veterans in the 1930 census.

Recording Veterans in the 1930 Census

237. *Column 30. Veterans.* Write "Yes" for a man who is an ex-service veteran of the U.S. forces (Army, Navy, or Marine Corps) mobilized for any war or expedition and "No" for a man who is not an ex-service veteran. No entry is to be made in this column for males under 21 years of age or for females of any age whatever.
238. *Column 31. What war or expedition.* Where the answer in column 30 is "Yes," give the name of the war or expedition in which the man served. The principal military activities in which service will be reported, together with a convenient abbreviation for each which you may use in this column, are listed below:

World War, WW
Spanish-American War, SP
Civil War, Civ
Philippine insurrection, Phil
Boxer rebellion, Box
Mexican expedition, Mex

239. Those men are to be counted as "veterans" who were in the Army, Navy, or Marine Corps of the United States during the period of any U.S. war, even though they may not have gotten beyond the training camp. A World War veteran would have been in the service between 1917 and 1921; a Spanish-American War veteran, between 1898 and 1902; a Civil War veteran, between 1861 and 1866.
240. Persons are not veterans of an expedition, however, unless they actually took part in the expedition. For example, veterans of the Mexican expedition must have been in Mexico or Mexican waters at the time of the expedition; veterans of the Boxer rebellion, in China or Chinese waters at the time of the rebellion, etc.
241. Persons in the military or naval service of the United States during peace times *only* are not to be listed as veterans.

1930 U.S. Census enumerator instructions from Integrated Public Use Microdata Series, available at http://usa.ipums.org/usa/voliii/inst1930.shtml.

State Censuses

Some states also conducted their own censuses, usually in the mid-decade years between censuses. In Illinois, for example, there are surviving state census records from 1855 and 1865. These are great sources for filling in gaps in the genealogical record. Ancestry.com has digitized some state censuses. Researchers can also check the Web sites of state archives or state historical societies for information about state censuses.

REFERENCES

"A Look at Cook," http://alookatcook.com/ (accessed August 1, 2007).

Ancestry.com. "Genealogy, Family Trees and Family History Records Online," http://ancestry.com/ (accessed August 10, 2007).

FamilySearch.org. "Census Search," http://www.familysearch.org/Eng/Search/frameset_search.asp?PAGE=census/search_census.asp (accessed August 1, 2007).

IPUMS. "Enumerator Instructions," http://usa.ipums.org/usa/voliii/tEnumInstr.shtml (accessed August 1, 2007).

Morse, Stephen P. "One-Step Webpages," http://www.stevemorse.org/ (accessed August 1, 2007).

4

Researching Vital Records

After the U.S. census, vital records are the most important resource for genealogy research. By *vital records*, I refer to birth, marriage, and death records kept by state and local governments. Like the census, vital records are useful for novice researchers because they record a large percentage of the population, and they provide detailed information about their subjects. Vital records are often more effective than the census in connecting one generation to a previous one.

However, vital records are more difficult to use than the census. Because state or local governments maintain vital records, access to them varies widely based on locality. Some counties have very complete records, whereas others have lost years of documents in fires or floods. Some states began requiring birth records in the 1870s, whereas others did not collect them until the 1920s. Some localities have put copies of their death records on the Internet, whereas others will not allow you to see them at all. Because of this patchwork terrain, helping novices locate vital records can be difficult. Obtaining vital records can also be expensive; typically, county clerks charge between $5 and $20 per document.

This chapter describes the kind of information found in birth, death, and marriage records and explains how to locate them. The end of the chapter discusses the Social Security Death Index (SSDI), which is similar to an index of death records in some ways.

DEATH RECORDS

Of the three vital record types, death records are the best starting point for novice researchers, for two reasons. First, most beginners can identify the rough place and date of death for a parent or grandparent, and this is the basic information necessary for locating a death record. They are often less sure of the date/place of birth or marriage for their ancestors.

Second, most governments are less restrictive with death records than marriage or birth documents. Because the individuals described are deceased, death records raise fewer privacy concerns than the other types of vital records.

Death records typically record:

- The locality where the deceased was born
- Names of the parents of the deceased
- The name of a spouse or next-of-kin
- The individual's most recent address
- Individual's occupation
- Date of death
- Cause of death
- Place of burial

Much of this information is hard to glean from the census. A census will tell us that an ancestor is from Poland, but the death record often records the name of the village in Poland. If your grandfather emigrated from Ireland, but his parents remained overseas, the census will not record the parents' names; a death record might.

Beyond connecting two generations, death records provide other information of interest to genealogists. Genealogists are interested in where their ancestors are buried, and finding the name of a cemetery in a death record is much easier than searching through numerous cemetery indexes. The cause of death is often of great interest to genealogists, not just as part of the story of their ancestors' lives but also as part of the family medical history.

Of course, the information on the death record is not infallible. The next-of-kin typically gives information at the time of death, and they may be misinformed or inaccurate. Even the cause of death may be inaccurate because doctors in the past sometimes falsified records to spare families embarrassment or shame.

My great-grandfather's death certificate (fig. 4.1) is fairly typical. It records that he died on March 8, 1924, in Uniontown, Pennsylvania, at his home address of 61 Cleveland Ave. He had been employed as a mine superintendent. He was 48 at the time of death because he was born on Dec. 5, 1876 in Jackson, Ohio. His parents were John W. Simpson and Martha Thompson. It records that both of his parents were also born in Jackson, Ohio. His cause of death is listed as "duodenal ulcer" with "acute cardiac failure" listed as a contributory cause. His place of burial is hard to read; it appears that "Wheeling W. Va." was written in and then crossed out and replaced with "Jackson, Ohio." The informant is listed as "Mrs. J.W. Simpson." From further research, I believe that several pieces of information here are wrong. The deceased's father was born in New York rather than Jackson, Ohio, and his mother's maiden name was Leach, rather than Thompson. Also, I have doubts about the cause of death; given the circumstances of my great-grandfather's death, I wonder if the cause listed is accurate.

MARRIAGE RECORDS

Most marriages since the mid-19th century were recorded with a civil certificate. Because recent marriage records might include information about living people, governments tend to be more restrictive about them than death records.

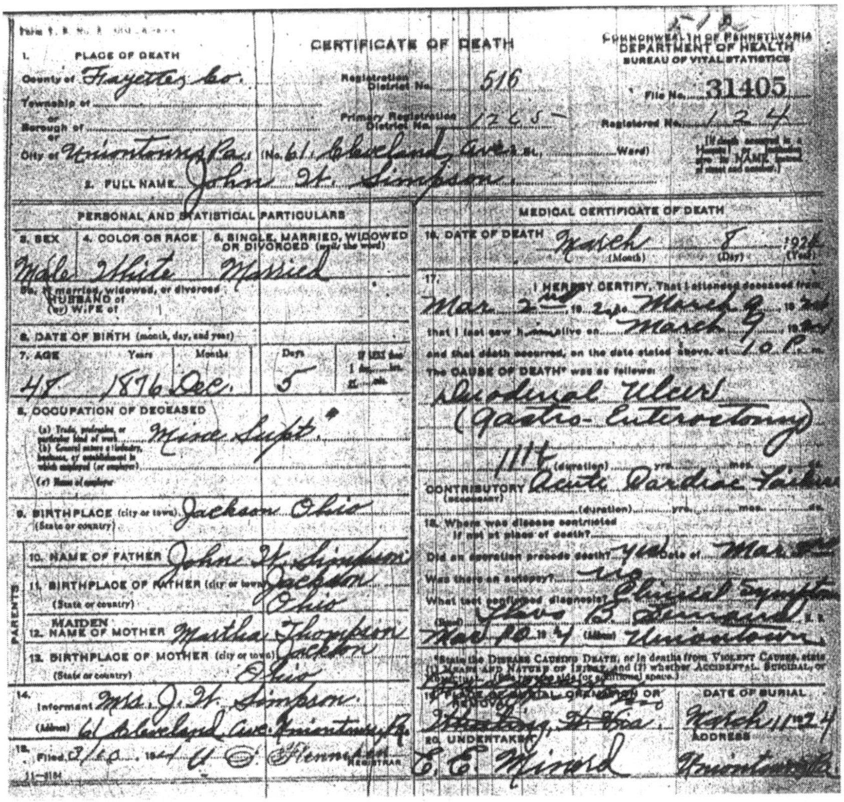

Figure 4.1. 1924 Death certificate for John Simpson. Death certificate no. 31405 (1924), Commonwealth of Pennsylvania, Bureau of Vital Statistics, Harrisburg.

Marriage records tend to record:

- Name of the groom
- Maiden name of the bride
- Date of marriage
- Official who performed the ceremony
- Age of bride and groom
- Parents of the bride and groom

The maiden name of a bride is a critical piece of information. A researcher can use the woman's maiden name to search for her on census records before her marriage, thereby connecting her to her parents. Knowing the date of the marriage is also useful. If a couple married in 1928, we know not to search for the bride under her maiden name on the 1930 census. We can also guess that the birth dates of a couple's children follow their marriage date (although this is not always the case). The name of the official who performed the marriage is important because it sometimes leads to a church record that might contain more information than the civil marriage record.

The case study of Jeanette Winter's ancestors gives us an unusual chance to compare two marriage records: one from Milwaukee, Wisconsin and one from Chicago,

Illinois. For some unknown reason, Jeanette's grandparents Ella Tischer and Adolphus Beaudette were married twice within four months, in two different ceremonies. In my experience, this is very unusual; most researchers can stop searching after they find one civil marriage for a particular couple. However, this anomaly gives us an opportunity to examine two different marriage records.

The marriage record from Chicago (fig. 4.2) shows that Adolphus Beaudette and Ella P. Tischer were married on August 17th, 1891, in Chicago.

Ella was 20 years old, and Adolphus was 25. A minister named W.W. Satterfield, of the Wicker Park M.E. Church, performed the ceremony. The certificate does not record the names of the parents. This record gives us a minimal amount of information, but it points us to more documents. For example, because we know the name of the church where the marriage was held, we can look for a church record of the marriage, which we will do in the next chapter.

The marriage record from Milwaukee (fig. 4.3) provides much more information. It records the names of the parents of Ella and Adolphus, including Ella's mother's maiden name. It records birth states for Ella and Adolphus. It describes Adolphus's occupation as real estate. It records that the person who performed the marriage is named Sabin, but it does not indicate if he was a minister. The license appears to misreport Ella's name as Ella Palmer Fisher, rather than Ella Palma Tischer.

The information from the Milwaukee marriage index allowed me to locate Adolphus Beaudette in the 1880 census. Equipped with the names of his parents, I searched for them in the 1880 census. I found no results for Stephen Beaudette, but I

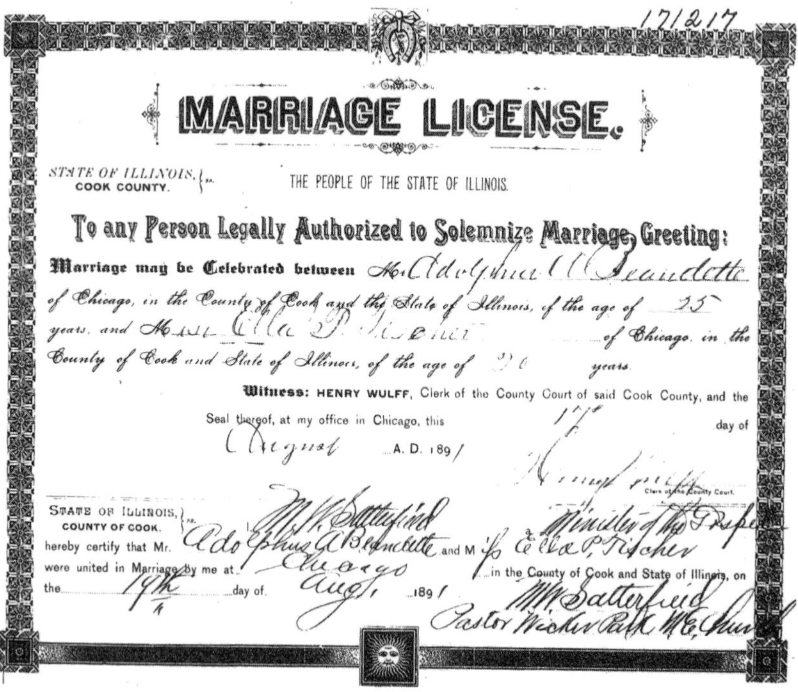

171217

MARRIAGE LICENSE.

STATE OF ILLINOIS, COOK COUNTY. } ss. THE PEOPLE OF THE STATE OF ILLINOIS.

To any Person Legally Authorized to Solemnize Marriage, Greeting:

Marriage may be Celebrated between Mr. Adolphus A. Beaudette of Chicago, in the County of Cook and the State of Illinois, of the age of 25 years, and Miss Ella P. Tischer of Chicago, in the County of Cook and State of Illinois, of the age of 20 years.

Witness: HENRY WULFF, Clerk of the County Court of said Cook County, and the Seal thereof, at my office in Chicago, this 17th day of August A. D. 1891

Henry Wulff, Clerk of the County Court.

STATE OF ILLINOIS, COUNTY OF COOK. } ss. I, W. W. Satterfield, Minister of the Gospel hereby certify that Mr. Adolphus A. Beaudette and Miss Ella P. Tischer were united in Marriage by me at Chicago in the County of Cook and State of Illinois, on the 17th day of Aug. 1891

W. W. Satterfield
Pastor Wicker Park M.E. Church

Figure 4.2. Beaudette-Tischer marriage certificate, Chicago. Cook County (Illinois) County Clerk.

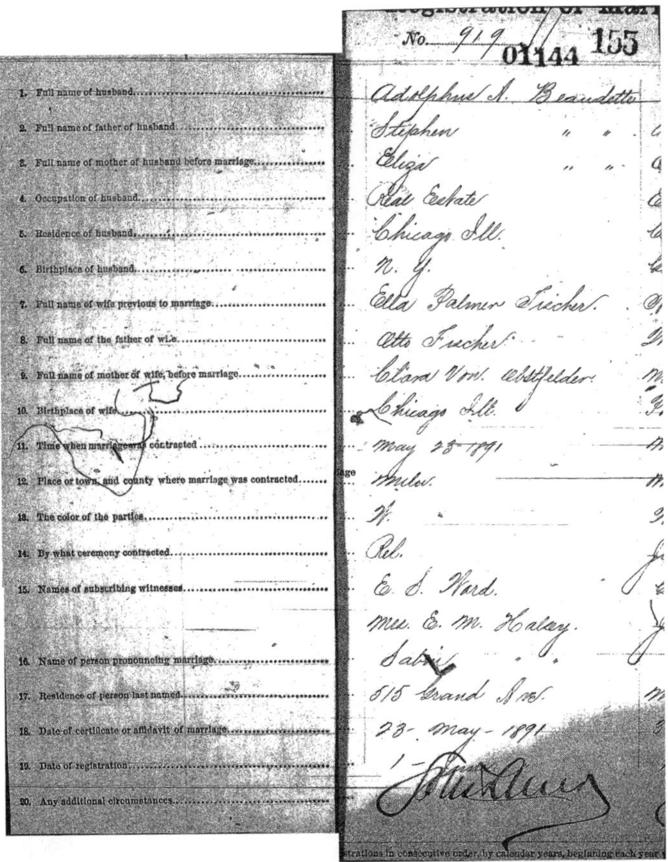

No. 919 01144 155

1. Full name of husband	Adolphus A. Beaudette
2. Full name of father of husband	Stephen " "
3. Full name of mother of husband before marriage	Eliza " "
4. Occupation of husband	Real Estate
5. Residence of husband	Chicago Ill.
6. Birthplace of husband	N. Y.
7. Full name of wife previous to marriage	Ella Palmer Tischer
8. Full name of the father of wife	Otto Tischer
9. Full name of mother of wife before marriage	Clara Von. Abstfelder
10. Birthplace of wife	Chicago Ill.
11. Time when marriage was contracted	May 23 1891
12. Place or town and county where marriage was contracted	Milw.
13. The color of the parties	W.
14. By what ceremony contracted	Rel.
15. Names of subscribing witnesses	E. S. Ward. Mrs. E. M. Haley.
16. Name of person pronouncing marriage	Sabin
17. Residence of person last named	515 Grand Ave.
18. Date of certificate or affidavit of marriage	23-May-1891
19. Date of registration	1-
20. Any additional circumstances	[illegible]

...strations in consecutive order, by calendar years, beginning each year...

Figure 4.3. Beaudette-Tischer marriage certificate, Milwaukee. Wisconsin Bureau of Vital Statistics.

did find two results for Eliza Beaudette, one in Wisconsin and one in New York. Examining the full census record, I found that the Eliza Beaudette in Fond-Du-Lac, Wisconsin had a 13-year-old son named Adolphus Beaudette. He is recorded in the Ancestry.com index as Adophues Beaudette, which is apparently why I did not locate the record in the census index.

BIRTH RECORDS

Birth records directly connect two generations; for that reason, they are very valuable genealogical evidence. However, birth records are often difficult to locate. Because even a birth record from 100 years ago might disclose information about a living person, governments often restrict access to them. Also, birth registration is a relatively modern phenomenon, and many states and counties did not require registration of births until the early 20th century. Ancestors born before the 1920s may not have received a civil birth certificate. (Church records of baptisms, however, were common in that period; we will discuss them in the next chapter.)

19th and 20th century birth records tend to record:

- Place of birth
- Date of birth
- Gender and race of child
- Name of father
- Maiden name of mother

Coleman Young's birth record is fairly typical. His birth was recorded in a ledger at the Tuscaloosa Probate Court, which is available as a microfilm from the Family History Library (FHL). The ledger records the birth of a boy named Coleman Alex Young on May 24, 1918 at 11:30 P.M. His mother's full/maiden name is recorded as Ida R. Jones, and his father is named as Wm. Coleman Young. His mother is described as 21 years old, but the portion of the ledger recording his father's age is illegible, probably due to water damage. Both his parents are described as "black," and both are recorded as being born in Alabama. The ledger records the father's occupation, but this portion is also illegible (fig. 4.4).

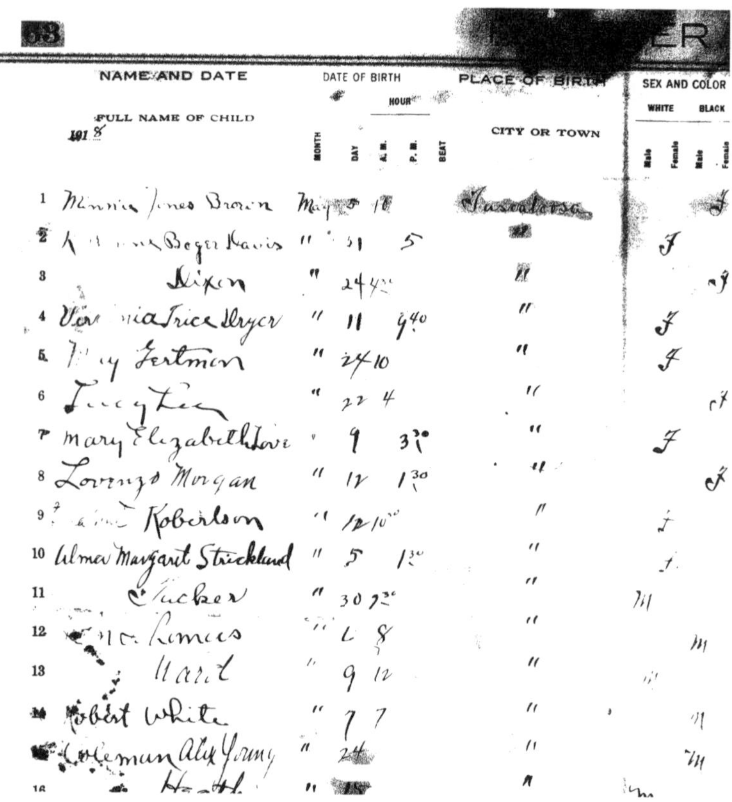

Figure 4.4. Portion of Coleman Young's birth record, Tuscaloosa, Alabama. Tuscaloosa County (Alabama) Probate Court.

LOCATING VITAL RECORDS USING INDEXES

We have seen that birth, marriage, and death records contain valuable information, so how can a researcher locate them? The first step is to look for an index to vital records. An index will confirm that a record exists and give specific information (a date or record number, for example) that will make obtaining the record easier. Statewide indexes are particularly useful because researchers are often uncertain about the county that their ancestors were from. There is no definitive source to indicate if a particular set of records is indexed, but there are a number of good places to start looking.

Indexes on Government Web Sites

Many state governments have started placing vital records indexes online. To find such indexes, a researcher might start with the state government Web site and navigate to the section on vital records, or he or she might visit the USGenWeb (see Chapter Nine) for the particular state the researcher is interested in because these pages often link to statewide indexes.

Illinois has been fairly aggressive in indexing its vital records online. The Illinois State Archives Web site has the following indexes online at http://www.cyberdrive illinois.com/departments/archives/databases.html:

- Illinois Statewide Marriage Index, 1763–1900
- Illinois Statewide Death Index, pre-1916
- Illinois Statewide Death Index, 1916–1950

I used the statewide index of Illinois marriages to locate the marriage record of Augustus Beaudette and Ella Tischer. I first searched on Beaudette, but I found only one Beaudette: a Robert Beaudette who married Johanna Brosman in 1908. Therefore, I tried just the surname Tischer, and the index returned the following entry:

BEANDETTE, ADOLPHUS A
TISCHER, ELLA P 08/19/1891
00171217
COOK

The surname of Adolphus Beaudette is misspelled, which is why a search for the groom did not produce the entry. The index entry indicates that the marriage occurred in Cook County on August 19, 1891, and that the Cook County Clerk had a certificate of marriage. Knowing the date and the certificate number (00171217) allowed me to obtain the original record.

Published Indexes

Many local governments and genealogy societies have published vital records indexes in print or microform. For example, the Mississippi State Board of Health published a Soundex index to pre-1926 marriage records in that state on 89 microfilm reels. Many genealogy societies publish print indexes to local vital records, usually at the county level. Libraries might be able to interlibrary loan such works for their patrons. To locate print indexes, search Online Computer Library Center (OCLC)'s WorldCat catalog under the subjects such as:

(County, state) genealogy
Marriage records (state, county)
Registers of birth, etc. (state, county)

Indexes on Free Web Sites

Similarly, many genealogy societies and hobbyists have placed vital record indexes on the Internet. Sites such as USGenWeb and Rootsweb, which I cover in Chapter Nine, are good places to look for such records. There are also other independent hobbyist sites with indexes. For example, my great-great-grandfather Simpson's Civil War pension indicated he was married in Lawrence County, Ohio. Using Google, I located a genealogical Web site covering Lawrence County, Ohio: http://www.lawrencecountyohio.com.

On the site, there is a series of indexes to vital records kept in numbered volumes, presumably in the County Clerk's office. My great-grandfather, the couple's oldest child, was born in 1876, so I checked the index for Volume 11, from 1875. There I found the following entry:

SIMPSON, John LEACH, Martha 139

This entry confirms that there is a record for the couple in the records of Lawrence County from 1875.

Indexes from the Family History Library

The Family History Library (FHL) in Salt Lake City, part of the Church of Latter Day Saints, has many vital records indexes available on microfilm. Some of these indexes are unavailable elsewhere. For example, the FHL has a marriage index for Cook County, Illinois that is otherwise unavailable. Currently, the FHL catalog is not part of OCLC's WorldCat but can be searched on the Internet at http://www.familysearch.org. The public can borrow material from the FHL at local Family History Centers. For more information about the FHL, see Chapter Ten.

Indexes on Subscription Sites

Commercial Web sites such as Ancestry.com and World Vital Records contain a wealth of vital records indexes. Some of these databases are copies of indexes freely available elsewhere on the Internet, whereas others are exclusively available on the commercial sites. Some examples from Ancestry.com include:

- Alabama Deaths, 1908–1959
- Maine Marriages to 1875
- Minnesota Birth Index, 1935–2002

- Oakland County, Michigan, Vital Records, 1800–1917
- Rockingham County, Virginia, Births, 1860–1865

OBTAINING VITAL RECORDS FROM REPOSITORIES

Whether or not you have success locating an index, the next step in vital records research is to contact the record holding institution to request a copy. If you have found a reference to a record (as I did with Ella Tischer and "Adolphus Beandette"), this process is fairly easy. If you did not find a reference in an index, it might be more difficult, but it is not impossible.

Using the Genealogist's *Handybook* and County Web Sites

To obtain the records, a researcher needs to discover who holds the records for a particular county. A basic tool for this research is the *Handybook for Genealogists* (Everton, 2006). The *Handybook* describes what records exist for a particular county and gives information about where the records are held. For example, the *Handybook* gives the following entry about Jackson County, Ohio, where I believed my great-grandfather was born:

County	Jackson
Date Created	12 Jan 1816
Parent County or Territory	Scotio, Athens, Gallia, Ross
Web Site	http://www.rootsweb.com/~ohjackso/jackson.htm
Address/Details	Jackson County; 226 E. Main St.; Jackson, OH 45640-000; phone 740.286.2006
Details:	(Pro Judge has b, m, & pro rec; Co Hlth Dept. has d and bur. Rec; Clk Cts ahs div & ct. rec; Co Rcder has land rec)

This entry shows that the county was formed in 1816 and indicates which county office holds which records. For example, to find whether a birth record exists for my great-grandfather, I might contact the Probate Judge's office, which holds birth, marriage, and probate records.

Obtaining Original Records from Repositories

The next step is to contact the office that holds the records to request a copy. Generally, it is a good idea to see if the record holder has information about obtaining records on their Web site. For Jackson County, I could not find an official county Web site that listed information about vital records. Instead, I checked the Web site listed in the *Handybook*, an unofficial genealogy Web site from Rootsweb. It gave the following information about obtaining birth records from Jackson County:

For Birth and Death Info (December 1908 thru present):
Jackson County Health Department
200 E. Main St.

Jackson, OH 45640
Phone: (740) 286-5094
Fax: (740) 286-8809
E-Mail: None
Hours: Monday thru Friday, 8:00 A.M. – 4:30 P.M.
The cost of copies of birth and death certificates as of October 2001 are:
Certified copies: $7.00 (seven dollars) each
Non-certified copies: $0.50 each
Postage is not required but it would be appreciated, especially for the non-certified copies.
For Birth and Death Info (approximately 1867 thru December 1908) and Marriages and Wills and Estate Probate Records:
Jackson County Probate Judge's Office
226 E. Main St.
Jackson, OH 45640
Phone: (740) 286-1401
Fax: (740) 286-4061
E-Mail: None
Hours: Monday thru Friday, 8:00 A.M. – 4:00 P.M.

The cost of copies is $0.10 per page. Birth and death records require two pages each because they are written across two facing pages. A self-addressed stamped envelope is not required but is appreciated.

Based on the information from his death certificate, I believe that my great-grandfather was born December 5, 1876, so I now know to contact the Probate Judge's office at the listed address for information and that they charge a dime a page. Whether this would give me a traditional birth certificate, as we described above, is unclear.

Obtaining Records from the FHL

Borrowing microfilmed vital records from the FHL is another method of obtaining vital records (for details on how to borrow from the FHL, see Chapter Ten). In the case of Jackson County, Ohio, the FHL appears to have the same birth records referenced on the Web site above. The FHL library catalog describes the following microfilm set:

Title:	Jackson County, Ohio, birth records, 1867–1909
Authors:	Ohio. Probate Court (Jackson County) (Main Author)
Notes:	Microfilm of original records in the Jackson County Courthouse, Jackson, Ohio. Some volumes have listed the births in alphabetical order.
Publication:	Salt Lake City, Utah: Filmed by the Genealogical Society of Utah, 1963
Physical:	2 Microfilm reels; 35 mm
Film Notes:	Note: Location [film]
Births, v. A-B 1867–1890:	FHL US/CAN Film [301032]
Birth records, v. C-D 1890–1908:	FHL US/CAN Film [301033]

In this case, it appears to be cheaper to obtain the records directly from the county because they charge only twenty cents for two pages of records, whereas borrowing a microfilm from the FHL costs $5.50. However, the situation is often reversed, with the FHL offering a cheaper alternative to purchasing the records from the county.

Because I had an opportunity to visit the FHL in Salt Lake in person, I checked the microfilm rather than write to the county. Unfortunately, I did not find a record for my great-grandfather in the microfilmed ledger. Later, other evidence indicated that his family probably moved to Jackson County when he was a child, and his likely birthplace was Lawrence County, Ohio.

Commercial Services

There are also commercial services that will procure vital records for a fee, such as VitalChek Network (http://www.vitalchek.com). In some situations, such a company might be a quicker way to obtain vital records. In the case of Jackson County, Ohio's birth records, VitalChek did not offer record searches prior to 1908.

SOCIAL SECURITY DEATH INDEX (SSDI)

Although there are no nationwide vital records indexes, the SSDI serves a similar function for genealogists. The SSDI indexes individuals in the Social Security system who have died. The bulk of records in the system date from the mid-1960s to the present. The SSDI is freely available on the Internet through Rootsweb (http://ssdi.rootsweb.com) or through Ancestry.com. Because most Americans are in the Social Security system, the SSDI is a very inclusive index; at the time of writing, it contained over 77 million entries. The index is name searchable, and researchers do not need to know the search subject's Social Security number (SSN) to search.

Entries in the index give the following information:

- Name
- Social Security Number (SSN)
- Last residence
- Birth date
- Death date (sometimes only the month is given)
- State where SSN was issued

When I first began to research my own family, the SSDI was an easy source to start with. I knew that my grandfather, John W. Simpson, died in Ypsilanti, Michigan in the late 1980s, and I knew his approximate age, but my knowledge was fairly imprecise.

I searched the SSDI for people named "John Simpson" whose last address was in Michigan, and I got 43 results. Among them was my grandfather's entry:

Name:	John W. Simpson
SSN:	301-12-9093
Last residence:	48197 Ypsilanti, Washtenaw, Michigan, United States of America
Born:	9 Sep 1906
Died:	2 Dec 1987
State (year) SSN issued:	Ohio (before 1951)

This gave me some very useful information about my grandfather. Knowing the exact dates of birth and death makes searching for vital records much easier. I also now knew that he should be about 3 years old in the census of 1910. Finally, I learned that he was in Ohio when he applied for Social Security, which probably would have been in the late 1930s (when the Social Security System was created).

If an entry is found in the SSDI, a researcher can request a copy of the deceased's original Social Security application. The original application records the following information, as the individual recorded when applying for Social Security:

- Full name
- Full name at birth (including maiden name)
- Present mailing address
- Age at last birthday
- Date of birth
- Place of birth (city, county, state)
- Father's full name "regardless of whether living or dead"
- Mother's full name, including maiden name, "regardless of whether living or dead"
- Sex and race
- Ever applied for SSN/Railroad Retirement before? Yes/No
- Current employer's name and address
- Date signed
- Applicant's signature

In the Jeanette Winter case study, the Social Security application for Vera Winter provided some important information. Figure 4.5 shows Vera Beaudette's Social Security application.

She applied for Social Security in September of 1948. She records her name as Vera Beaudette. She appears to have originally written "Vera Beaudette Winter,"

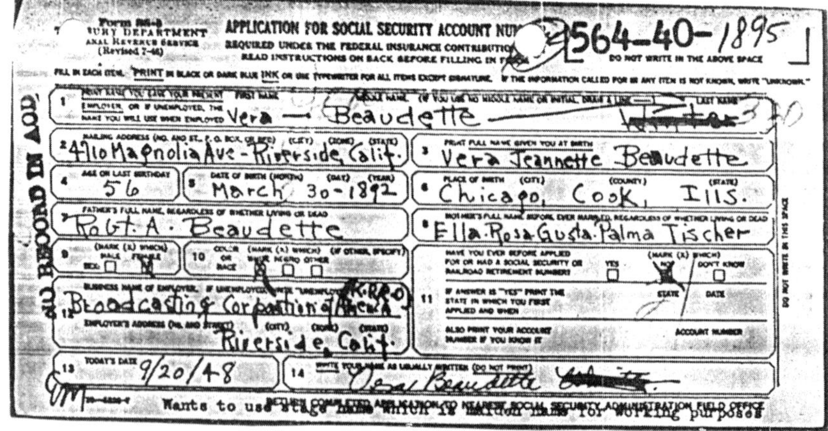

APPLICATION FOR SOCIAL SECURITY ACCOUNT NUMBER 564-40-1895

REQUIRED UNDER THE FEDERAL INSURANCE CONTRIBUTIONS ACT

READ INSTRUCTIONS ON BACK BEFORE FILLING IN FORM

DO NOT WRITE IN THE ABOVE SPACE

FILL IN EACH ITEM. PRINT IN BLACK OR DARK BLUE INK OR USE TYPEWRITER FOR ALL ITEMS EXCEPT SIGNATURE. IF THE INFORMATION CALLED FOR IN ANY ITEM IS NOT KNOWN, WRITE "UNKNOWN."

1. Vera — Beaudette ~~Winter~~
2. MAILING ADDRESS: 4710 Magnolia Ave - Riverside, Calif.
3. PRINT FULL NAME GIVEN YOU AT BIRTH: Vera Jeannette Beaudette
4. AGE ON LAST BIRTHDAY: 56
5. DATE OF BIRTH: March 30-1892
6. PLACE OF BIRTH: Chicago, Cook, Ills.
7. FATHER'S FULL NAME, REGARDLESS OF WHETHER LIVING OR DEAD: Robt. A. Beaudette
8. MOTHER'S FULL NAME BEFORE EVER MARRIED, REGARDLESS OF WHETHER LIVING OR DEAD: Ella Rosa Gusta Palma Tischer
9. SEX: FEMALE [X]
10. COLOR OR RACE: WHITE [X]
11. HAVE YOU EVER BEFORE APPLIED FOR OR HAD A SOCIAL SECURITY OR RAILROAD RETIREMENT NUMBER? NO [X]
12. BUSINESS NAME OF EMPLOYER: Broadcasting Corporation of America K.P.R.O.
EMPLOYER'S ADDRESS: Riverside, Calif.
13. TODAY'S DATE: 9/20/48
14. WRITE YOUR NAME AS USUALLY WRITTEN (DO NOT PRINT): Vera Beaudette ~~Winter~~

RETURN COMPLETED APPLICATION TO NEAREST SOCIAL SECURITY ADMINISTRATION FIELD OFFICE

Wants to use stage name which is maiden name for working purposes

Figure 4.5. Vera Beaudette/Winter's application for Social Security.

and then she crossed out the last name. At the bottom of the page, a typewritten note explains the change, indicating that she "wants to use stage name which is maiden name for working purposes." She was working for the Broadcasting Corporation of America, at a station called KRRO. At that time, she lived at 4710 Magnolia Avenue in Riverside, California. The document records her birth date and birthplace, her race, and her gender. It also records the names of both of her parents. Interestingly, her father is listed here as Robert Beaudette, when all previous records recorded him as Adophus Beaudette. This document helped uncover a previously unknown fact; her father changed his first name after divorcing her mother.

To obtain the original application, a researcher must send a Freedom of Information Act request to the Social Security Administration. The SSDI databases at Ancestry and Rootsweb allow users to generate a letter to print out and send to the Social Security administration. At the time of writing, copies of the original records cost $27.

The SSDI is an extremely useful database for patrons who do not know a great deal about their parents or grandparents. Patrons who start with very little information can search across the U.S. for death information, and this can lead to a variety of other records.

The Future of Vital Records Research

Two trends may change vital records research in the near future: digitization and new privacy laws. Digitization is changing every kind of research, and vital records are no exception. Some localities have scanned their original vital records and made them available directly online. For example, the State of Missouri has put images of its death records for the years 1910–1928 in a free online database: http://sos.mo.gov/archives/resources/deathcertificates/.

Digitization removes some of the cost and labor of vital records research and will allow more casual researchers to view vital records. However, although some state and local governments are making vital records more accessible, others are restricting access. In an attempt to combat identity theft, some state governments have become more restrictive with vital records. Similarly, the federal government passed a law in 2004 (the Intelligence Reform and Terrorism Prevention Act) that contained provisions restricting access to vital records. So far, the government has not enforced those provisions. Nevertheless, citizen access to vital records remains a contested issue.

REFERENCES

Cook County (Illinois) County Clerk. *Marriage Licenses, 1871–1920* (Salt Lake City, UT: Genealogical Society of Utah), FHL US/CAN film 1030205. Microfilm, 1980.

Everton, George B. *The Handybook for Genealogists: United States of America.*. Logan, UT: Everton Publishers, 2006.

Illinois State Archives. "Illinois State Archives Databases," http://www.cyberdriveillinois.com/departments/archives/databases.html (accessed August 1, 2007).

The Lawrence Register. "History of Lawrence County, Ohio," http://lawrencecountyohio.com/ (accessed August 1, 2007).

Missouri Digital Heritage. "Missouri State Archives: Death Records Certificates," http://sos.mo.gov/archives/resources/deathcertificates/ (accessed August 1, 2007).

Mississippi State Board of Health. *Mississippi Index (Soundex) to Marriage Records Prior to 1926*. Microfilm, 1985.

Rootsweb. "Jackson County Ohio (USGenWeb)," http://www.rootsweb.com/~ohjackso/jackson.htm (accessed August 1, 2007).

Tuscaloosa County (Alabama) Probate Court, *Births and Deaths, 1895–1922: Microfilm of Originals in the Tuscaloosa County Courthouse in Tuscaloosa, Alabama* (Salt Lake City, UT: Genealogical Society of Utah, 1989).

VitalChek. "VitalChek Express: Birth Certificates, Death Certificates, Marriage Records, Divorce Records and Vital Records," http://www.vitalchek.com/ (accessed August 1, 2007).

Wisconsin Bureau of Vital Statistics. *Milwaukee County Registration of Marriages; Microfilm of Records in the Department of Vital Statistics at Madison, Wisconsin, 1837–1907* (Salt Lake City, UT: Genealogical Society of Utah, 1980). FHL US/CAN Film 1292267.

WorldCat. "WorldCat.org," http://www.worldcat.org/ (accessed August 1, 2007).

5

Basic Published Sources

There are a wide variety of useful sources of genealogy information beyond the census and vital records. This chapter describes some of the most important published sources: newspapers, city directories, local histories, family histories, and genealogy periodicals.

NEWSPAPERS AND OBITUARIES

Newspapers, always an important genealogical source, have become more useful to genealogists in the digital era. Although genealogists have long mined newspaper obituary columns, recent digitization efforts have made the other parts of the newspaper easily searchable as well.

Obituaries

Obituaries usually contain a wealth of genealogy information. Here is the obituary for Otto Tischer, Jeanette Winter's great-grandfather, published in the Chicago *Tribune* on July 9, 1931:

Otto Tischer Dead; Veteran of Civil War

Funeral Services for Otto Tischer, 89 years old, who died Tuesday in the Edward Hines hospital, will be conducted Saturday in the Graceland cemetery chapel. The body will be cremated.

Mr. Tischer was one of four veterans remaining on the membership roll of the Benjamin S. Butler post, No. 754, G.A.R. He had been in good health until the recent hot wave.

Mr. Tischer was born in Leydenburg, Schwartzburg, Germany, March 10, 1842, and came to this country as a youth. He entered the Union army on March 8, 1865, enlisting in company C, 35th New Jersey state volunteers. Out of the army, he came to Chicago, married Clara von Obstfelder, and engaged in the real estate business. The great fire of 1871 wiped him out financially and in later years he became a general contractor.

Mrs. Tischer died in 1915 and since that time he has made his home with his daughter, Mrs. Winona F. Warnock, 1524 Jonquil Terrace. Two other daughters also survive – Mrs. E. Palma Neal, Gary and Mrs. Ada C. Posthuma, 1008 North Shore avenue.

This example is somewhat more detailed than many obituaries from the early 20th century, but most describe the following basic information:

- Date of death
- Place of burial
- Place where memorial services were held (usually a house of worship or the home of a next-of-kin)
- Organizations the individual belonged to
- Maiden name of woman
- Names of surviving relatives and children

The death notice for Otto Tischer that ran in the *Chicago Daily News* on July 10, 1931 (fig. 5.1) is more typical.

Obituaries and death notices are particularly helpful in tracking married female ancestors. Female ancestors are often difficult to trace forward in time. Women typically changed their name when married, and marriage records are often difficult to locate. In this case, Otto Tischer's obituary reveals the married names of his three daughters. Before seeing this obituary, I did not know that Ella Palma, (Jeanette's grandmother, formerly Ella Palma Beaudette) was married to a man named Neal after divorcing her first husband.

Ancestors in the News

In the past, genealogists generally accessed newspapers by date; a researcher would find a date of death in an index and would then look at that date in the newspaper for an obituary. In recent years, information companies have digitized many

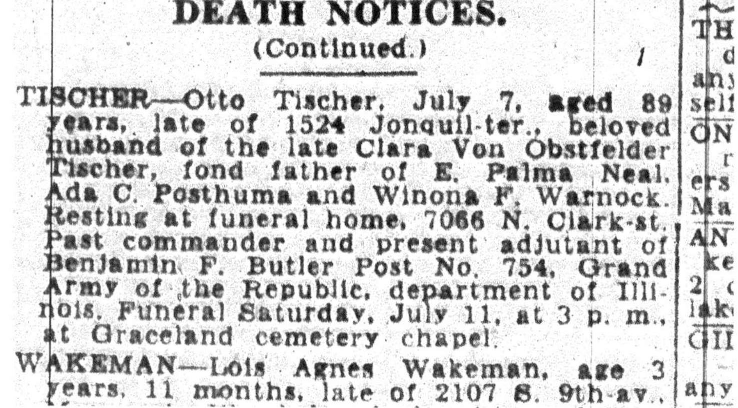

DEATH NOTICES.
(Continued.)

TISCHER—Otto Tischer, July 7, aged 89 years, late of 1524 Jonquil-ter., beloved husband of the late Clara Von Obstfelder Tischer, fond father of E. Palma Neal, Ada C. Posthuma and Winona F. Warnock. Resting at funeral home, 7066 N. Clark-st. Past commander and present adjutant of Benjamin F. Butler Post No. 754, Grand Army of the Republic, department of Illinois. Funeral Saturday, July 11, at 3 p. m., at Graceland cemetery chapel.

WAKEMAN—Lois Agnes Wakeman, age 3 years, 11 months, late of 2107 S. 9th-av.,

Figure 5.1. Death notice for Otto Tischer from the *Chicago Daily News*, July 10, 1931. Newberry Library.

newspapers and created full-text searchable databases of newspaper content. Digitization has surfaced newspaper information from news articles that was previously inaccessible to genealogical researchers because most newspapers were not indexed.

To take an example from the case study of Jeanette Winter, when I first researched Jeanette's grandmother, Ella Palma Beaudette, I had difficulty. She was considered a colorful character in family lore, but I could not find substantive information about her beyond her divorce record. She spent most of her life in the Chicago area, but none of Chicago's newspapers were name-indexed, so I was unable to locate any articles about her, other than her parents' obituaries. Several years after I began researching her, ProQuest created the digital *Chicago Tribune Historical Archive.* I searched for various combinations of her name, and found the following articles:

- *Causes Teamster's Arrest in Burnham* (September 1, 1913)
  This article, accompanied by a photograph, detailed how "Mrs. Palma E. Beaudette" complained about two teamsters who were driving crippled horses, leading to charges against the drivers.
- *She Carries Razor to Protect Herself* (May 8, 1915)
  According to this article, E. Palma Beaudette was fired upon with a pistol by political rivals in the Chicago suburb of Burr Oak and was only saved because she fell, "hampered in her flight by her hobble skirt."
- *Evanston "Stung" by Woman; Mad; Alleged Swindler is Arrested After Asking Wrong Man for Advertising Money* (September 15, 1912)
  Here, Ella Palma Beaudette was arrested for selling advertisements for a history of St. Mary's church, without the permission of the church.

Finding Newspapers

There are a number of methods for locating local newspapers. For many towns, the easiest way to get an obituary or news article is to contact the local public library. For example, I contacted the Uniontown Public Library and successfully requested a copy of my great-grandfather's obituary at a modest price.

The U.S. Newspaper Program (USNP) is another source of information about newspaper holdings. The USNP is a cataloging project of the Library of Congress. For years, catalogers with the project have been scouring libraries across the country and inventorying their newspaper holdings. The inventory is accessible as a statewide database of newspaper holdings in many states; the catalog records are also entered into the OCLC WorldCat catalog. For state-by-state information on the project, visit the USNP Web site, http://www.neh.gov/projects/usnp.html.

Digitized newspapers are available in a number of ways. First, there are a few free digitized newspapers on the Internet. For example, the Brooklyn Public Library has digitized the *Brooklyn Eagle* for the years 1841–1902, http://www.brooklynpubliclibrary.org/eagle/. However, the expense of newspaper digitization has meant that most digitalized newspapers are fee-based commercial products.

ProQuest, the information and research company, has digitized a number of major newspapers, including the *Chicago Tribune*, the *New York Times*, and the *Washington Post*. These digitized historical archives are available as subscriptions, and many major urban libraries and academic libraries subscribe. For remote patrons, accessing these databases is difficult unless researchers live in the locality they are researching; genealogists in California will have difficulty finding access to the *Historical Chicago Tribune*. However, most of these newspapers allow users to search the historical archives on their Web sites. For example, researchers can search the New York Times Historical Archives (1851–1980) on the New York Times Web site, http://www.nytimes.com/. Users can see only a brief summary of the result and must pay a fee to view the full article.

Other commercial services, including Ancestry.com and GenealogyBank, also offer digitized newspapers as part of their genealogy products.

CITY DIRECTORIES

Before telephones were popular, urban dwellers used city directories instead of telephone books to locate people, business, and other local information. Directories help genealogists track down ancestors in the years between census reports. They also provide a snapshot of a city in a particular year and can answer many urban research questions.

Like telephone books, city directories were published annually for most cities and contained a brief listing for individuals. These listings contained more information than modern phone books. In addition to the names of individuals, city directories typically listed people's occupation, work address, and home address.

The directory companies employed canvassers who walked the city and collected information about individuals. In 1892, the *Chicago Tribune* (July 22, 1892, p. 1) described how the R.H. Donnelly Company created the directory that year.

The work on the book was commenced the first Monday in May. Two hundred canvassers were employed five weeks ... Mr. Donnelly tells many amusing stories of the people met by the canvassers ... Some send names of the entire family. Others want their names left out on all manner of pleas. Divorce cases cause many people to request that their names be suppressed. This year, particularly, there were many who said they did not want their names to appear on account of the World's Fair. They say they don't want their country cousins to find them in 1892. A few refused to answer the questions and the canvasser located them at the neighboring stores.

In the 1900 city directory, Otto Tischer's entry is very sparse:

Tischer, Otto h 831 N Robey

Tischer lives at 831 N. Robey Street; the "h" stands for home. Because no work address is listed, it is not clear whether Otto is employed. In the same directory, Otto's son-in-law Adolphus Beaudette's entry (fig. 5.2) is equally spare:

Beaudette Adolphus A. Salesman 13 Lasalle

It indicates that he works as a salesman at 13 Lasalle, but no home address in given. It is characteristic of the city directory that both Tischer and Beaudette's names, botched on many other sources, are spelled correctly in the directory. Directories seemed to do a better job of recording names than the census or the newspaper.

In contrast to the sparse Chicago listings for Beaudette and Tischer, my grandfather's family is well documented in the 1923 Uniontown, Pennsylvania directory. Both his parents are listed:

Beauclerk, Bigelow & Co (Harry W Beauclerk and Gordon Bigelow) cement 1635, 84 Vanburen
Harry W (Beauclerk, Bigelow & Co) 1635, 84 Vanburen
Beaucock Isaac painter h 815 Clifton av
Lucy J Miss dressmkr h 1148 Wellington
Beaud Frank grocer 6556 Wentworth av h 6550 Wentworth av
Beaudette Adolphus A salesman 13 Lasalle
Arthur S shoemkr h 375 Lincoln av
Beaudoin Edouard grocer 869 Grand av h 101 N Claremont av

Figure 5.2. Adolphus Beaudette's entry in the 1900 Chicago City Directory. Newberry Library.

WESLEY CHURCH—1003-1009 N. Halsted. Pastor, Rev. N. H. Axtell.
WESTERN AVENUE CHURCH—Cor. W. Monroe and Western av. Pastor, Rev. Lewis Curts.
WICKER PARK CHURCH—N. Robey cor. Evergreen av. Pastor, Rev. M. W. Satterfield.
WINTER STREET CHURCH—Winter cor. 44th. Pastor, Rev. Edward W. Drew.

Figure 5.3. Church Listing from the 1928 Chicago City Directory. Newberry Library.

Simpson John W (Clara B.) mgr h 61 Cleveland Av

The listing indicates that John W. Simpson has a wife name Clara B. Simpson, he is a manager, and they live at 61 Cleveland Avenue. Somewhat unusually, my grandfather is also listed, although he was in high school at the time:

Simpson Wm J student res 61 Cleveland Av

Housewives were typically not listed in directories, but women who were employed are often listed. Therefore, Ella Palma Beaudette is not listed in the 1900 Chicago city directory during her marriage to Adolphus Beaudette. However, following their divorce and her entry into the shady side of the publishing business, she is listed. In the 1917 Chicago directory, she appears:

Beaudette, E. Palma author h 4429 N Lamon av

In addition to these individual listings, city directories typically had a front section of information about the city for that year: city boundaries, city officials, schools, churches, organizations, and a street guide. For genealogy researchers, the front matter can answer many questions. For example, in the Chicago marriage record of Augustus Beaudette and Ella Tischer, the descriptions of the pastor and his church were not very legible. I could make out that the minister's last name was Satterfield and that "Wicker Park" was part of the church name. Browsing the list of churches in the 1891 directory, I found a Wicker Park Methodist Episcopal Church with a minister named Satterfield (fig. 5.3).

Using Directories to Locate Addresses

City directories can also be used to find the location of city addresses, even when street names and address numbers have changed. Finding where an address was

Robey N. (W. D. and L. V.) fr. 772 W. Lake n. to city limits.

Even nos. e. s. P25

Lake	2
Walnut	24
Fulton	48
Carroll av	72
Kinzie	96
Austin av	128
Ferdinand	148
Grand av	158
Emerson av	178
Ohio	198
Erie	222
Huron	246
Superior	270
Lee pl	275
Chicago av	294
Rice	325
Iowa	354
Cornelia	
Augusta	414
Cortez	445
Thomas	474
Haddon av	507
Division	534
Crystal	565
Potomac av	592
Evergreen av	620
Fowler	665
Wicker Park	
LeMoyne	687
Park	712
Ewing pl	725
Milwaukee av / North av	758
Raymond	793
Wabansia av	814
Wilmot av	839
Peterson	865
Bloomingdale av	876

Figure 5.4. Listing for Robey Street, 1900 Chicago City Directory.

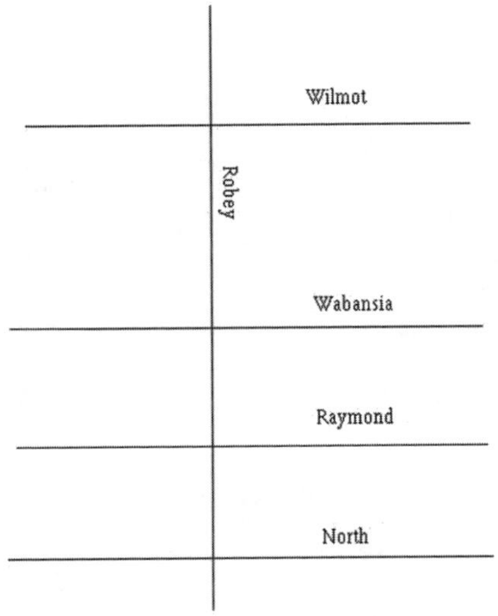

Wilmot
Robey
Wabansia
Raymond
North

Figure 5.5. Graph showing east-west streets crossing Robey Street, based on 1900 Chicago City Directory.

located is an important task for genealogists because it helps identify nearby churches and census enumeration districts.

Let us take the example of Otto Tischer in Chicago in 1900. He is listed at 831 N. Robey. If you type this address into a map search such as Google maps or search for it on a current atlas of Chicago, you will not find it because there is no Robey Street today. So, where was Tischer's house located that year?

Turning to the street guide in the front of the city directory, we find a listing for N. Robey. It indicates that Robey is a north-south street in the city's West division. It begins at Lake Street and runs north. Even numbers are on the east side, and odd numbers are on the west. The directory lists the address at each cross street (fig. 5.4). Therefore, Tischer's address of 831 N. Robey was between Wabansia and Wilmot on Robey (fig. 5.5).

If we pick a major cross street in the 1900 directory, we can see where Robey St. crossed it. If we look at the recognizable current day thoroughfare of North Avenue in the 1900 directory, we find the following progression of cross streets (fig. 5.6). Thus, we can create a grid of streets surrounding the Tischer home in 1900 (fig. 5.7). Looking at a present day map of Chicago, you will find that a number these of streets still exist in the same order (fig. 5.8).

We find one street between Hoyne and Winchester along North Avenue: Damen Avenue. We can guess, then, that Robey became Damen. Looking at the north-south cross streets, we find North Avenue is still there, as is Wabansia one block north, then St. Paul and Willow. St. Paul becomes Wilmot slightly west of Damen. Bloomingdale is visible to the east, a bit north of Willow, but it does not cross through Damen Avenue. We can make the assumption that Wilmot became St. Paul, and Peterson became Willow. Therefore, Tischer's house was on the present day block of Damen between Wabansia and St. Paul. Even if we are not exactly correct, we are probably not off by

North av. W. (W. D.) fr. the River w. to city limits. Even nos. s. s. R23

The River..........	1
Fleetwood.........	47
McHenry..........	87
Wright.............	107
Elston av..........	129
Noble..............	142
Coventry..........	147
R. R. Crossing.....	165
Holt...............	191
Dickson...........	217
Ashland av........	241
Marshfield av......	271
Paulina...........	297
Hermitage av......	327
Wood..............	353
Girard.............	379
Lincoln............	405
Elk Grove av......	406
Winchester av.....	437
Robey.............. } Milwaukee av.... }	471
Hoyne av..........	527
Hoyne ct..........	
Leavitt............	587
Irving av..........	613
Oakley av.........	639
Claremont av......	665
Western av........	691
Artesian av........	717
Campbell av.......	743
Maplewood av.....	775

Figure 5.6. Listing for North Avenue, 1900 Chicago City Directory.

more than a few blocks. Knowing the rough location of the house is helpful in locating census records, church records, and other source material.

Some city directories are available online through Ancestry.com and Heritage Quest. Many urban public libraries and major research libraries also have collections of city directories. The Newberry Library in Chicago has a nationwide collection of directories, inventoried at http://newberry.org/genealogy/dirholdings.html.

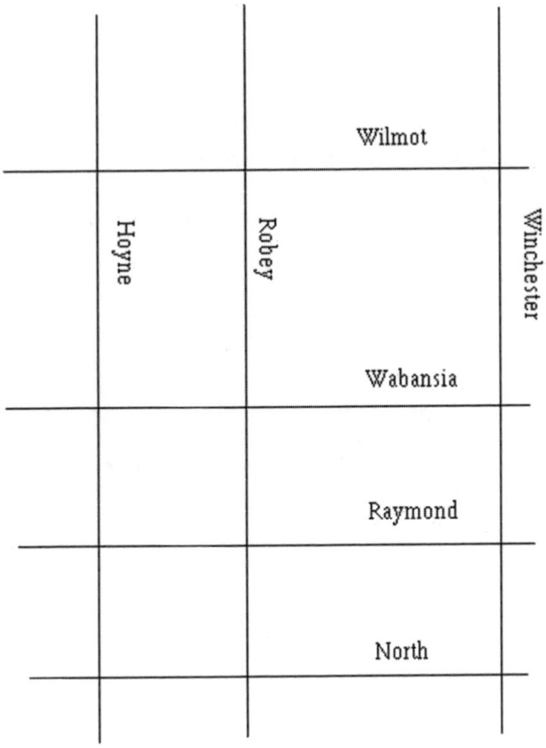

Wilmot
Hoyne
Robey
Winchester
Wabansia
Raymond
North

Figure 5.7. Grid of streets surrounding Tischer home, based on 1900 Chicago City Directory.

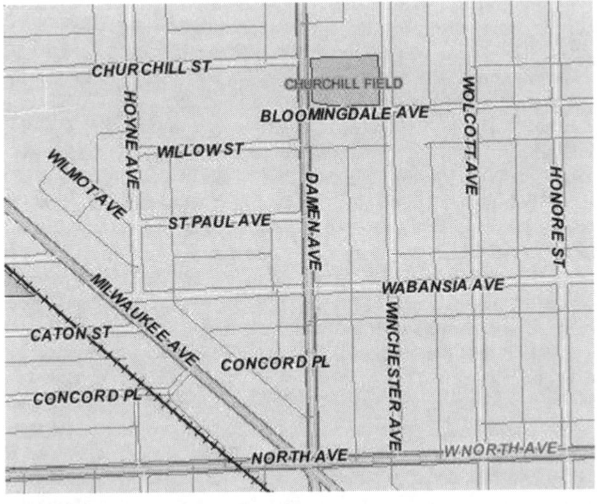

Figure 5.8. Current map of streets surrounding 1900 location of Tischer home. Courtesy of the City of Chicago.

LOCAL HISTORIES

Genealogists often overlook local histories because researchers assume that their ancestors would not merit mention in a history. This is a misperception because local histories often describe even the most mundane lives of local residents.

This is particularly true of the subscription-based county histories published in the late 19th and early 20th centuries. At that time, most Americans did not have access to bookstores, and books were often sold door-to-door by subscription. Salesmen would

6 BIOGRAPHICAL:

—Pauline, Carl, Mattie, Ellen, Libbie, Lula, Bernice and Philip, Jr. Is a Republican.

ANTONI BAPST, retired blacksmith, Naperville, was born September 25,1817, in Alsace, Germany; is a son of Joseph and Ursal Bapst. He came to this county in 1846, and worked at the blacksmith's trade at Naperville, which he began at the age of sixteen. In 1862, he abandoned the business and moved on his present farm of eighty acres, near the village, in Naperville Township. He was for a few years engaged in a grocery store in Naperville; was married in 1849 to Caroline Cooney, who blessed him with nine children, viz.: Mary, Fannie, Joseph, Antoni, Carrie, Frank, Louisa, Annie and Helen. He and wife are the artificers of their own fortune, having started their married life with $20. They are members of the Catholic Church.

HON. HIRAM H. CODY, P. O. Naperville, is a native of Vernon Center, Oneida Co., N. Y. He was born June 11, 1824, and is the son of Hiram Cody and Huldah, née Hitchcock. His paternal grandparents, Samuel Cody and Susannah, née Carroll, were among the pioneers of Oneida County. The former was a soldier in the Revolutionary army; the latter, with pardonable pride, traced her lineage to Charles Carroll, of Carrollton. His maternal grandparents, David Hitchcock and Mercy, née Gilbert, formerly of Connecticut, but during many years residents of Hamilton, Madison Co., N. Y., were universally respected for their many virtues. Hiram's parents took a deep interest in his early eduaction, and intended to give him the advantage of a thorough course of study in Hamilton College, five miles from their home. Their design was that he should enter the legal profession, and in all his instruction, both at school and under private tuition, this purpose was kept in view, and, being well known to him, made a very deep impression upon his hopes and aspirations for the future. A sad disappointment, however, awaited him. His father, who was engaged in mercantile business, was by a sudden reverse of fortune compelled to resume the occupation of his early life, that of shoemaking. Hiram, the eldest of the five children, then about sixteen years of age, was expecting to enter an advanced class in college the following year, instead, however, he voluntarily left his school and assisted his father in the support of the family, pursuing his studies afterward to some extent under private instruction. This circumstance, though it seemed a great calamity, and the destroyer of his highest hopes and aspirations proved to him a blessing in disguise, by inducing his removal to the West and settlement in Illinois. In 1843, with his father's family, he removed to Lisbon, Kendall Co., Ill., and one year later the family settled at Bloomingdale, Du Page County. In 1847, Mr. Cody removed to Naperville, having been elected Clerk of the County Commissoners' Court of Du Page County. Two years later, upon the adoption of the constitution of 1848, he was nominated by acclamation, and in 1849 elected the first County Clerk of said county, and during the six years he held the office he applied himself to the study of law, and finally, was admitted to the bar, after which he retired from public life and devoted himself to his profession. Politically, his views were Democratic, but during the war of the rebellion his earnest efforts and eloquent appeals in behalf of the Union cause will ever be remembered by his fellow-citizens, and it was to these that Du Page County was largely indebted for her brilliant record made during the war. In 1861, in a convention assembled without distinction of party, he was nominated and afterward almost unanimously elected County Judge of Du Page County. In 1869, he was elected a delegate to the Constitutional Convention, and was one of its most useful members, being elected by votes irrespective of party. He acted with a small number of independents who in the convention really held the

Figure 5.9. Page from *History of Du Page County, Illinois, 1882*. Courtesy ProQuest.

pitch a forthcoming book to subscribers before the book was printed. Local histories were a popular genre for subscription-based publishers. Canvassers would gather historical information about the county while simultaneously selling the publication. As a result, these large histories are packed with biographical information about local residents. For example, figure 5.9 shows a page from Rufus Blanchard's 1882 *History of Du Page County, Illinois*, featuring biographical entries on residents of Naperville, Illinois.

These county histories, sometimes called "mug books," were particularly popular in the Northeast and Midwest from 1870–1920. There are similar books for urban areas such as the *Notable Men of Pittsburgh and Vicinity* (Smith, 1901) and ethnic groups, such as *The Jews of Baltimore: An Historical Summary of Their Progress and Status As Citizens* (Blum, 1910).

Later local histories are usually not as detailed as the 19th century mug books but are nevertheless worth searching out. Many county historical/genealogical societies continue to publish county histories with significant biographical/genealogical information. For example, I found a detailed history of my Simpson ancestors, including a photograph of my great-grandfather in a 1991 history of Jackson County. This source was my major breakthrough in researching this family.

Researchers can find local histories in a number of ways. To locate a print history of a county, researchers can search WorldCat for the subject headings:

(name) county, (state): history
(name) county, (state): biography

Some examples include:

Jackson County (Ohio): history
Fayette County (Pa.): biography

Many county histories are also available digitally, through both commercial and noncommercial Web sites. Both Ancestry.com and HeritageQuest have digitized large collections of local histories. Researchers will also find transcriptions of some county histories on http://USGenWeb.com and other noncommercial sites. These online sources for digitized histories are described in more detail in Chapter Nine.

PUBLISHED FAMILY HISTORIES

Novice researchers often approach the library looking for "a book of their family history." These beginners expect that someone has written a history of their family and that they just need to find it. Unfortunately, this is rarely the case. A published family history can be a treasure trove of information, but many families are not documented in family histories. Even when such a history exists, it can be difficult to find. I do not discourage researchers from looking for these books, but I caution them that it is not easy, and they are not a good starting point.

Researchers studying Anglo-American families who arrived in the colonial period are more likely to find a family history than, say, descendants of an Italian-American family that arrived here in 1910. Part of this is simply mathematics; colonial families have more American descendants researching them than more recent immigrants. Beyond this, the bulk of genealogies published before the 1970s described

Anglo-American families, and many focused on the colonial and revolutionary period. As a result, these families are better documented by published histories than other groups.

To find a printed family history, researchers should search WorldCat for the following subject heading: *(name) family*; for example, *Beaudette family*. Family histories are usually self-published in small runs, so if a family history exists, it is often held by only a few libraries. Family histories also are usually well catalogued by the major family documented; for example, most Beaudette family histories are catalogued with the subject heading above. These two characteristics make WorldCat a great tool for finding family histories, as searching by subject across the vast catalog is very effective.

Researchers should also check the holdings of the Family History Library (FHL) in Salt Lake City, which is not part of WorldCat. See Chapter Ten for more information about searching the FHL catalog.

Using these catalogs, I searched for five families from our case studies, with mixed results.

- Beaudette: A search of WorldCat shows no published history for this name, although there is a Canadian Beaudette family newsletter. The FHL shows two titles, including a history titled *The Bodett-Bodette-Beaudette Family* by Thomas Bodett. The catalog record indicates that the book describes a family from Minnesota and Illinois, which is promising.
- Kubrick: WorldCat or FHL do not have titles for this name.
- Simpson: There are many published histories of various Simpson families in WorldCat and FHL because it is a common name. I have yet to locate one that includes information about my particular family, however.
- Tischer: WorldCat shows one Tischer family history, *An Inheritance* by Martha Geitz Tischer. Because this book appears to involve a family of Germans from Russia, it does not seem to be closely related to the Tischer family I am researching because they were not from Russia. Searching for the spelling "Tisher" locates several additional records in WorldCat; whether they are related families is unclear. A search of the FHL catalog reveals one Tischer genealogy by Patricia Kasten. The catalog record indicates that this is a family that came from Prussia to Wisconsin, which might match our Tischer family.
- Young: Like Simpson, there are many published histories of families with this name. However, it is difficult to see a connection between any of the titles in WorldCat and the FHL catalog and Coleman Young's ancestors.

These examples are not very impressive, but this should not discourage researchers from seeking out family histories. If we traced these families further back in time, we would probably find connections in published works. In other parts of my own family that I did not use as case studies, I have found valuable information in published genealogies. For example, my grandmother's maiden name was Chenoweth. The most widely held Chenoweth family history is *The Chenoweth Family, Beginning 449 A.D.*, by Cora Chenoweth Hiatt, published in 1925. This book contains information about my ancestors and includes a letter to the author from my great-great-grandfather Chenoweth, in which he relates his father's childhood memories of traveling west in a wagon train. Although this information is invaluable to me, I found that Cora Chenoweth Hiatt made errors and leaps of faith in her research, and contemporary Chenoweth researchers reject some of the lineages she constructed. Therefore, a family history can be a great source of unusual family information but must be viewed with skepticism.

Finding a family history is not as easy as some researchers expect. If you do happen to locate a published genealogy, it can provide a treasure trove of information. Looking for a family history should not be the researcher's first task, though. The more a researcher has gleaned from census and other basic search sources, the easier it will be to determine whether a particular family history describes the researcher's ancestors.

There are several online archives of digitized family histories worth mention. First, HeritageQuest Online has digitized many family histories, including the aforementioned Chenoweth history. The full-text searchable genealogies and local histories are available by selecting the "search books" option from the front page of the site. The Brigham Young University Library is also creating an online archive of digitized genealogies, available at: http://www.lib.byu.edu/fhc/.

GENEALOGICAL PERIODICALS AND PERIODICAL SOURCE INDEX (PERSI)

Many genealogical organizations publish journals and newsletters that contain local record transcriptions, brief family histories, and other articles of interest to genealogy researchers. These journals range from *The New England Historical and Genealogical Register*, which began publishing in 1847 to *Internet Genealogy,* which printed its first issue in 2006. There are single-family newsletters such as *About Towne* (which documents the Towne family), local history journals such as *Footprints in Williamson County, Illinois History*, and ethnic-specific publications such as the *Swedish Pioneer Historical Quarterly*.

The best tool for accessing articles in genealogy and local history journals is the PERSI. PERSI is maintained by the Allen County Public Library. Originally issued as a print periodical, it is now available through HeritageQuest Online. PERSI allows users to search for articles by surname or by locality. For example, a search for the surname Beaudette returned two results:

1. Carlton Beaudette photo, 1924, MN
   Hennepin History. Minneapolis, MN: Summer 1996. Vol. 55 Iss. 3
2. Walter Beaudette (Fr.) at the Front, WWI
   Wisconsin Magazine of History. Madison WI: Spring 1996. Vol. 79 Iss. 3

A search for the locality of Jackson County, Ohio returned 380 results. The first three were:

1. Jackson newspaper excerpts, 1894–1957
   Researcher. Jackson OH: Jun 2005. Vol. 13 Iss. 2
2. County creeks overview, n.d.
   Researcher. Jackson OH: Mar 2005. Vol. 13 Iss. 1
3. Dr. D.A. Hoffman reminiscences of old settlers, 1820s–1860s
   Researcher. Jackson OH: Mar 2005. Vol. 13 Iss. 1

When a researcher locates an article, he or she can check local libraries for the periodical. Because many of these small journals are not widely available, researchers may have difficulty locating some of them. In these cases, researchers can send a photocopy request to the Allen County Public Library. There is information about this service on the ACPL Web site, http://www.acpl.lib.in.us/genealogy/persi.html.

REFERENCES

Allen County Public Library. "Allen County Public Library: Genealogy," http://www.acpl.lib.in.us/genealogy/persi.html (accessed August 1, 2007).

Allen County Public Library. *Periodical Source Index*. Fort Wayne, IN: Allen County Public Library Foundation, 1986.

Blum, Isidor. *The Jews of Baltimore: An Historical Summary of their Progress and Status as Citizens of Baltimore from Early Days...* Baltimore: Historical Review Pub. Co., 1910.

Brigham Young University. "Family History Archive," http://www.lib.byu.edu/fhc/ (accessed August 1, 2007).

Brooklyn Daily Eagle Online. "Historic Newspaper: Brooklyn Daily Eagle Online (1841–1902)," http://www.brooklynpubliclibrary.org/eagle/ (accessed August 1, 2007).

Family History Library. http://www.familysearch.org (accessed August 13, 2007).

GenealogyBank. "GenealogyBank.com: Find Ancestors/Family History Records," http://www.genealogybank.com/gbnk/keyword.html (accessed August 1, 2007).

"Growth of Chicago: What Is Shown by New City Directory," *Chicago Tribune*, July 22, 1892.

Hiatt, Cora Chenoweth. *History of the Chenoweth Family, Beginning 449 A.D.*. Winchester, IN: Winchester Pub. Co., 1925.

The Lakeside Annual Directory of the City of Chicago. Chicago: Chicago Directory Co., 1875.

Newberry Library. "Newberry Library: Genealogy Collections," http://newberry.org/genealogy/collections.html (accessed August 14, 2007).

New England Historic Genealogical Society. *The New England Historical and Genealogical Register*. Boston: S.G. Drake, 1847.

New York Times. "The New York Times: Breaking News, World News & Multimedia," http://nytimes.com/ (accessed August 1, 2007).

"Obituary." *Chicago Daily News*, July 10, 1931.

Ohio Genealogical Society. *Jackson County, Ohio: History and Families, 175th Anniversary, 1816–1991*. Paducah, KY: Pub. Co., 1991.

Otto Tischer Dead; Veteran of Civil War." *Chicago Tribune*, July 9, 1931.

"ProQuest," http://www.proquest.com/ (accessed August 1, 2007).

ProQuest Information and Learning Co. "ProQuest Historical Newspapers," http://hn.umi.com/pqdweb?RQT=306&TS=1026331051 (accessed August 1, 2007).

Smith, Percy. *Notable Men of Pittsburgh and Vicinity*. Pittsburgh: Pittsburgh Print. Co., 1901.

Swedish Pioneer Historical Society. *The Swedish Pioneer Historical Quarterly*. Chicago: Swedish Pioneer Historical Society, 1950.

Towne Family Association. *About Towne*. Asheville, NC: Towne Family Association, 1981.

Uniontown (Fayette County, Pa.) City Directory. Boston: R.L. Polk & Co., 1923.

"U.S. Newspaper Program," http://www.neh.gov/projects/usnp.html (accessed August 1, 2007).

Williamson County Historical Society (Williamson County, Ill.). *Footprints in Williamson County, Illinois*. Marion, IL: Williamson County Historical Society, 1998.

6

Basic Archival Sources

This chapter presents three more valuable types of genealogical sources: church, cemetery, and military records.

CHURCH RECORDS

Church records are an important source for birth, marriage, and death information and provide an alternative to civil vital records. They are sometimes difficult to locate; researchers typically need to know the denomination their ancestors belonged to and then must determine the congregation they attended before finding the records. Not all denominations place the same importance on record-keeping, so church records range from the detailed vital records kept by many Roman Catholic churches to the sparse membership records of some Protestant congregations. Although church research can be difficult, it is often rewarding; a church record of a baptism or burial might provide information that is otherwise difficult or impossible to find.

The first step in locating church records is to determine which congregation your ancestors attended. Other documents may answer this question. For example, civil marriage records typically record the minister who performed the ceremony, and a city directory for the year of the marriage will usually indicate which church the minister led. An obituary will usually tell where a memorial service was held, which might be the congregation the deceased attended.

To locate a church record of the marriage of Ella Palma Tischer and Adolphus Beaudette, I first used the Illinois marriage index to locate a civil marriage record from Cook County. I obtained the civil marriage record, and it indicated that the marriage was held at Wicker Park Methodist Episcopal Church. I searched for records of this church in the catalog of the Family History Library (FHL) in Salt Lake City and found the following record:

Title:	Church records, 1881–1935
Authors:	Wicker Park Methodist Episcopal Church (Chicago, Illinois) (main author)
Notes:	Microreproduction of original manuscripts at the Northern Illinois Conference, United Methodist Church, Evanston, Illinois
Physical:	On one microfilm reel; 35 mm
Film Notes:	
Statistical record	
Record of official members:	1912–1913, 1923
Alphabetical record:	1887–1903
Members in full connection:	1891–1895
Alphabetical record of members ca.	1887–1904
Record of probationers:	1881–1904
Record of marriages:	1887–1904
Record of baptisms:	1887–1904
Record of official members:	1888–1897
Pastoral and statistical record (financial data)	
FHL US/CAN Film [1927962 Item 5]	

I borrowed a copy of the microfilm from the FHL (see Chapter Ten for more information about this process). The microfilmed ledger record (Fig. 6.1) shows that Adolphus Beaudette and Ella Tischer were married in the church on August 19, 1891. It gives their ages, addresses, and the name of the minister but does not provide any other information.

In contrast, consider the 1829 marriage of David Simpson in the Parish of Kirkcaldy, Church of Scotland. I found this record through an index of parish records in Scotland. The marriage records the names of the bride and groom, the name of each party's father, and the home parish of each father (fig. 6.2). Although this particular example is from Scotland, many American congregations kept similar records at that time.

Researchers who are unable to locate referring information from a civil record or other source can look geographically for churches near their ancestors' homes. For rural ancestors, this might not be difficult; a small town might only have one or two churches of a particular denomination. To find what church records exist for a rural area, researchers can search the library catalog of the FHL.

202 VI. RECORD OF MARRIAGES.

Figure 6.1. Winter-Beaudette marriage record from Wicker Park Methodist Episcopal Church.

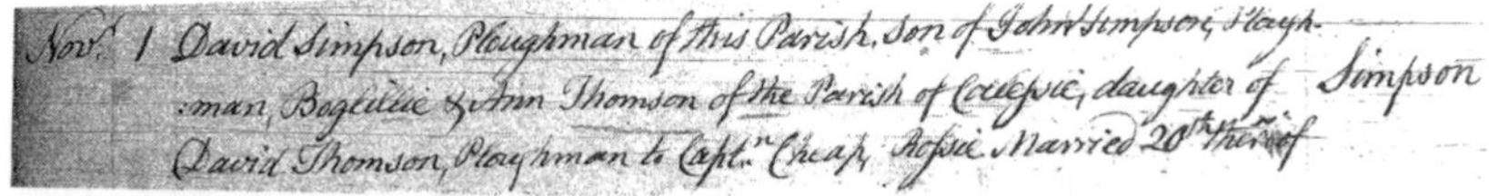
Nov.r 1 David Simpson, Ploughman of this Parish, Son of John Simpson, Plough- Simpson
-man, Bogellie & Ann Thomson of the Parish of Collessie, daughter of
David Thomson, Ploughman to Capt.n Cheap, Rossie. Married 20th thereof

Figure 6.2. Simpson-Thomson marriage record, Parish of Kirkcaldy, Church of Scotland.

Locating the right congregation is more difficult in an urban area because there might be many churches of a particular denomination. Researchers can survey the existing churches of a particular year by checking a city directory for that year. They might find churches that are close to the address that their ancestors lived and then search for that church in the FHL catalog. This is a painstaking process, however.

If the FHL does not hold films of the records, researchers might search to see whether the church still exists using the yellow pages or Internet search engines. If the congregation is still active, they might contact the church to see whether it holds its historical records, or the church could direct researchers to the repository where the records are kept.

Alternatively, researchers might start by contacting church archives. Catholic archdioceses often have a historical archive or records center, and many Protestant congregations have nationwide historical repositories. Elizabeth Crabtree Wells' chapter on church records in the third and most recent edition of *The Source* lists major American religious archives.

CEMETERY RECORDS

Genealogy researchers are typically interested in finding where their ancestors are buried. For many genealogists, finding graves is part of a memorializing element of genealogy; finding places where ancestors are buried fulfills an emotional need to remember them. Beyond the desire to memorialize ancestors, genealogists use cemeteries as a source of information. There are two kinds of records available at cemeteries. First, most cemeteries have gravestones or other markers with information. Because people are often buried in family plots, finding an ancestor's grave marker often reveals collateral information about other family members. Second, some cemeteries keep paper records, including ledgers of burial records and plot purchases.

The first step in locating this information is to determine which cemetery an ancestor is buried in. Unfortunately, for most localities, there is no cross-index of burials. There is no database of people buried in Chicago, for example, so researchers need to cull burial information from other sources.

Generally, civil death records give the place of burial. For example, the 1917 death certificate of John W. Simpson (the Civil War veteran) shows that he is buried in Fairmount Cemetery, Jackson County, Ohio. His son, John W. Simpson, died in Uniontown, Pennsylvania, in 1924. The son's death certificate's burial information is difficult to decipher. "Wheeling, W. Vir" is clearly written in the box labeled "Place of Burial or Removal" and then crossed out. It appears that an illegible location ending in "Ohio" (possibly Jackson) has been written in correction.

Obituaries are another good source of information about burials. For example, Otto Tischer's obituary indicates that his services were held at Graceland Cemetery in Chicago and that he was cremated. The younger John Simpson's obituary indicates that interment would be in Wheeling, West Virginia, but a cemetery was not named.

There are some helpful online resources for locating what cemeteries exist in a particular locality. The Geographic Names Information System is a geographical database maintained by the U.S. Department of the Interior. It records names and locations of geographical features in the United States, including cemeteries. The database is freely available online at http://geonames.usgs.gov/pls/gnispublic.

Researchers can search for all of the cemeteries in a particular county using the database. A search of the database for Cemeteries in Jackson County, Ohio returns 119 results. The database gives the names of the cemeteries and their exact longitude and latitude but otherwise does not give information about the cemeteries.

FindAGrave (http://www.findagrave.com) is a popular Web site for cemetery research. This Web site began as a hobbyist site for sharing photographs and information about famous burial sites but has grown to become a major source of information on cemeteries across the United States. For example, a search for Fairmount Cemetery in Jackson County, Ohio, returns a page with a map of the cemetery location, a photograph of the cemetery, and 141 user-submitted entries on individuals buried there. Unfortunately, John Simpson was not among those submitted. For the famous individuals in our case studies, there is more information on the site. Coleman Young's FindAGrave entry includes a photograph of his grave marker, which is inscribed with the names of his parents, the political offices he held and his unit from World War II. There is no photograph for Stanley Kubrick, but his entry indicates that he is buried at Childwickbury Manor, Hertfordshire, England.

USGenWeb, the cooperative genealogy Web site, is also worth searching when researching cemeteries. USGenWeb has a page for every state and every county, and the county pages often include cemetery directories or transcriptions. For example, the page for Jackson County, Ohio (http://www.rootsweb.com/~ohjackso/jackson.htm) contains a link to a transcription of burials in Fairmount Cemetery, the burial location listed on the death certificate for the elder John William Simpson. The cemetery transcription, on the Jackson County government Web site, http://www.jacksonohio.us, lists John W. Simpson:

Name	Burial Date	Section	Space
Simpson John W.	1917 Mar 28	N 1/2 Lot 59 Sec J	1st on West Line

A few lines down, a Martha Simpson is listed:

Simpson Martha E.	1933 Sep 6	N 1/2 59 Sec J	2nd from West Line

Given that I knew that John's wife was named Martha, and because this Martha is buried next to John, I can assume they are one and the same.

There are also many print resources for cemetery research. Many genealogy societies have published gravestone transcriptions. Typically, these works are cataloged with subject headings:

- (Locality) - genealogy
- cemeteries - (Locality)

For major urban cemeteries, historical and descriptive books often exist. For example, Barbara Lanctot's *A Walk Through Graceland Cemetery* (1988) describes the cemetery where Otto Tischer was memorialized and cremated. The book does not list individual burials, except of famous individuals or people with notable grave markers.

Visiting a cemetery to view grave markers and look for paper records is often worthwhile, but cemeteries are idiosyncratic, so researchers should be prepared for a variety of possibilities. Some cemeteries are well maintained, and some are abandoned. Some have friendly services for researchers, whereas others do not welcome genealogists. Tracking down cemetery records requires some patience but can be very rewarding.

MILITARY RECORDS

At various points in American history, conflicts drew many citizens into the military. The records of their service are a major source for genealogical information. The records documenting each conflict are complex and distinct.

The American Revolution

Many ancestors of modern-day Americans were not involved in the American Revolution because they were busy raising sheep in rural Ireland or fishing in the Mediterranean. In other words, the bulk of immigration to the United States occurred after the Revolutionary period, so a low percentage of our ancestors were in North America in 1776. Although revolutionary records cover a small group in comparison with later conflicts (especially the Civil War), participation in the Revolution is a popular topic for genealogical inquiry.

Three sets of records are good starting points for researching soldiers in the Revolution: military service records, pension records, and bounty land records. Service records record some basic information about each soldier, including the unit served in, birthplace and date, rank achieved, and dates of service. An index to these records was microfilmed by the National Archives, and National Historical Publishing published a print index by Virgil White in 1995, entitled *Index to Revolutionary War Service Records.*

After the Revolution, some veterans received a pension, whereas others chose to be paid for their service with bounty land. The pension and bounty land records are indexed by microfilms M805 and M804 from the National Archives. HeritageQuest Online has an online index to these records, and a print index by Virgil White was published by National Historical Publishing in 1990. Once a record is identified in an index, researchers can request copies of the full pension or bounty record using the National Archives and Record Administration (NARA)'s online request form, http://www.archives.gov/research/order/orderonline.html, or by mailing NATF form 85 to the Archives (the Archives will mail researchers a form if requested).

Civil War

Americans are likely to have ancestors who fought in the Civil War. A huge number of Americans participated in the conflict, and there are well-kept records on both Union and Confederate soldiers.

Civil War Soldiers and Sailors System (CWSSS)

A basic starting source for Civil War genealogical research is the CWSSS, an online database maintained by the National Park Service, http://www.itd.nps.gov/cwss/.

The CWSSS compiles rosters of both Union and Confederate sources and is a first step in researching a soldier. It indicates which unit the soldier served in, which is a basic piece of information for further research.

Union Service and Pension Records

The U.S. Government created two sets of records on soldiers of great genealogical interest: military service records and pension records.

Military service records document what soldiers did during the war: the battles they fought in, the ranks they achieved, the injuries they sustained, and other details of their service. Once you have determined what unit a soldier served in, you can request the military service record from the National Archives in Washington, DC. Researchers can request copies using NARA's online request form, http://www.archives.gov/research/order/orderonline.html, or by mailing NATF form 86 to the Archives (the Archives will mail researchers a form if requested). For more information about the ordering these records, visit the NARA Web site, http://www.archives.gov/genealogy/military/civil-war/index.html.

For genealogical research, a soldier's pension file is often more useful than his service record. A Union soldier received a pension for the rest of his life that could be passed on to his widow. The pension file is an unusually valuable genealogy record because it traces a veteran and his widow forward from the 1860s for the rest of their lives, documenting when they moved, their marriages, medical information, and death information.

The National Archives has a microfilmed index to the pension files, *Microfilm T288, General Index to Pension Files*. The index is also available on Ancestry.com. The index is searchable by the name of a veteran or the name of his spouse. Once a researcher obtains an entry from the index, he or she can obtain the pension file from the National Archives in Washington, DC. Researchers can request copies using NARA's online request form, http://www.archives.gov/research/order/orderonline.html, or by mailing NATF form 85 to the Archives.

Unfortunately, the high cost of copies of the pension records may dissuade beginners from seeking them out; at the time of writing, the Archives charges $125 for a complete file. That is a shame, because as you can see from the Otto Tischer and John Simpson case studies, the pension files are an unusually rich source of information.

Confederate Service and Pension Records

After the Civil War, the official service records of the Confederate Army were preserved and are now held by the National Archives. The process of searching for these records is similar to that of Union soldiers. To find a soldier's unit, the first place to check is the Soldiers and Sailors System online. Once a record is found in CWSSS, researchers can request a copy of the service record from the National Archives using the online ordering system or by sending in NATF Form 86. Certain states also kept service records of soldiers from the war; the respective state archives of the former confederate states are the best place to research these records. Confederate soldiers did not receive Federal pensions, but some states did issue pensions.

1890 Veteran's Schedule of the Census

In 1890, the U.S. Census included a special schedule for veterans and their widows. Although most of the 1890 census was destroyed in a fire, the Veteran's Schedule remains for the following states: Kentucky (part), Louisiana, Maine, Maryland, Massachusetts, Michigan, Minnesota, Mississippi, Missouri, Montana, Nebraska, Nevada, New Hampshire, New Jersey, New Mexico, New York, North Carolina, North Dakota, Ohio, Oklahoma and Indian Territories, Oregon, Pennsylvania, Rhode Island, South Carolina, South Dakota, Tennessee, Texas, Utah, Vermont, Virginia, Washington, West Virginia, Wisconsin, and Wyoming. The schedule records basic information about the service of veterans, including the units they served in.

Regimental Histories

Many Civil War units have been described in unit histories. For example, one of my predecessors at the Newberry Library, the late David Thackery, wrote a history of the Sixty-Sixth Ohio Volunteer Infantry (Thackery, 1999). The best bibliography of regimental histories is Charles E. Dornbusch's *Regimental Publications and Personal Narratives of the Civil War* (1961). Given the popularity of this genre, though, new regimental publications appear every year.

Researchers will also find brief unit histories for Union regiments in Frederick Dyer's *A Compendium of the War of the Rebellion*, originally published in 1908. Dyer's histories are also available online at http://www.civilwararchive.com/.

Memorials and Reunions

After the Civil War, soldiers on both sides memorialized the conflict with reunions, monuments, and veterans' organizations. For Union soldiers, the Grand Army of the Republic (GAR) was the largest veterans' organization. GAR posts published rosters and memorial books, and genealogists have compiled statewide indexes of GAR records. These organizational records provide another source of information on Civil War soldiers. On the confederate side, the United Confederate Veterans was similar to the GAR. *The Confederate Veteran*, a monthly published from 1893–1932, is a good source for information of veterans; Broadfoot Publishing issued a name index to the entire run in 1986.

Two Civil War Case Studies: John Simpson and Otto Tischer

John Simpson

I believed that my great-great-grandfather, John Simpson, was a Civil War soldier, but I had trouble finding him in the Soldiers and Sailors system because there were too many other soldiers with the same name. I knew that he was from Ohio, but I did not find a clear match in searches of that state's soldiers.

Luckily, the 1890 Veteran's Schedule for Ohio was preserved. I searched this schedule years before Ancestry indexed and digitized it, but it was not difficult. There were only a limited number of veterans in Jackson County, Ohio, and it was not hard to browse the county until I found John Simpson (fig. 6.3).

The census showed that he served as a private in Company F of the 2nd Maryland Infantry. This surprised me; I knew he lived in Ohio after the war and assumed that he had served from an Ohio unit. I checked the Soldiers and Sailors System again, and found a John W. Simpson who served as a private in the 2nd Potomac Home Brigade, Maryland Infantry.

Dyer's *Compendium* gives a brief history of the 2nd Potomac Home Brigade. Its primary duty during the war was guarding the Baltimore and Ohio railroad. The

Special Schedule.—Surviving Soldiers, Sailors, and Marines, and Widows, etc.

S. D.: 4 ; E. D.: 105 ; Minor Civil Division: — Page 7

Line	House No. (1)	Family No. (2)	Names of Surviving Soldiers, Sailors, and Marines, and Widows (3)	Rank (4)	Company (5)	Name of Regiment or Vessel (6)	Date of Enlistment (7)	Date of Discharge (8)	Length of Service Yrs. (9)	Mos.	Days
27	324	327	[illegible] widow of George W. Smedley	P	G.	193 O.V.I.	20 Feb. 186[illegible]	18 Dec. 186[illegible]		9	28
28	326	329	Oliver Hiram	P.	H.	91 O.V.I.	14 Aug. 1862	24 Aug. 1864	2	9	15
29	3[illegible]	332	~~Young George W.~~	P.	[illegible] Artillery (Va)		15 June 1861	Apl. 186[illegible]	3	6	
30	332	335	Snyder Theodore C.	P.	I	78 Pa. Inf.	16 Sept. 1861	4 Nov. 1864	3	1	8
31	332	335	Snyder Theodore C.	P.	K.	100 Pa. Inf.	3 Feb. 1863	24 July 1864	1	5	21
32	337	340	Simpson John W.	P.	F.	2 Md. Inf.	28 Aug. 1861	24 Aug. 1864	3	0	0
33	342	345	Hommes John W.	P	K	63 O.V.I.	4 Jan. 1862	186			
34	340	343	Hommes John W.	P	B.	12 O. Cav.	186	186			
35	342	345	McGinnis Thomas B.	P.	K	4 W. Va. Inf.	July 1861	Sept. 1862	1	2	
36	342	345	McGinnis Thomas B.	P.	A.	7 W. Va. Inf.	Dec. 1862	July 1865	2	6	
37	349	352	Ray David	P	C.	33 O.V.I.	10 Aug. 1861	1 Sept. 1864	3		2[illegible]
38	353	356	Howe Jefferson	P.	I	18 O.V.I.	24 Apl. 1861	28 Aug. 1861		4	4
39	353	356	Howe Jefferson	Corp.	H.	2 W. Va. Cav.	1 Sept. 1861	21 Nov. 1863	2	2	20
40	353	356	Howe Jefferson	Sergt.	C.	2 W. Va. Cav.	22 Nov. 1863	17 June 1865	1	6	21

Line	Post-Office Address (10)	Disability Incurred (11)	Remarks (12)
27	Coalton, Ohio	Catarrh of head.	
28	Coalton, Ohio	Wounded in left arm and right foot.	
29	Jackson, Ohio		
30	Jackson, O.	Wounded in left hip.	
31	Jackson, Ohio	Dyspepsia and Scurvy.	
32	Jackson, Ohio	Crippled left foot resulting from Typhoid fever.	
33	Jackson, Ohio	Eyes effected.	
34	Jackson, Ohio		
35	Jackson, Ohio	Wounded left foot, breast, right hand	
36	Jackson, Ohio,		
37	Jackson, Ohio	Wounded in right leg.	
38	Jackson, O.	Piles and Throat Trouble	
39	" "		
40	" "		

Figure 6.3. John Simpson in the Veteran's Schedule of the 1890 Census. U.S. Federal Census, 1890. Veteran's Schedule. 1890; Census place: Coal, Jackson, Ohio; roll, 68; page, 7; enumeration district, 105.

history notes that Company F was involved in skirmishes at Perryville and Point of Rocks, Maryland in June 1863.

Knowing the unit he served with, I requested a copy of his military service record from the National Archives. The service record showed that he mustered in to "Lieut. Summer's Co., 2 Reg't Potomac Home Brigade Vols" on August 31, 1861, near Hancock, Maryland. The rest of the record is a series of muster cards showing when he was present for duty. For much of the war, he was reported "absent in hospital" in Sandy Hook, Maryland. Yet, he appeared to be present during the fighting at Perryville and Point of Rocks mentioned in Dyer's unit history.

I also searched for a pension record for John Simpson. I started by searching the index to pensions at Ancestry.com, searching on "John Simpson" with a widow "Martha." I located an index entry for John Simpson's record, and this allowed me to order the original pension file from the National Archives. The record is very lengthy, over 100 pages. It primarily consists of correspondence between Simpson and the Bureau of Pensions, with Simpson submitting affidavits to prove that he injured his left leg during the war and that he only had one wife. The bulk of the affidavits are medical reports from doctors confirming the injury to his leg, but the file also provided me with information I did not otherwise know. In an affidavit submitted in 1881, he recorded the places he lived throughout his life. He describes what he did in the years before the war: "four years in Fayette Co. Penn hauling cord wood and working in coaling."

An 1885 affidavit by A. S. Gallion, a fellow soldier in Company F, records the circumstances where John Simpson took ill. "(W)hile my company was stationed at Harper's Ferry West Va (we had no tents they having been captured from us at Charlestown W. Va) we were exposed to the weather for some time during which time from exposure said Simpson contracted Typhoid fever and he was sent to the Hospital near Sandy Hook Maryland." Other affidavits gave the exact date of his marriage to Martha Leach, the names and birth dates of his children, and a copy of his death certificate.

Otto Tischer

According to Otto Tischer's obituary, he served in Company C, 35th New Jersey State Volunteers. When I checked the Soldiers and Sailors System, though, I did not find an Otto Tischer or Tisher. Because I knew this name is often mangled, I entered "Otto Fischer" and found him listed under that name. Despite this, the National Archives was unable to locate a service record for him.

Although I was unable to find a service record, I did find him listed in the pension index under his real name. I was able to obtain his pension record. Like John Simpson's pension, Otto's file was large and consisted mostly of correspondence regarding medical benefits. It also provided some valuable genealogical information that would be difficult to discover otherwise. It recorded the date and place of his marriage to Clara Von Obstfelder: Nov. 20, 1867, in Chicago. This information is difficult to locate otherwise because all of the official marriage records from Chicago were destroyed in the fire of 1871. Most interestingly, the file contains a 1925 photograph of the elderly Otto Tischer, posed by an automobile at what appears to be the

Chicago waterfront. His doctor enclosed the picture to illustrate Otto's withered right hand.

The pension record also contains a letter from Otto to the Bureau of Pensions explaining why his name was confused in the official records of the war. He wrote:

> *... at the first Alphabetical Roll Call at Trenton, New Jersey, the name of Otto Fischer was called three (3) times, I did not answer as there were some "Bounty Jumpers." I wanted to have my name correct, at the end of the Roll Call the officers stuck their heads together exchanging their ideas of what had become of Otto Fischer and suppose came to the conclusion that he had "jumped." I then stepped in front of the line and saluted, being asked if I wanted to say something, I stated that my name was not called that my name was Otto Tischer that the name of Otto Fischer was called but that was not my name - you should have seen how their faces brightened up, finding nobody was missing - but I was ordered and as a soldier of course had to obey, to answer to the name of Otto Fischer, until correction could be made, which seems to have been done only in some books...*

Later Conflicts

It often surprises researchers to learn that soldiers in the World Wars and later conflicts are more difficult to research than participants in the Civil War. There are several reasons for this. First, a major fire in a National Archives repository destroyed 80% of the Army service records for soldiers discharged between 1912 and 1960 and a number of other military personnel records from that period. Second, privacy concerns limit access to records of recent conflicts.

Recently, some major record sets have become accessible. Draft records from the First World War were microfilmed by the National Archives and are now available through Ancestry. These records do not give information about military service, and many men recorded in the draft records did not serve. Nevertheless, these records provide some valuable information about men of military age during the First World War. In the case study of Coleman Young, his father's draft card provided information that helped identify his parents and town of origin.

The National Archives recently released a database of World War II Enlistment Records, available as part of the Access to Archival Databases system, http://aad.archives.gov/aad/. A search for Coleman Young located his record, showing some basic information (fig. 6.4).

Nevertheless, finding detailed information about these conflicts can be difficult. The Web site of the National Archives provides good information about researching these conflicts, http://www.archives.gov/genealogy/military/.

There are also several good books on 20th century military research. *How to Locate Anyone Who Is or Has Been in the Military* by Richard S. Johnson and Debra Knox (1999) is a useful guide for 20th century research. *U.S. Military Records: A Guide to Federal and State Sources, Colonial America to the Present.* (Neagles, 1994) provides a broader look at military sources.

Field Title	Meaning
ARMY SERIAL NUMBER	3.6E+07
NAME	YOUNG#COLEMAN#A#########
RESIDENCE: STATE	MICHIGAN
RESIDENCE: COUNTY	WAYNE
PLACE OF ENLISTMENT	FT CUSTER MICHIGAN
DATE OF ENLISTMENT DAY	3
DATE OF ENLISTMENT MONTH	2
DATE OF ENLISTMENT YEAR	42
GRADE: ALPHA DESIGNATION	Private
GRADE: CODE	Private
BRANCH: ALPHA DESIGNATION	Branch Immaterial - Warrant Officers, USA
BRANCH: CODE	Branch Immaterial - Warrant Officers, USA
FIELD USE AS DESIRED	#
TERM OF ENLISTMENT	Enlistment for the duration of the War or other emergency, plus six months, subject to the discretion of the President or otherwise according to law
LONGEVITY	###
SOURCE OF ARMY PERSONNEL	Civil Life
NATIVITY	ALABAMA
YEAR OF BIRTH	18
RACE AND CITIZENSHIP	Negro, citizen
EDUCATION	4 years of high school
CIVILIAN OCCUPATION	MILLWRIGHT
MARITAL STATUS	Single, without dependents
COMPONENT OF THE ARMY	Selectees (Enlisted Men)
CARD NUMBER	#
BOX NUMBER	1041
FILM REEL NUMBER	5.103

Figure 6.4. Coleman Young's Army enlistment record from the National Archives Database.

REFERENCES

Church of Scotland, Parish Church of Kirkcaldy (Fifeshire). *Old Parochial Registers for Kirkcaldy, 1614–1867* (Salt Lake City, UT: Genealogical Society of Utah, 1951–1979), microfilm of original records in the New Register House, Edinburgh, FHL BRITISH film 1040187.

Confederated Southern Memorial Association (U.S.). *Confederate Veteran*. Nashville: S.A. Cunningham, 1893.

Dornbusch, C. *Regimental Publications and Personal Narratives of the Civil War: A Checklist*. New York: New York Public Library, 1961.

Dyer, Frederick. *A Compendium of the War of the Rebellion*. New York: T. Yoseloff, 1959.

"Find A Grave-Millions of Cemetery Records," http://www.findagrave.com/ (accessed August 13, 2007).

General Index to Pension Files, 1861–1934 T288. Washington, DC: National Archives and Records Service, 1993.

Index to Revolutionary War Service Records. Waynesboro, TN: National Historical Publishing Co., 1995.

"Jackson County Ohio (USGenWeb)," http://www.rootsweb.com/~ohjackso/jackson.htm (accessed August 13, 2007).

Johnson, Richard. *How to Locate Anyone Who Is or Has Been In the Military: Armed Forces Locator Guide*. Spartanburg, SC: MIE Publishing, 1999.

Lanctot, Barbara, and Chicago Architecture Foundation. *A Walk Through Graceland Cemetery*. Chicago: Chicago Architecture Foundation, 1988.

Manarin, Louis. *Cumulative Index, the Confederate Veteran Magazine, 1893–1932*. Wilmington, NC: Broadfoot Publishing Co., 1986.

National Archives and Records Administration. Office of Records Services, Washington, DC. Modern Records Programs. Electronic and Special Media Records Services Division. *World War II Army Enlistment Records, 1938 – 1946*. Washington, DC: National Archives, 1998–.

National Park Service. "Civil War Soldiers and Sailor System," http://www.itd.nps.gov/cwss/ (accessed August 13, 2007).

Neagles, James. *U.S. Military Records: A Guide to Federal and State Sources, Colonial America to the Present*. Salt Lake City: Ancestry, 1994.

Szucs, Loretto. *The Source: A Guidebook to American Genealogy*. Provo, UT: Ancestry, 2006.

Thackery, David. *A Light and Uncertain Hold: A History of the Sixty-sixth Ohio Volunteer Infantry*. Kent, OH: Kent State University Press, 1999.

United States Geographic Survey. "Geographic Names Information System," http://geonames.usgs.gov/pls/gnispublic/ (accessed August 13, 2007).

United States Census Office. *Eleventh Census of the United States, 1890 Schedules Enumerating Union Veterans and Widows of Union Veterans of the Civil War: Ohio*. Washington, DC: United States Census Office, 1890.

White, Virgil. *Genealogical Abstracts of Revolutionary War Pension Files*. Waynesboro TN: National Historical Publishing Co., 1990.

Wicker Park Methodist Episcopal Church (Chicago, Illinois). Church Records. *Microfilm of Original Manuscripts at the Northern Illinois Conference, United Methodist Church, Evanston, Illinois* (Salt Lake City: Genealogical Society of Utah, 1994), FHL US/CAN film 1927962 item 5.

7

Immigration Records

"Where did my ancestors live before they came to the United States?"

Answering this question is the primary goal of many genealogy researchers. There are two major groups of documents that help answer this question: ship passenger lists and naturalization records. In this chapter, we will examine both kinds of records and will also suggest some alternative sources for information.

PRELIMINARY RESEARCH

Before searching for immigration and naturalization documents, researchers should cull clues about immigration from the documents mentioned in earlier chapters. The U.S. Census is particularly useful. In the years 1900–1930, the census asked immigrants the year that they arrived in the United States and their naturalization status. The answers to these questions help researchers narrow their search. The town of origin for a person is sometimes recorded on death records or in an obituary, so these sources are also worth exploring before searching for immigration documents.

PASSENGER LISTS

Passenger lists record the passengers on board a particular ocean-crossing vessel. These lists are also referred to as *manifests*. The availability of passenger lists varies by port and time period. Researchers will find that the passenger arrival records for New Orleans are different from those for New York, and records from the 1860s are unlike those from the 1920s. Understanding a rough outline of passenger ship records by time period is helpful in directing researchers.

- Colonial era: 1820

  In this early period of immigration, passenger lists were fairly spare; they did not record a great deal of information about the immigrants. Many of the manifests from this era have been lost or destroyed. Therefore, researching during this time period is hit-or-miss.

However, because this era has been thoroughly researched by generations of genealogists, what information exists has been fairly well transcribed and indexed.

- 1820–1880

  More manifests exist from this time period, and many were preserved and microfilmed by the National Archives. The records tend to be somewhat sparse in the information they provide, usually listing the passenger, name, age, and country of origin. Many of these records were indexed in print publications and microfilm or are available digitally through Ancestry.com and other Web sites.
- 1880–1957

  For this period, detailed manifests exist for most U.S. ports. Many of the records are available digitally through commercial and free Web sites. Passenger lists in this period became increasingly detailed, often listing the passenger's birthplace, final U.S. destination, and sometimes the address of an American relative.

For the post-1820 era, researchers can see the original passenger lists on microfilm. The National Archives' Web site lists what records are available on microfilm: http://www.archives.gov/genealogy/immigration/passenger-arrival.html#film.

These are the original lists of passenger arrival, organized by port, date, and ship. Researchers can use these microfilm at branches of the National Archives or can borrow them through the Family History Library (FHL). The original lists are organized by date and are often difficult to read, so researchers are better off starting with a passenger list index, when possible.

Passenger List Indexes

Many overlapping passenger indexes exist in print, microfilm, and online. When searching for an immigrant ancestor, it is worth checking multiple indexes because sometimes the indexing of a particular passenger record will vary. The following indexes, organized in a rough chronology of the time periods they cover, are some of the most useful.

Passenger and Immigration Lists Index (Filby and Meyer, 1981)

This set of indexes, published periodically, extracts passenger information from passenger lists transcribed in secondary books or journals. For example, if a genealogical journal publishes a transcription of the ship *Majestic*, which arrived in Boston in 1827, the Filby and Meyer *Index* will extract the name of the passengers and other details and include them in their index. Researchers who are looking for a particular passenger but do not know the exact date or the ship name can look in Filby and Meyer, which will direct them to the relevant print source describing the passenger arrival. This index is now available as a database on Ancestry. It is especially useful for finding immigrant ancestors before the mass immigration of the late 19th century. It rounds up many of the scattered records of earlier ship arrivals. Researchers are sometimes confused because it directs them to a secondary print resource rather than an original list, so it often requires some explanation for novice genealogy patrons.

Ethnic Passenger Lists

There are a number of ethnicity-specific passenger list indexes. The best known of this genre is *Germans to America*, which indexes German names from the lists of heavily German shipping routes for the period 1840–1900. Similar works include *Italians to America*, *Migration from the Russian Empire*, and *The Famine Immigrants* (which covers Irish immigrants). These works share the problem of most genealogical indexes; they are not complete, and they contain errors. However, they offer a good starting place for genealogists researching immigrant ancestors. If you know your great-great-grandfather emigrated from Germany in 1868, but you do not know the port or the exact year, browsing the volumes of *Germans to America* for that period is a good starting step. Many of these works overlap with other indexes; researchers will find some passengers listed in both *Germans to America* and the Ellis Island database described below. Because of the difficulty of transcribing handwritten manifests, duplicate indexing benefits researchers. A name indexed with one spelling on *Germans to America* may be transcribed differently on the Ellis Island Web site, and researchers should consult both. These indexes are now available on the Web site of the National Archives at http://aad.archives.gov/aad.

Castle Garden and Ellis Island Indexes

Castle Garden and Ellis Island were arrival stations for international passengers traveling to New York City. Castle Garden was active from 1855–1890, and Ellis Island served from 1892–1954. Indexes to records from both locations are freely available on the Internet. Because New York is the country's major port of arrival, these databases are very useful.

The Ellis Island index, http://www.ellisisland.org, is the much larger of the two (it contains about 22.5 million records, about twice as many as the Castle Garden), and more widely used. The Ellis Island Foundation, in collaboration with the FHL, digitized and indexed Ellis Island passenger arrival records from 1892–1924. Use of the database is free but requires registration. Users can search for a particular passenger name, and the database will return a list of matches. They can then choose to view a digital image of the original manifest, a partial transcription of the list, or an image of the ship.

Novice users often give up on the Ellis Island index before fully exhausting the search possibilities because they do not find results with their initial search. As with census records, spelling variation and indexing errors often distort ancestors' names, causing many basic searches to fail. Currently, the Ellis Island database also has some particular problems that confuse users. Rather than show the entire two-page original manifest, the database generally links only to the second page, which lists information about the passengers but does not show their names. Also, there are many mismatched entries where the database record for a particular passenger is linked to the wrong manifest image.

The genealogist Stephen P. Morse has created tools for navigating the Ellis Island database more easily, available at http://stevemorse.org/. A more user-friendly search interface Morse created allows users to devise more complex searches. By truncating names or searching fields such as age at arrival, year of arrival, and country of origin, users can overcome name variations. Morse also created a tool to browse the Ellis Island manifest images by date of arrival, which allows users to locate passenger manifests that are incorrectly linked.

The Castle Garden database, http://www.castlegarden.org, is smaller than the Ellis Island database and does not link to digitized images. However, it is a large database that covers the Castle Garden era and also includes some earlier and later New York arrival records, including records from 1820–1913.

Passenger Records on Ancestry.com

Ancestry has been aggressively digitizing the microfilmed passenger lists from the National Archives, covering the period of 1820–1957. These records are similar to those included in the Ellis Island database but also cover other ports such as New Orleans, Boston, Philadelphia, and San Francisco.

Foreign Port Departure Records

Some countries kept records of emigrants' departures. For example, records of passengers leaving Sweden were recorded and have been transcribed and released on compact disc. Similar records from Denmark have been placed online by the Danish Emigration Archives, at http://www.emiarch.dk. Also, similar records for emigrants from Finland are available at the Finnish Institute of Migration, at http://www.migrationinstitute.fi. A good overview of such lists is available from the Web site German Roots, at http://home.att.net/~wee-monster/onlinelists.html.

NATURALIZATION RECORDS

Naturalization is the legal process whereby immigrants become citizens. The naturalization process changed over time in the United States; early in the country's history, naturalization was a fairly informal process and produced only cursory documentation. In recent times, naturalizing immigrants were required to file detailed applications at a court. As with passenger records, understanding a rough chronology of naturalization records is useful:

- Colonial Period

  Naturalization was uncommon in this period. British subjects did not need to naturalize when coming to the American colonies. Some non-British immigrants did take an oath of allegiance to the British crown, and scattered records of those oaths exist.
- 1790–1906

  During this period, naturalization records were filed at a local court. Naturalization documents typically recorded the applicant's name, date of birth, port of entry, and date of entry, but documents vary depending on the court. Some courts recorded more information, such as the applicant's place of birth. Women automatically assumed their husband's naturalization status during this period, so few women are well documented in the naturalization records of this era.
- 1906–1922

  In 1906, the Federal government standardized the naturalization process under a new administrative body, the Bureau of Immigration and Naturalization. Naturalization records from this period contain a great deal of information, including place of birth, date of birth, port and date of entry, name of ship, and names of spouses and children.

- 1922–2002

  In 1922, Congress passed a law ending the automatic naturalization of women married to naturalized citizens. This motivated more immigrant women to naturalize than in previous years. Otherwise, the naturalization process remained largely the same until 2002, when immigration and naturalization were placed under the authority of the Department of Homeland Security.

Finding Naturalization Records

Generally, naturalization documents were filed at local courts and are still kept by local courts. Christina Schaefer's *Guide to Naturalization Records of the United States* is an essential reference work for locating where the records of a particular county or state are held. Researchers who are uncertain of the date or place of naturalization are best off starting by searching naturalization indexes.

Currently, there is no national database or index of naturalization records. However, there are many regional indexes to naturalizations in print, on microfilm, or online. The Filby and Meyer *Index* includes some early naturalization records. Other print indexes cover naturalizations for a particular region, such as *Index to Naturalization Records of Bexar County, Texas through 1906*, published by the San Antonio Genealogical Society. The regional branches of the National Archives have some microfilmed naturalization indexes for regional courts. For instance, the National Archives branch in Chicago holds a Soundex index to naturalization petitions for the U.S. district and circuit courts, in northern Illinois for the years 1840–1950. There are a number of naturalization indexes online, some on free sites and others on commercial sites. For example, the Jewish Genealogy Society maintains a database of Brooklyn naturalizations, http://www.jgsny.org/.

IMMIGRATION RESEARCH: THREE CASE STUDIES

Below are three examples from our case studies. In each case, I started with domestic documents (such as vital records and the census) and attempted to trace immigration routes.

Elias Kubrick

In the case study of Stanley Kubrick, I found him living with his parents Jack and Gertrude in the 1930 U.S. Census. Ten years earlier, the census of 1920 shows Jack living with his parents, "Alias" and Rose; their last name is spelled "Kubrik" in that census. The same record shows that Alias Kubrik was born in Austria, arrived in the United States in 1902, and was naturalized in 1911. Going back ten years further, the 1910 census record for the family shows Jack's father listed as "Elias Kubrick" and confirms that he arrived in 1902 and was not yet naturalized. Therefore, before I even began searching for immigration documents, I had the sense that Alias/Elias Kubrik/Kubrick arrived in 1902 and naturalized in 1911.

I started my search for Elias's immigration records by searching the Ellis Island database. My initial search for "Elias Kubrick" showed no results. I tried searching

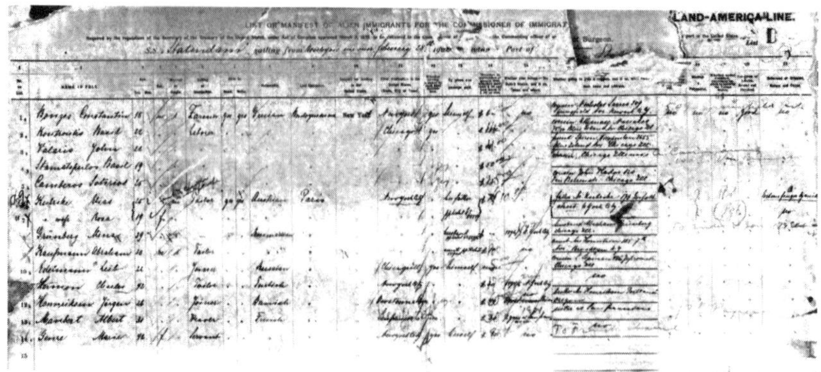
LAND-AMERICA LINE.

Figure 7.1. Passenger arrival for Elias Kubrike. *Passenger and Crew Lists of Vessels Arriving at New York, New York, 1897–1957*; National Archives microfilm roll, T715_258; year, 1902; line, 21.

for all immigrants named "Kubrick," but I only got four results. None had a first name similar to "Elias."

Because I had no quick results using the simple search form, I tried a more complex search on Stephen P. Morse's "One-Step" interface. I searched for a passenger whose first name started with "E" and whose last name sounded like Kubrick, using the "Soundex" option on the last name. Because I had reason to believe Elias arrived in 1902, I limited the search to 1900–1903. This returned 19 records, among them an Elias Kubrike who arrived in 1902. The original manifest image is shown in figure 7.1.

The manifest shows the 25-year-old Elias Kubrike arriving with his wife Rosa, who is 19 years old. They sailed on the *Statendam*, which arrived March 10, 1902, having sailed from Boulogne-sur-Mer, France. Both Elias and Rosa list their nationality as "Austrian" but record Paris as their most recent residence. Elias describes his profession as "tailor." The manifest asks whether the passenger is going to join a relative, and Elias records that he is going to join his father (illegible) Kubrike, who lives at 173 Norfolk, New York City. Under the "deformed or crippled" column, Elias's entry appears to read "lost one finger by accident." Therefore, the passenger list tells us quite a bit about Elias and Rosa. However, it does not list where either of them was born, exactly.

After researching Elias Kubrick's passenger list, I searched for his naturalization record. I started with the Stephen P. Morse Web site. Morse has created a one-step search that queries a set of online naturalization indexes for New York (http://stevemorse.org/natural/naturalization.html), but I did not find a match for a name similar to Elias Kubrik. I then searched Ancestry's immigration and naturalization records and got a hit: an Elias Kubrick is listed in the New York Supreme Court Naturalization Petition Index. The index entry indicates that he submitted a petition on Feb. 10, 1911, which was recorded in volume 24, page 20 of the court's records.

I searched the FHL catalog (http://www.familysearch.org) to see whether the FHL held the New York Supreme Court naturalization records on microfilm. Selecting the "place" search, I chose "New York" as the place and browsed the subject headings. Under the heading "New York, New York: Naturalization and Citizenship," I found

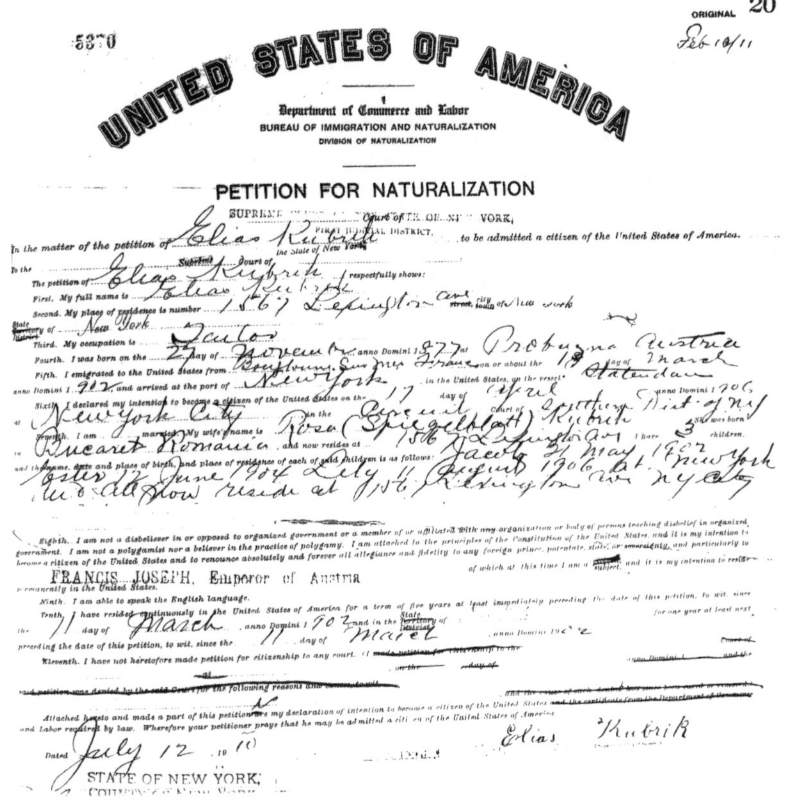

ORIGINAL 20

Feb 10/11

5370

UNITED STATES OF AMERICA

Department of Commerce and Labor
BUREAU OF IMMIGRATION AND NATURALIZATION
DIVISION OF NATURALIZATION

PETITION FOR NATURALIZATION

In the matter of the petition of Elias Kubrik to be admitted a citizen of the United States of America.

To the Supreme Court of the State of New York, First Judicial District.

The petition of Elias Kubrik respectfully shows:

First. My full name is Elias Kubrik

Second. My place of residence is number 1567 Lexington ave street, city of New York, State of New York

Third. My occupation is Tailor

Fourth. I was born on the 27 day of November anno Domini 1877 at Probuzna Austria

Fifth. I emigrated to the United States from Boulogne Sur Mer France on or about the 1? day of March anno Domini 1902, and arrived at the port of New York, in the United States, on the vessel Statendam

Sixth. I declared my intention to become a citizen of the United States on the 17 day of April anno Domini 1906 at New York City in the Circuit Court of Southern Dist of N.Y.

Seventh. I am married. My wife's name is Rosa (Spiegelblatt) Kubrik. She was born in Bucarest Romania, and now resides at 1567 Lexington Ave. I have 3 children, and the name, date and place of birth, and place of residence of each of said children is as follows: Jacob 21 May 1902, Ester 12 June 1904, Lily 11 August 1906 at New York and all now reside at 1567 Lexington Av NY City

Eighth. I am not a disbeliever in or opposed to organized government or a member of or affiliated with any organization or body of persons teaching disbelief in organized government. I am not a polygamist nor a believer in the practice of polygamy. I am attached to the principles of the Constitution of the United States, and it is my intention to become a citizen of the United States and to renounce absolutely and forever all allegiance and fidelity to any foreign prince, potentate, state, or sovereignty, and particularly to FRANCIS JOSEPH, Emperor of Austria of which at this time I am a subject, and it is my intention to reside permanently in the United States.

Ninth. I am able to speak the English language.

Tenth. I have resided continuously in the United States of America for a term of five years at least immediately preceding the date of this petition, to wit, since the 11 day of March, anno Domini 1902, and in the State of ... for one year at least next preceding the date of this petition, to wit, since the 11 day of March anno Domini 1902.

Eleventh. I have not heretofore made petition for citizenship to any court.

Attached hereto and made a part of this petition are my declaration of intention to become a citizen of the United States and the certificate from the Department of Commerce and Labor required by law. Wherefore your petitioner prays that he may be admitted a citizen of the United States of America.

Dated July 12 1910

Elias Kubrik

STATE OF NEW YORK,

Figure 7.2. Naturalization record for Elias Kubrike.

a set of records that matched the index: *Petition and Record of Naturalization, 1907–1924 New York. Supreme Court (New York County).*

Clicking on "View Film Notes," I browsed the listing of microfilms. I selected the film that corresponded to volume 24 (FHL microfilm no. 1435856). Upon receiving the microfilm, I scrolled forward to volume 24, page 20, and found Elias Kubrick's naturalization (fig. 7.2).

The naturalization petition confirms information we got from other documents, such as his occupation (tailor) and his address (1567 Lexington). However, it also provides a great deal of elusive information. It gives Elias's exact birth date (November 27, 1887) and gives a place of birth (Probuzna, Austria). It records his wife's maiden name (Spiegelblatt) and her place of birth (Bucharest, Romania). It records the names and birth dates of his three children: Jacob, born May 21, 1902, Hester, born June 12, 1904, and Lily, born August 11, 1904; all of the children were born in New York. It indicates that he had lived in the country since March 11, 1902. The document is witnessed by two individuals, one of whom, Morris Speigelblatt, is presumably Rosa's relative.

By locating Elias Kubrik's passenger list and naturalization record, I found how he got to the United States and where he came from. However, it was not a straightforward search; my initial searches for "Elias Kubrick" failed. As with census and vital records research, immigration research requires a patient trial-and-error approach. In the next chapter, I will try to trace Elias to Probuzna, Austria.

Otto Tischer

In the case study of Renata Winter, I searched for immigration records for Renata's grandfather, Otto Tischer. Otto died in Chicago in 1931. His obituary provides some basic information about his origins:

Mr. Tischer was born in Leydenburg, Schwartzburg, Germany, March 10, 1842, and came to this country as a youth. He entered the Union army on March 8, 1865, enlisting in company C, 35th New Jersey state volunteers. Out of the army, he came to Chicago, married Clara von Obstfelder, and engaged in the real estate business.

Otto's entry in the censuses of 1900 through 1930 consistently record that he arrived in 1862. Because he gives his birth year as 1842, he would have been 20 at the time of immigration.

I checked volume 14 of *Germans to America*, which covers January 1861 to May 1863. Unfortunately, I did not find an Otto Tischer, Tisher, Thisher, or Tisch. I did find two immigrants listed named Otto Fisher, but both seemed too young; one was 14, and the other was 10. Because "Otto Fisher" is a fairly common German name, I decided that these two records did not match closely enough to warrant further research. I then searched the New York passenger list database on Ancestry.com for men named Otto born in 1842 who arrived in the years 1860–1864. I found one close match; the index showed an Otto Tischer, born in 1842, who arrived on July 15, 1863. Could this be our Otto? A close examination of the digitized manifest makes it appear that this passenger's name is Fischer, rather than Tischer. Also, his year of arrival does not match what Otto later recorded. Because I cannot find an exact match, I will hold onto this record and continue to look for further information in other documents. In a sense, though, we have already learned a rough account of Otto's immigration from census and obituary records; he most likely came to the United States in the early 1860s, as a young adult. We can guess that he initially settled in the New York area because he served in the Army from New York or New Jersey. In the next chapter, I will try to find records of Otto from Germany.

David Simpson

This example comes from the John W. Simpson case study. My grandfather was raised in Uniontown, Pennsylvania. Using the census, I traced my grandfather's father, also John W. Simpson, from Uniontown back to his birthplace of Coalton, Ohio. His father was a Civil War veteran, also named John W. Simpson. I located a Jackson county, Ohio history from 1977 that traced the origins of the elder Simpson:

John W. Simpson was born in New York City in 1835 to David W. and Ann Kathryn (Thompson) Simpson, who had come from Scotland the same year. Family tradition says that in Scotland, David had worked for Ann's family who was wealthy. When she married David, the family disowned her, so she came to America to start a new life. David settled his family in Powell's Fort Valley in northwest Virginia where he worked at different furnaces and was said to have engineered a railroad in the mountains to haul iron ore to the furnaces. He died at the age of 52 from pneumonia during the Civil War. The family could not get a doctor for him because the Union Army was in the Shenandoah Valley. (page 198.)

Basic genealogical records on David Simpson and his family do not give much information about his origins. I have not been able to find a record of his death in Shenandoah, and census records in that period did not ask about immigration or naturalization. However, the census record showing the family in 1850 seems to confirm the information in the family history. It shows David and Ann born in Scotland. Their two oldest children also list Scotland as a birthplace: son David is 20 years old, and daughter Margaret is 18. The next oldest child, 15-year-old John, lists New York as his birthplace. He is followed by Ann, 13 years old and born in Virginia. This suggests that 18 years earlier (1832), the family was in Scotland. By the time John was born in 1835, they were in New York, and by the time Ann was born (1837), they were in Virginia (U.S. Federal Census, 1850; census place, district 58, Shenandoah, Virginia; roll, M432_976; page, 140; image, 282).

I checked Filby and Meyer's *Passenger and Immigration Lists Index* to see whether it records a David Simpson arriving in New York in that period. We do not really know that David and his family arrived in New York, but it seems likely because their child was born there. The index has one entry for a David Simpson arriving in New York in 1835:

Name:	David Simpson
Year:	1835
Place:	New York, New York
Source Publication Code:	8208
Primary Immigrant:	Simpson, David
Annotation:	Date and place of declaration of intention or naturalization, a few reflect date and port of arrival or date and place of first mention of residence in the New World. Extracted from vols. 5–16 of the naturalization records for the Marine Court

Filby and Meyer's *Index* often confuses novice researchers because it is essentially an index of published indexes. In this case, it indicates that a passenger named David Simpson is recorded in an index of New York naturalizations compiled by author Kenneth Scott. David Simpson's entry is on page 118 of Scott's book. At the Newberry Library, we have a copy of this book, and so I was able to view the entry on David Simpson: *Simpson, David, subject of the kin of U.K.; rec. by James Dicks - 15 June 1835 (543).*

Because this record did not provide much information, I decided to look at the original naturalization record myself. I checked the FHL catalog under New York (City): Naturalizations, and I found that they had microfilm of the Marine Court Records. I borrowed the microfilm (FHL film no. 1710968) that covered 1835. Unfortunately, naturalizations in that time period did not record much information; the original record essentially contained the same information as Scott's index. Therefore, the naturalization record did not provide me with the town of origin for the Simpson family, nor did it name the ship they arrived on.

REFERENCES

CastleGarden.org. "Castle Garden," http://www.castlegarden.org/ (accessed August 1, 2007).

"The Danish Emigration Archives," http://www.emiarch.dk/home.php3 (accessed August 1, 2007).

Family History Library. "FamilySearch.org" (accessed August 1, 2007).

Filby, William P., and Mary Meyer. *Passenger and Immigration Lists Index: A Guide to Published Arrival Records of 500,000 Passengers Who Came to the United States and Canada*. Detroit: Gale Research Co., 1981.

Glazier, Ira, ed. *The Famine Immigrants: Lists of Irish Immigrants Arriving at the Port of New York, 1846–1851*. Baltimore: Genealogical Publishing Co., 1983.

Glazier, Ira, ed. *Germans to America: Lists of Passengers Arriving at U.S. Ports*. Wilmington, DE: Scholarly Resources, 1988.

Glazier, Ira A., ed. *Migration from the Russian Empire: Lists of Passengers Arriving at the Port of New York*. Baltimore: Genealogical Publishing Co., 1995.

Glazier, Ira A., and P. William Filby, eds. *Italians to America: Lists of Passengers Arriving at U.S. Ports, 1880–1899*. Wilmington, DE: Scholarly Resources, 1992.

"Jewish Genealogical Society, Inc.," http://www.jgsny.org/ (accessed August 10, 2007).

National Archives. "Access to Archival Databases" http://aad.archives.gov/aad (accessed May 26, 2008).

New York Marine Court (New York City). *Naturalization Records for Marine Court, 1827–1845* (Salt Lake City: Genealogical Society of Utah, 1990), microfilm of original records at New York Municipal Archives, New York City. Microfilm no. 1710968, Family History Library, Salt Lake City, Utah.

New York Supreme Court (New York County). *Petition and Record of Naturalization* (Salt Lake City: Genealogical Society of Utah, 1986), microfilm of original records in the County Clerk's Office, New York City, New York. Microfilm no. 1435856, Family History Library, Salt Lake City, Utah.

Ohio Genealogical Society. *Jackson County, Ohio: History and Families, 175th Anniversary, 1816–1991*. Paducah, KY: Turner Publishing Co, 1991.

"One-Step Webpages by Stephen P. Morse." http://www.stevemorse.org/.

National Archives. *Passenger and Crew Lists of Vessels Arriving at New York, New York, 1897–1957* (Washington, DC: National Archives), microfilm publication T715, 8892 rolls, Records of the Immigration and Naturalization Service, National Archives.

San Antonio Genealogical and Historical Society. *Index to Naturalization Records of Bexar County, Texas through 1906*. San Antonio, TX: The Society, 1998.

Schaefer, Christina. *Guide to Naturalization Records of the United States*. Baltimore, MD: Genealogical Publishing Co., 1997.

Scott, Kenneth. *Naturalizations in the Marine Court, New York City, 1827–1835, Vol. XIII, Collections of the New York Genealogical and Biographical Society*. New York: New York Genealogical and Biographical Society, 1990.

"Siirtolaisuusinstituutti: Institute of Migration," http://www.migrationinstitute.fi/index_e.php (accessed August 10, 2007).

The Statue of Liberty-Ellis Island Foundation, Inc. "Ellis Island Port of New York Passenger Records Search," http://ellisisland.org/ (accessed August 1, 2007).

"What Passenger Lists Are Online?" http://home.att.net/~wee-monster/onlinelists.html (accessed August 10, 2007).

8

Ethnic Records and International Research

Because this book is a very general overview of American genealogy records, most chapters focus on records that are common to most Americans, such as census schedules and vital records. In this chapter, I want do the opposite and focus on records and research strategies that are specific to an ancestor's ethnic group. This chapter explores two distinct but related kinds of research: ethnic sources in the United States and international sources.

There is not room in this book to explore genealogy sources for every American ethnic group and country of origin. Instead, I want to demonstrate the variety of ethnic research resources and strategies by looking at some specific examples of ethnic research. First, I will discuss ethnic records created in the United States. Second, I will discuss the next step: looking for genealogical records from the home countries of immigrant ancestors. Third, I will examine examples of sources and strategies for particular immigrant groups. Finally, I will discuss strategies for researching African-American and Native American ancestors.

ETHNIC RESEARCH IN THE UNITED STATES

For a number of years, I lived in a Chicago neighborhood heavily populated by Polish immigrants. Polish immigrants in that neighborhood spoke Polish while shopping for Polish food in the nearby Polish market, subscribed to a local Polish-language newspaper, and watched Polish language television. They worshiped at churches that were primarily Polish, and they belonged to Polish ethnic organizations. They went to Polish nightclubs and listened to Polish music. Although my Polish neighbors and I lived next to each other, in a sense, we inhabited different communities.

The same is true of most immigrant ancestors: they lived in émigré communities and built their own institutions. To a great extent, this is also true of African-American ancestors, who lived in heavily segregated communities for much of the recent past and created their own newspapers, social organizations, and other institutions.

These ethnic institutions are important to researchers because they often create informative genealogical records. At the Newberry Library, researchers often search the *Chicago Tribune* or other English-language newspapers for obituaries of their Polish immigrant ancestors. When they are unsuccessful, we often suggest they check the index of obituaries in the *Dziennik Chicagoski,* Chicago's Polish Daily; the index is available on the Web site of the Polish Genealogical Society of America (http://www.pgsa.org/database.htm). More often than not, we locate entries for their ancestors in the index. Because these Polish ancestors may have lived in a largely Polish-speaking community, an obituary in the Polish-language daily was a more effective way to inform their friends and neighbors of the funeral. Learning about the institutions of a particular ethnic group will help locate information about ancestors who inhabited that community.

Ethnic Books

There are many reference books about genealogy research on particular ethnic groups, and these are great starting points for researching ethnic records. For example, there is an excellent guide to Swedish genealogy: *Your Swedish Roots: A Step by Step Handbook* by Per Clemmenson (2004). Typically, these will be cataloged with Library of Congress subject headings such as these for *Swedish Roots*:

- Swedes - genealogy - handbooks, manuals, etc.
- Swedish Americans - genealogy - handbooks, manuals, etc.
- Sweden- genealogy - handbooks, manuals, etc.

Checking WorldCat for such headings for the particular ethnic group you are researching will locate reference books to interlibrary loan or purchase.

There are also books about ethnic communities in particular localities. Many 19th century and early 20th century ethnic groups published biographical and historical books about their communities similar to the subscription-based local histories discussed in Chapter Five. For example, here are some titles held by the Newberry Library:

Blum, Isidor. *The Jews of Baltimore: An Historical Summary of Their Progress and Status As Citizens of Baltimore from Early Days to the Year Nineteen Hundred and Ten.* Baltimore: Historical Review Publishing Co,, 1910.

Droba, Daniel D., and University of Chicago. *Czech and Slovak Leaders in Metropolitan Chicago; a Biographical Study of 300 Prominent Men and Women of Czech and Slovak Descent.* Chicago: Slavonic Club of the University of Chicago, 1934.

Geschichte Der Deutschen in Albany Und Troy Nebst Kurzen Biographien Von Beamten Und Hervorragenden Buergern: Illustrirtes Handbuch Wissenswerthen Inhaltes. Albany, NY: Albany Taeglicher Herold, 1897.

Some of these out-of-print works are now available digitally through HeritageQuest, Google Books, or the Internet Archive. (Note: when studying immigrant communities, researchers will encounter sources in foreign languages. Although this is off-putting to novice genealogists, this is not an insurmountable problem. Genealogists are primarily hunting for names, and as long as the sources use a script that is readable to the researcher, sources can be scanned for information. For example, if a researcher has a date of death and a name, he or she can search for an obituary in a German newspaper.)

There are also many contemporary books about local ethnic communities: genealogy indexes, community histories, or ethnographical academic monographs. Although not all of these are specifically aimed at assisting genealogical research, any source about the specific community might lead to valuable information. Here are some titles from the Newberry that show the variety of these works available:

Fretheim, Richard, and Park Genealogical Books (Firm). *Norske I Montana*. Roseville, MN: Park Genealogical Books, 2003.

Szymarek, Gene Stachowiak. *Polish Marriage Applicants, St. Joseph County, Indiana, 1905–1915*. Bowie, MD: Heritage Books, 1988.

University of Texas Institute of Texan Cultures at San Antonio. *The Greek Texans*. San Antonio: University of Texas at San Antonio, Institute of Texan Cultures, 1974.

Wong, Marie Rose. *Sweet Cakes, Long Journey: The Chinatowns of Portland, Oregon*. Seattle: University of Washington Press, 2004.

Typically, both the older biographical books and the recent ethnic studies are cataloged with subject headings such as:

- Germans: New York (State): Albany
- Norwegian Americans: Montana: Genealogy
- Greek Americans: Texas
- Chinese Americans: Oregon: Portland: History

Ethnic Newspapers

Ethnic newspapers were popular in the United States, especially in the late 19th and early 20th centuries, and the ethnic press is still vibrant in areas with large immigrant populations. An obituary in an ethnic newspaper might contain details left out of English-language notices, so they are well worth seeking out. Unfortunately, locating ethnic newspapers is not easy. The U.S. Newspaper Program, a major nationwide cataloging effort led by the Library of Congress, is a good place to start. Researchers can browse statewide newspaper holdings linked from the U.S. Newspaper Project Web site, http://www.neh.gov/projects/usnp.html. The OCLC WorldCat catalog is also a good resource for tracking down ethnic newspapers.

Ethnic Sources on the Internet

There are many sources for ethnic research on the Internet, particularly the Web sites of ethnic genealogy or community organizations. Cyndi's List, http://www.cyndislist.com, is a good tool for locating these sites. Cyndi's List is a directory of genealogical Web sites organized into categories. Some ethnic groups and international research categories are listed in the site's front-page "main category index," including Norway, Poland, and Acadian-Cajun-Creole. Other ethnic groups are listed as subcategories. Therefore, although Albania is not listed on the main page, there are Albanian links in the following categories: Eastern Europe, Languages and Translation, Unique Peoples (links about Italians of Albanian ancestry), and the

Library of Congress (links to Albanian collections at the Library). If you do not see a particular ethnicity or country listed in the main category, use the site's search engine to locate categories with links about that group.

INTERNATIONAL RESEARCH

This book is primarily about research in records from the United States, but because genealogy patrons are curious about researching the foreign places their immigrant ancestors came from, I want to offer some suggestions for beginning this process.

Family History Library (FHL) Resources

The FHL is the most important genealogy research institution in the world. The scope of the FHL is international, and it has created many useful tools for international research. First, the FHL catalog itself is a useful resource. When researching a particular foreign place, it is worth simply searching the FHL holdings for that place. Second, the FamilySearch Web site has many helpful "research helps" and guides for specific countries available online. See Chapter Ten for more information about querying the FHL catalog and using its research guides.

Other Online Sources

Two Web sites are particularly useful for international research. First, WorldGenWeb is a site that helps researchers collaborate in international genealogy research. It has volunteer-run pages for regions, nations, provinces, and localities. As with other volunteer-run Web sites, WorldGenWeb is uneven, with some regions having very useful pages and others nearly abandoned. Nevertheless, it is often a good starting point for research. A second online resource for international research is Cyndi's List (http://www.cyndislist.com), mentioned above. Many of the same categories for ethnic research in the United States also serve as useful guides to research abroad.

Geographical Resources

Locating the geographical and political location of places is one of the difficult research tasks in international research. A modern gazetteer, or place-name dictionary, is a helpful starting point. There are several major print gazetteers for international research, including the *Columbia Gazetteer of the World* (Cohen, 1998). Online, the GeoNet Names Server is a searchable database of international place names (http:gnswww.nga.mil/geonames/GNS). For more information about place name research, see *Walking With Your Ancestors*, by Melinda Kashuba (2005).

There is also an extraordinary online resource for researching Central and Eastern European place names in history: the ShtetlSeeker database maintained by JewishGen, http://www.JewishGen.org. JewishGen is a noncommercial Web site created for Jewish genealogical research. It features a database of current and historical communities in Europe. Users can search for a town name and see results that match on an online map. The database uses the Daitch-Mokotoff Soundex system, a coding system developed for use with Eastern European languages. Using this option allows researchers to find towns names that sound similar to the name entered. Although ShtetlSeeker was created by a Jewish research group, it is useful for any researcher studying communities in Central and Eastern Europe. The power of the database is demonstrated in the case studies below.

Three Case Studies in International Research

Three examples from the case studies illustrate the complexity of international research.

Elias Kubrike and Probuzna

In the case of Stanley Kubrick's grandfather Elias Kubrike, I found a birthplace located on his naturalization certificate (fig. 8.1). I read this as Probuzna, Austria. I first checked the FHL catalog for a town with this name, but I found no results. I searched the JewishGen ShtetlSeeker database for the town of Probuzna, using the Daitch-Mokotoff Soundex option. This returned 53 results from across Europe. None were in current-day Austria, but because the borders have changed completely since then, the current country location is not particularly significant. When researching places in Central or Eastern Europe, it is wise to focus on the locality and not to place too much importance on the country, due to the frequent and significant border changes.

I found one community that had a very similar name (fig. 8.2). Looking at the linked map, I saw that this town was in an area that is now western Ukraine. Although I suspected that this was the town Kubrike came from, I was unsure. I then tried another search option as part of the ShtetlSeeker page: "search for Jewish communities." This provided more information on the same town (fig. 8.3). This figure shows that Probuzna (now officially spelled Probezhna) was part of the Austrian Empire before World War I; then, it was part of Poland between the World Wars, and it is now part of the Ukraine. Clicking on the icon brought up a page of basic information about the Probezhna: a map of the area, a list of nearby Jewish communities, and several important links. One link is to a catalog of Yizkor books, which are memorial histories of Jewish towns, typically written by former residents. It shows that there is a history of this community entitled *Sefer Probezhna*, or *The Book of Probezhna*, published in 1887, and it names two libraries in Israel that hold it.

A second link is to a page from the JewishGen ShtetLinks page for the town. The ShtetLinks page helps researchers studying the same Jewish communities connect. The page gives more information about the Shtetl: the administrative districts it was a part of over the years, the Jewish population before the Holocaust, and some basic information about the destruction of the community in the Holocaust. The page also describes the *Landsmanshaftn* (home town clubs) established by emigrants from the town in the United States and where those clubs purchased burial plots in the New

Fourth. I was born on the 27 day of November anno Domini 1877 at Probuzna Austria

Figure 8.1. Elias Kubrike's birthplace, from his naturalization record.

Probezhną Probuż na, Probuzhna, Probezhnaya	49°02' 25°59'	E M U G	Ukraine	224.2 miles WSW of Kyyiv 50°26' 30°31'

Figure 8.2. Entry for town of Probezhna in the ShtetlSeeker database.

Modern Town & Country	Other Names	c. 1950 After WWII Town / Country	c. 1930 Between Wars Town / District / Province / Country	c. 1900 Before WWI Town / District / Province / Country	# of JGFF Entries
Probezhna, Ukraine 49°02' 25°59' 361 km WSW of Kyyiv	Probezhna [Ukr], Probuż na [Pol], Probuzhne, Probuzhna, Probezhnaya	Probezhna Soviet Union	Probuż na Kopyczyń ce Tarnopol Poland	Probuż na Husiatyń Galicia Austrian Empire	19

Figure 8.3. Entry for town of Probezhna in Jewish Communities database of JewishGen.

York area. A third link connects to 19 researchers studying ancestors from Probuzna in JewishGen's FamilyFinder database. Although I have not yet found any information about Elias Kubrike, I have new leads to follow up on: a plausible town of origin and a number of fellow researchers to contact.

Otto Tischer and Leydenburg

The *Chicago Tribune* obituary for Otto Tischer indicates a place of birth:

Mr. Tischer was born in Leydenburg, Schwartzburg, Germany, March 10, 1842, and came to this country as a youth.

I searched for "Leydenburg" in the FHL catalog but found no results. This suggested to me that the name had changed or was no longer used. To get suggestions for similar names, I searched ShtetlSeeker. I used a Soundex search and found that there is a town in Germany called Ladenburg, which seemed to be a fairly close name match (fig. 8.4).

I went back to the FamilySearch catalog and searched for this spelling, and one town was listed (fig. 8.5). However, I was puzzled; if this Ladenburg is in Baden, why does Tischer's obituary describe him from being from Schwartzburg? Is Schwartzburg now part of Baden? To get more information before attempting further research, I looked into the location of Schwartzburg.

Town (Native names in BOLD)	Coordinates	Maps	Country	Distance/Direction from reference point
Ladenburg	49°29' 8°36'	E M U G	Germany	295.7 miles SW of Berlin 52°31' 13°24'

Figure 8.4. Entry for town of Ladenburg in ShtetlSeeker database.

To get trustworthy information about the states of Germany, *Encyclopedia Britannica* or the *Oxford Atlas of World History* (O'Brien, 2002) would be ideal sources. However, because I was simply testing out a theory, I used Wikipedia as my first resource. Although Wikipedia is fallible, I often use it when I need a suggestion, rather than a rock-solid reference. At the time of writing, the Wikipedia entry for Germany included an extensive description of the states that made up the German Confederation from 1815–1866. Among them are Baden (now part of the state of Baden-Württemberg) and the principalities of Schwarzburg-Sondershausen and Schwarzburg-Rudolstadt (both now part of the state of Thuringia). Because the areas of Schwarzburg and Baden are not near each other, it seems unlikely that Tischer was from Baden, so perhaps there was another town with a name like "Leydenburg" in what is now Thuringia. To test this out, I went back to the ShtetlSeeker database and ran a search for places with names like Leydenburg near the town of Rudolstadt, the former capitol of the principality of Schwarzburg-Rudolstadt.

Using the longitude and latitude for Rudolstadt town found on Wikipedia (50°43′ N 11°20′ E), I chose the "Search for Towns by Location" option in ShtetlSeeker. I searched for towns beginning with "L" within 30 miles of Rudolstadt. I found a town that was a fairly close match (fig. 8.6). Checking the FHL for this location, I found two entries: *Germany, Schwarzburg-Rudolstadt, Leutenberg* and *Germany, Thüringen, Leutenberg*.

Unfortunately, both of these entries point to the same set of church records, which end too early to record Otto's birth: *Kirchenbuch, 1637–1763 Evangelische Kirche Leutenberg (AG. Leutenberg)*.

Nevertheless, locating this town as a subject for further study advances the research task. Later on in my research, I obtained Tischer's Civil War pension

Place	Germany, Baden, Ladenburg
Topics	Germany, Baden, Ladenburg - Church records
	Germany, Baden, Ladenburg - Genealogy
	Germany, Baden, Ladenburg - Jewish records
	Germany, Baden, Ladenburg - Public records

Figure 8.5. FHL catalog entry for Ladenburg.

Leutenberg	50°33'N 11°27'E	E M U G	Germany	12.6 miles SSE

Figure 8.6. Entry for town of Leutenberg in ShtetlSeeker database.

record, which confirmed that this was the correct town. In a Bureau of Pensions form Otto filled out in 1911, he recorded his birthplace as "City of Leutenberg, Schwarzburg, Rudolstadt Germany."

David Simpson and Kirkcaldy

As I mentioned in the previous chapter, what I know about my great-great-great grandfather David is based upon a brief history of my family:

John W. Simpson was born in New York City in 1835 to David W. and Ann Kathryn (Thompson) Simpson, who had come from Scotland the same year. Family tradition says that in Scotland, David had worked for Ann's family who was wealthy. When she married David, the family disowned her, so she came to America to start a new life. David settled his family in Powell's Fort Valley in northwest Virginia here he worked at different furnaces and was said to have engineered a railroad in the mountains to haul iron ore to the furnaces. He died at the age of 52 from pneumonia during the Civil War. The family could not get a doctor for him because the Union Army was in the Shenandoah Valley. (page 198.)

I found an 1835 New York naturalization record for him, but it did not name his birthplace or previous home. I was not able to locate a death certificate for him or an obituary. I continued to search for information about the family on the Internet and eventually found a posting by a researcher studying the family. The researcher had found an 1829 marriage record for a David Simpson and Ann Thomson by using the International Genealogical Index. The marriage record showed that this couple was married in Kirkcaldy, Scotland, and indicated where Ann and David's parents lived. I tried to find information that might confirm that this couple is the same one that emigrated to New York and Virginia; for example, baptismal records for their oldest children. However, I was unable to locate such records. Nevertheless, I suspect that this is the same couple, and I now have more leads to follow.

ETHNIC CHALLENGES AND STRATEGIES

Because this book is a broad overview, I do not have room to examine many ethnic groups in depth. Instead, I have selected a few ethnic groups as examples. As another caveat, each example is a very brief description of challenges and tools related to each ethnicity and is more an impressionistic overview than definitive guide. For a more in-depth look at any of these ethnic groups, see the print reference sources described in each example.

Irish

Many Americans trace their ancestry to Ireland, and Irish genealogy research is quite popular. Some Americans trace their ancestors to Protestant Irish who primarily came from the area that is now Northern Ireland, and many more have Irish Catholic forbears, who are more commonly from the area that is now the Republic of Ireland. It is important to determine whether a patron is researching Catholic or Protestant ancestors because it defines where you will find church and cemetery records. Most researchers know the denomination of their Irish ancestors, so it is worth asking when assisting researchers.

Irish Naming Tradition

The naming traditions of Irish Catholics can make genealogy research difficult. Historically, Irish and Irish-American Catholics favored a narrow range of first names, such as John, James, and Michael for boys and Mary, Anne, and Catherine for girls. The result is that index searches for Irish ancestors locate numerous individuals with the same name. For example, if I search for men with the exact name "James Murphy" in Cook County, Illinois using Ancestry's 1930 census index, I get 263 results, too many to browse through.

To get around this problem, researchers can consider ways to limit their search. If you know the occupation of an ancestor, you might look for sources that will include this information. For example, if James Murphy was a lawyer, we might scan the Chicago city directory for men named "James Murphy" who list that occupation. Another tactic is to locate another family member with an unusual name. I have an Irish immigrant ancestor named Mary Colfer who was difficult to trace because there are a number of women with the same name of roughly the same age, all from County Wexford. In her obituary, I discovered that she had a brother with an atypical first name: Moses. Tracing Moses Colfer proved much easier.

Irish Immigration Records

Irish people have been immigrating to North America since colonial times and continue to do so today. The Famine of the 1840s caused a large spike in the number of Irish immigrants, but it is important to remember that many Irish immigrants arrived before and after the famine. Because the Famine is a well-known event, some patrons may assume that their ancestors left during that period, when in fact they came decades before or after. Immigrants who left during the Famine are documented in a seven-volume index entitled *The Famine Immigrants* (Glazier, 1983). However, many more Irish immigrants appear in the other passenger indexes described in the previous chapter.

Discovering Towns of Origin

Researchers are typically seeking the towns their ancestors came from, but this can prove surprisingly difficult for Irish researchers. Lucky researchers will find an Irish townland or county name in a death certificate or obituary. Others may locate towns of origin on a naturalization record (after 1906) or ship manifest (after 1883). Other sources that might provide this information include church records and military records.

Irish Censuses and Griffith's Valuation

The absence of Irish censuses prior to 1901 makes searching for towns of origin more difficult. Nationwide censuses for 1901 and 1911 are available through the FHL. Censuses were taken in earlier years, but they were subsequently destroyed.

Although there are no census records available from the 19th century, Griffith's Valuation serves a similar purpose. Griffith's Valuation was a tax assessment survey taken by the British government between 1847 and 1864. Its official name was the Primary Valuation of Tenements, but it is universally known as Griffith's Valuation today after Richard Griffith, the director of the survey. Griffith's Valuation lists landowners and tenants across Ireland but provides no family information. Compared with the U.S. Census of 1850, it is not very informative, but it is widely used because of the scarcity of other sources. It was published as a microfiche set, which is held by many research libraries. It is also available online through a subscription Web site, Irish Origins (http://www.irishorigins.com).

Family History Research Centers

The Irish Family History Foundation (http://www.irish-roots.net) coordinates a network of county-based genealogy centers in the Republic of Ireland and Northern Ireland. These centers provide genealogy research services for overseas customers, from searching for a single record to a family research report. The high price of these services has limited their use by American researchers, however.

Basic Print Reference Sources

There are a number of general guides to Irish research, such as John Grenham's *Tracing Your Irish Ancestors* (1993) and region-specific works such as *A Guide to Tracing Your Cork Ancestors* by Tony McCarthy and Tim Cadogan (1998). Several geographical reference works are helpful for Irish research: Brian Mitchell's *New Genealogical Atlas of Ireland* (1986) is a user-friendly guide to Irish geographical divisions throughout history. The *General Alphabetical Index to the Townlands and Towns, Parishes, and Baronies of Ireland* (1984) is a gazetteer of Irish localities based on the census of 1851, which is useful for determining where an obscure place named in a document was located.

Online Sources

The *Irish Research Outline* from the FHL gives a good overview of sources for Irish research: http://www.familysearch.org/Eng/Search/RG/guide/Ireland10.asp. Irish Origins (http://www.IrishOrigins.com) is part of the Origins Network, a for-profit genealogy company. It has digitized some of the major resources for Irish research, including Griffith's valuation, census extracts, and maps. Researchers can pay for single searches or take out a personal subscription and libraries can purchase institutional subscriptions.

Polish

Most Polish Americans trace their ancestry to immigrants who arrived between the 1880s and the 1930s. This relatively recent migration is an advantage for

Polish-American researchers because many of their ancestors arrived in a period when immigration and naturalization documents contain considerable personal description. In discussing Polish immigrants here, I am referring to people who considered themselves ethnically Polish. There were many Jews who also emigrated from Poland in the same period, but I discuss them separately because they created separate institutions from ethnic Poles.

Mangled Names

In Chicago, we have a large Polish-American community, and many patrons visit the Newberry Library researching Polish ancestry. One difference between Polish and Irish or even, say, Italian research is the extent to which Polish names are misrecorded in American documents.

The way sounds are recorded in English and Polish differ greatly. In Rosemary Chorzempa's *Polish Roots* (1993), she gives the following example of this gulf in language. In Polish, the consonant combination "Rz" indicates a sound that would be best approximated by "zh" in English. The Polish consonant combination "ów" at the end of a name indicates the sound that would be spelled "oof" in English. Therefore, the Polish place name Rzeszów is pronounced "zhe-shoof." Imagine how an immigration official who spoke only English might spell this sound, and you can see how this is a problem. Polish immigrants often are recorded under unrecognizable surnames in the census and passenger lists. To get around this problem, researchers must try to search using criteria other than surnames.

Border Changes

As noted above, national borders in central Europe changed often, and this is particularly true for Poland. To get a sense of how that impacts American records, consider the changing instructions given to U.S. census takers. In 1900, census enumerators were directed to record nativity as follows:

In case the person speaks Polish, as Poland is not now a country, inquire whether the birthplace was what is now known as German Poland or Austrian Poland, and enter the answer accordingly as Poland (Ger.), Poland (Aust.), or Poland (Russ.).

In 1930, more difficult directions were given:

Since it is essential that each foreign-born person be credited to the country in which his birthplace is now located, special attention must be given to the six countries which lost a part of their territory in the readjustments following the World War. These six countries are as follows: Austria, which lost territory to Czechoslovakia, Italy, Yugoslavia, Poland, and Rumania. Hungary, which lost territory to Austria, Czechoslovakia, Italy, Poland, Rumania, and Yugoslavia. Bulgaria, which lost territory to Greece and Yugoslavia. Germany, which lost territory to Belgium, Czechoslovakia, Danzig, Denmark, France, Lithuania, and Poland. Russia, which lost territory to Estonia, Finland, Latvia, Lithuania, Poland, and Turkey … If the person reports one of these six countries as his place of birth or that of his parents, ask specifically whether the birthplace is located within the present area of the country; and if not, find out to what country it has been transferred. If a person was born in the

Province of Bohemia, for example, which was formerly in Austria but is now a part of Czechoslovakia, the proper return for country of birth is Czechoslovakia. If you can not ascertain with certainty the present location of the birthplace, where this group of countries is involved, enter in addition to the name of the country, the name of the Province or State in which the person was born, as Alsace-Lorraine, Bohemia, Croatia, Galicia, Moravia, Slovakia, etc., or the city, as Warsaw, Prague, Strasbourg, etc.

The result is that the birthplace of a Polish immigrant may be recorded a variety of ways in the U.S. Census, depending on the year and how well the enumerator followed instructions. When searching for Polish Americans in the census, entering "Poland" as a birthplace may exclude some Polish immigrants.

There are a number of geographical reference tools that describe the shifting borders. First, as shown in the Stanley Kubrick case study, the ShtetlSeeker database is a powerful tool for locating current locations of historical places in Central and Eastern Europe. Second, a general historical atlas, such as the *Oxford Atlas of World History* (O'Brien, 2002), is helpful in showing shifting borders. Third, there are Poland-specific gazetteers and geographical reference works, such as George Kay's *Postal Place Names in Poland* (Kay, 1992).

Basic Print Resources

There are a number of general guides to Polish research, including Rosemary Chorzempa's *Polish Roots* (1993). *Migration from the Russian Empire*, edited by Ira Glazier, is a basic index for Polish immigration, covering the period 1875–1891 in six volumes. A Polish-English dictionary is important to have available for genealogists, and there are also specific translation guides, such as Judith Franzin's *Translation Guide to 19th-Century Polish-Language Civil-Registration Documents* (1984).

Other American Sources

There are many records produced by Polish-American institutions that are helpful for genealogical research: marriage records and jubilee books from Polish congregations, obituaries from Polish-American newspapers, and insurance records from Polish-American fraternal organizations. The Web site of the Polish Genealogical Society features indexes of a number of such documents (http://www.pgsa.org/database.htm).

Polish Sources

There are many records from Poland that provide more information; for example, civil records, church records, and military records. For researchers who do not plan to travel to Poland, the FHL has microfilmed many Polish records, particularly Roman Catholic parish records.

Mexican

Like the other groups mentioned, Mexican-American genealogy varies greatly from family to family. Some researchers will trace their genealogy to ancestors who lived in the American Southwest before that region was part of the United States. Others are first or second generation Americans who have living memories of hometowns in Jalisco or Veracruz.

Helping Recent Immigrants

Although there are Mexican Americans who trace their ancestry back to the colonial era, heavy immigration since the 1970s means that many Mexican-American researchers are first or second generation Americans. Such relatively recent immigrants have different research needs than third or fourth generation immigrants. Some of the cornerstone documents of American genealogy research will not be useful for recent immigrants. They will not have ancestors in the 1930 census and might not have family members recorded on American death certificates. On the other hand, unlike many American researchers, recent immigrants tend to know the towns of origins for their ancestors. Therefore, although it might be difficult to find American sources for first or second generation Mexican Americans, you might be able to assist them in finding records from Mexico.

Mexican Records

Strong sets of civil vital records and Catholic parish records exist for most Mexican localities, and the FHL has filmed a large number of these records. Civil registration of births, marriages, and deaths began in 1860. Catholic parish records go back much further, to the 1500s in some cases. Both are most easily accessed by searching the FHL catalog for localities. The International Genealogical Index created by the FHL indexes many of these records. The FHL has digitized the 1930 census of Mexico; researchers can browse it by locality at http://labs.familysearch.org.

Published Reference Sources

There is an excellent reference book by George and Peggy Ryskamp entitled *Finding Your Mexican Ancestors: A Beginner's Guide* (2006). This book explains the basic strategies and sources for Mexican and Mexican-American research in a user-friendly and clearly written narrative.

Jewish

Judaism fits somewhat uncomfortably with the groups above because it is a religion and not a nationality of origin. Nevertheless, because Jewish Americans built distinctive Jewish institutions, for our genealogical purposes, Judaism functions like an ethnicity.

Basic Print Sources

There are a number of useful Jewish genealogy titles in print, many published by Avotaynu (http://www.avotaynu.com). The most important recent reference book is *The Avotaynu Guide to Jewish Genealogy*, edited by Sallyann Sack and Gary Mokotoff (Avotaynu, 2004). Avotaynu also offers translation guides, surname dictionaries, gazetteers, and nationality-specific guides to Jewish genealogy research. Estelle Guzik's *Genealogical Resources in New York* (2004) also merits mention. Although it is not solely focused on Jewish sources, it is very useful for researching Jewish institutions in New York City.

Online Sources

The most important online resource for Jewish genealogy research is JewishGen.org, a nonprofit site for Jewish research. I have already discussed the ShtetlSeeker database, but JewishGen has many other useful features. For example, the site maintains Family Finder, a very active database of family researchers. It is searchable by family name and town of origin. Beyond JewishGen, there are a number of other useful sites for Jewish research. The genealogist Stephen Morse maintains a site containing search tools, including a number of tools for Jewish research. Many regional Jewish genealogy societies maintain excellent Web sites. For example, the Jewish Genealogical Society, Inc. of New York (http://www.jgsny.org) has created a number of useful databases, including a large database of Brooklyn naturalizations.

Holocaust Research

The tragedy of the Holocaust affected most Jewish families from Europe, and researching the Holocaust is a basic task for many Jewish genealogists. There are a number of resources for genealogical research on the victims and survivors of the Nazi genocide. Yad Vashem, the Israeli museum of Holocaust remembrance, maintains a massive database of Holocaust victims: the Central Database of Shoah Victims Names (http://www.yadvashem.org). JewishGen maintains a registry of Holocaust survivors, available at http://www.JewishGen.org/registry. Many Jewish communities in Europe were destroyed in the war, and survivors from these towns often wrote communal histories known as Yizkor books. As mentioned in the Kubrick case study, JewishGen maintains a directory of these books at http://www.JewishGen.org/yizkor.

AFRICAN-AMERICAN AND NATIVE AMERICAN RESEARCH

I have grouped African-American and Native American research apart from the immigrant groups above because their histories in the United States are very different from the immigrant groups above. (By African-American, I am referring to descendants of American slaves, as opposed to recent immigrants from Africa.) Native Americans never immigrated, and African Americans were brought to North America forcibly as property. Nevertheless, like other ethnic groups, African Americans and Native Americans created records unique to their communities. Successful genealogical research means learning about these distinctive records and strategies.

African-American Research Basics

There are several misperceptions about African-American genealogy that sometimes affect novice researchers. First, novices are often overly pessimistic about beginning research on African-American ancestors, expecting to find very little information. Although African-American genealogy before the Civil War is exceedingly difficult, research since emancipation is not more difficult than other kinds of genealogical research. In fact, a number of factors make initial African-American genealogy research easier than some other ethnic research.

The census tends to record African Americans fairly well from 1880 on because African Americans do not have the name problems faced by some other ethnic groups; Anglophone surnames typical for African Americans did not cause difficulties for census takers compared with immigrants. African Americans did not use a limited number of first names in the way that Irish Americans did; therefore, they less commonly face the "James Murphy" problem mentioned in the Irish section above. Also, researching African Americans since emancipation rarely requires researching places outside of the United States. I mention this misperception because expectation of success affects how much effort a researcher is willing to expend and, therefore, their chances of success. If a researcher feels that the task before them is nearly impossible, it is easy to become discouraged by difficulties. Therefore, it is important to reassure novices that success is possible. I find that showing people how to find ancestors in the census is often the best way to encourage novices.

On the other hand, African American research before emancipation *is* extremely difficult. Because enslaved African Americans had no legal rights, they are rarely recorded on documents and only identified with first names where they appear. Occasionally, I have assisted patrons who expected that it would be much easier to research slave ancestors than it turned out to be. It is important to prepare researchers for the difficulty of this task. Researchers should prepare for researching antebellum ancestry by exhausting the available postemancipation records first.

Getting Started: Census and Vital Records

African Americans are well recorded in the U.S. Census and in vital records, and those are the best starting points for research. In using the census, if the patron knows what county a family came from, it sometimes helps to narrow the search to that county and search for the surname. This strategy will help get around variable recording of the first name, which might be a nickname, a middle name, or initials.

Racial designation is sometimes a problem in the census because census takers were sometimes asked to distinguish between "Negroes" of "full blood" and "mulattos" or "having some proportion of white blood" (this phrasing is taken from the instructions to enumerators of 1920). This means that the race of an individual will be recorded differently depending upon the instructions given the census taker and the interpretation of the instructions. Coleman Young's father is recorded as a "Negro" in the census of 1930, a "mulatto" in 1920 and 1910, and "black" in 1900, for example. Considering this, it is important to be careful when using census indexes; if you search for search for people classified as "Negro" in some databases, you may exclude people recorded as "mulatto," even though they later considered themselves "Negro" or "black."

Researchers should also be cautious using the 1870 census for African Americans. This is the first census taken after emancipation, and it is considered to be flawed in its recording of African Americans. Many families are enumerated with incorrect surnames, and there are many other errors. Researchers should keep this in perspective in evaluating its data.

Reconstruction-Era Records

Once researchers have traced their ancestry back to the 1870s, it is worth examining the records of two postwar agencies: the Freedmen's Bureau and the Freedman's Bank. The Freedmen's Bureau was created by the Federal government to assist the freed slaves and other refugees in the South following the Civil War. The Bureau assumed many of the responsibilities of civil government: it attempted to maintain order, performed marriages, and negotiated labor contracts between former slaves and former owners. The Bureau only existed from 1865–1872, but in those years, it created some of the first records of former slaves. The records of the Freedmen's Bureau were kept in Washington, DC and ultimately transferred to the National Archives. The National Archives has microfilmed most of these records, and http://www.Ancestry.com has digitized some of them. They have not been well indexed, however, so they can be difficult to use for novice researchers. There is a free volunteer site, Freedmen's Bureau Online, http://freedmensbureau.com, devoted to transcribing and indexing these records.

The records of the Freedmen's Bank are smaller and less informative than the Freedmen's Bureau records, but they are much better indexed. A group of investors chartered the Freedmen's Bank to provide freed slaves and refugees a way to save money. Account records from the bank provide valuable genealogy information, showing family relationships. Over 105,000 bank records have been digitized and indexed. The index is freely available at http://www.familysearch.org, and the index and fully digitized records are available at HeritageQuest Online.

Slavery Research

Researching the lives of enslaved African Americans prior to emancipation is very difficult. There are few records that document slaves, and those that do give scant information on individuals. Slaves are enumerated on special "slave schedules" in the censuses of 1850 and 1860. These schedules list slave holders and the age and gender of each slave. However, they do not name the slaves, so using them requires some guesswork on the part of researchers. For an interesting history of the slave schedules, see Margo Anderson's *The American Census: A Social History* (1988). Figure 8.7 shows a slave schedule for the slave owner Richard Napier, who is probably Coleman Young's great-great-grandfather. Based on the family history related in Young's autobiography, Richard Napier's white son, Robert, was the father of Virginia Napier, Coleman Young's grandmother. Virginia Napier's mother, Sarah, may be one of the slaves enumerated on the slave schedule (but not in the pictured portion).

Other sources that document slave ancestors include plantation records and the wills of slave owners. These records often give the first names of slaves. However, using them requires identifying a slave owner, which is sometimes more difficult than researchers expect because freedmen did not always take the surname of their owners. If a researcher can determine or guess at the identity of a slave owner, they can look for these kinds of records.

Page No. 31 110

SCHEDULE 2.—Slave Inhabitants in The Western Division of the County of Marengo State of Ala, enumerated by me, on the 30 day of June, 1860. [illegible] Ass't Marshal.

	Names of Slave Owners.	Number of Slaves.	Age.	Sex.	Color.	Fugitives from the State.	Number manumitted.	Deaf & dumb, blind, insane, or idiotic.	No. of Slave houses.	Names of Slave Owners.	Number of Slaves.	Age.	Sex.	Color.	Fugitives from the State.	Number manumitted.	Deaf & dumb, blind, insane, or idiotic.	No. of Slave houses.	
	1	2	3	4	5	6	7	8	9	1	2	3	4	5	6	7	8	9	
1	Richd Bryan [illegible]	1	15	f	B					Richd Napier [illegible]	1	9	m	B					1
2		1	2	f	B						1	9	m	B					2
3		1	19	f	B						1	8	m	B					3
4		1	26	f	B						1	6	m	B					4
5		1	45	f	B						1	6	m	B					5
6		1	19	f	B						1	6	m	B					6
7		1	17	f	B						1	3	m	B					7
8		1	2	f	B						1	2	m	B					8
9		1	7	f	B						1	2	m	B					9
10		1	16	f	B						1	9/12	m	B					10
11		1	18	f	B						1	7/12	m	B					11
12		1	30	f	B						1	9	m	B					12
13		1	21	f	B						1	2/12	f	B					13
14		1	17	f	B						1	10/12	f	B					14
15		1	[illegible]	[illegible]	[illegible]						1	11/12	f	B					15

Figure 8.7. Slave schedule for Richard Napier, 1860.

Wills or probate records of Southern counties are often available on microfilm through the FHL. Lexis-Nexis has published a set of microfilmed plantation records: *Records of Ante-Bellum Southern Plantations from the Revolution through the Civil War,* edited by Kenneth M. Stampp. Jean Cooper's *A Genealogical Index to the Guides of the Microfilm Edition of Records of Ante-Bellum Southern Plantations* (2003) is a user-friendly guide to this set. Patrons should be warned, though, that plantation records are difficult to read and interpret. Also, the existing records of plantations cover relatively few slave owners; records of most plantations or small slave owners are lost. For a general overview of slavery research, see *Slave Genealogy: A Research Guide With Case Studies* by David H. Streets (1986).

Free Blacks

It is important to remember that there were significant populations of free blacks in both the Northern and Southern states before the Civil War. Free blacks appeared in the regular schedule of the U.S. Census and in legal documents such as marriage and probate records.

Basic Reference Resources

There are many useful guides to African-American genealogy. Several general guides worth owning are Tony Burroughs' *Black Roots* (2001), the *African-American Genealogical Sourcebook* edited by Paula Byers (1995) and Curt Witcher's *African-American Genealogy* (2000).

The recent Public Broadcasting Service (PBS) documentary *African-American Lives*, hosted by Henry Louis Gates, is also worth recommending to novice researchers. Consisting of a series of case studies, it does a great job of conveying the complexity and excitement of African-American genealogy research. PBS maintains a Web site for the series, http://www.pbs.org/wnet/aalives/index.html.

Native American Research Basics

Native American research is very complex because the term "Native American" encompasses a variety of ethnic groups. The sources and strategies for researching Cherokee ancestors from the southeastern United States are entirely different from those for researching Northwestern tribes such as the Nez Percé. Family connections to Native American ancestors also differ greatly from researcher to researcher. Some researchers may belong to a tribal group or have grandparents who enrolled in a tribe. For other researchers, "Indian ancestors" is part of a vague story of distant family origins.

Getting Started

For most researchers with an interest in Native American ancestry, the best starting points are the basic sources of the census and vital records. Although some patrons are well informed about their Native American ancestry, many are uncertain about the details. For the latter, it is best not to start with the complicated and less accessible tribal records and rather to begin with standard genealogical research.

Tribal Research

If the researcher knows that their ancestors lived on a reservation or were enrolled in a tribe, it is worth exploring the basic records kept by the U.S. government on Native Americans: enrollment cards and reservation censuses.

The government required tribal enrollment for official tribal membership at certain points, and records that individuals submitted contain a great deal of genealogical information. The most widely used set of enrollment cards is the Dawes Rolls, which cover the "five civilized tribes": the Cherokee, Choctaw, Chickasaw, Creek, and Seminole. In 1893, Congress voted to allot the tribal lands of these tribes to individual tribal members. To complete this task, Congress created a committee led by Henry Dawes to determine tribal membership. The records collected as part of this process contain valuable genealogical data on thousands of individuals. The Dawes Rolls are just one example of enrollment cards; the National Archives holds enrollment records for other tribal groups.

The Bureau of Indian Affairs also required Indian agents to take a census of residents on reservations. Many of these records have been microfilmed by the National Archives, and many are available at the regional branches of the National Archives.

The Archives page on Native American genealogy is a good starting point for research in these tribal records: http://www.archives.gov/genealogy/heritage/native-american/index.html. The National Archives also created a helpful print reference work, *Guide to Records in the National Archives Relating to American Indians* (1984).

Basic Print Resources

There are several general Native American genealogical reference sources, including the *Native American Genealogical Sourcebook*, edited by Paula Byers (1995), and Curt Witcher's chapter on Native American research in *The Source* (2006).

There are also many other tribe-specific guides and record indexes, such as *Cherokee Roots* by Bob Blankenship (1992).

REFERENCES

Anderson, Margo. *The American Census: A Social History*. New Haven, CT: Yale University Press, 1988.

"Avotaynu," http://www.avotaynu.com/ (accessed August 1, 2007).

Blankenship, Bob. *Cherokee Roots*. Cherokee, NC: B. Blankenship, 1992.

Burroughs, Tony. *Black Roots: A Beginner's Guide to Tracing the African American Family Tree*. New York: Fireside Book, 2001.

Byers, Paula, ed. *African American Genealogical Sourcebook*. New York: Gale Research, 1995.

Byers, Paula, ed. *Native American Genealogical Sourcebook*. New York: Gale Research, 1995.

Chorzempa, Rosemary. *Polish Roots = Korzenie Polskie*. Baltimore: Genealogical Publishing Co., 1993.

Clemensson, Per. *Your Swedish Roots: A Step by Step Handbook*. Provo, UT: Ancestry, 2004.

Cohen, Saul. *The Columbia Gazetteer of the World*. New York: Columbia University Press, 1998.

Cooper, Jean. *A Genealogical Index to the Guides of the Microfilm Edition of Records of Ante-bellum Southern Plantations from the Revolution through the Civil War*. Bloomington, IN: 1stBooks, 2003.

Droba, Daniel, and University of Chicago. Czech and Slovak Leaders in Metropolitan Chicago: A Biographical Study of 300 Prominent Men and Women of Czech and Slovak Descent. Chicago: Slavonic Club of the University of Chicago, 1934.

FamilySearch. "FamilySearch.org: Family History and Genealogy Records," http://www.familysearch.org/ (accessed August 1, 2007).

"Family Search Labs." http://labs.familysearch.org/ (accessed June 4, 2008).

Frazin, Judith R. and Jewish Genealogical Society of Illinois. *A Translation Guide to 19th-century Polish-language Civil-registration Documents: (Birth, Marriage, and Death Records)*. Niles, IL: Jewish Genealogical Society of Illinois, 1984.

Freedmen's Bureau. "The Freedmen's Bureau Online: Black History: American History," http://freedmensbureau.com/ (accessed August 1, 2007).

Fretheim, Richard. *Norske i Montana*. Roseville, MN: Park Genealogical Books, 2003.

Geschichte der Deutschen in Albany und Troy nebst Kurzen Biographien von Beamten und hervorragenden Buergern. Illustrites Handbuch wissenswerthen Inhalts. Albany, NY: 1897. Publisher: Albany Taeglicher Herold.

Glazier, Ira. *The Famine Immigrants: Lists of Irish Immigrants Arriving at the Port of New York, 1846–1851*. Baltimore: Genealogical Publishing Co., 1983.

Grenham, John. *Tracing Your Irish Ancestors: The Complete Guide*. Baltimore: Genealogical Publishing Co., 1993.

Griffith, Richard, and Ireland. *General Valuation of Rateable Property in Ireland*. Dublin: Irish Microforms Ltd., 1978.

Guzik, Estelle, and Jewish Genealogical Society (New York). *Genealogical Resources in New York*. New York: Jewish Genealogical Society, 2003.

"HeritageQuest Online Index," http://heritagequestonline.com/ (accessed August 1, 2007).

Howell, Cyndi. "Cyndi's List of Genealogy Sites on the Internet," http://www.cyndislist.com/.

Integrated Public Use Microdata. "Enumerator Instructions," http://usa.ipums.org/usa/voliii/tEnumInstr.shtml (accessed August 1, 2007).

Integrated Public Use Microdata. "1900 Enumerator Instructions," http://usa.ipums.org/usa/voliii/inst1900.shtml (accessed August 1, 2007).

Integrated Public Use Microdata. "1930 Enumerator Instructions," http://usa.ipums.org/usa/voliii/inst1930.shtml.

Ireland. *General Alphabetical Index to the Townlands and Towns, Parishes, and Baronies of Ireland: Based on the Census of Ireland for the Year 1851*. Baltimore: Genealogical Publishing Co., 1984.

"Irish Family History Foundation: Genealogy in Ireland," http://www.irish-roots.net/ (accessed August 1, 2007).

"Irish Origins," http://irishorigins.com/ (accessed August 1, 2007).

JewishGen. "JewishGen: The Home of Jewish Genealogy," http://www.JewishGen.org/ (accessed August 1, 2007).

JewishGen. "The JewishGen ShtetlSeeker," http://www.JewishGen.org/ShtetlSeeker/ (accessed August 1, 2007).

Kashuba, Melinda. *Walking With Your Ancestors: A Genealogist's Guide to Using Maps and Geography*. Cincinnati: Family Tree Books, 2005.

Kay, George. *Postal Place Names in Poland*. Edinburgh: Kay, 1992.

McCarthy, Tony. *A Guide to Tracing Your Cork Ancestors*. Dublin: Glenageary Co., Flyleaf Press, 1998.

Mitchell, Brian. *A New Genealogical Atlas of Ireland*. Baltimore: Genealogical Publishing Co., 1986.

National Archives. "Native American Records at the National Archives," http://www.archives.gov/genealogy/heritage/native-american/index.html (accessed August 1, 2007).

O'Brien, Patrick. *Oxford Atlas of World History*. New York: Oxford University Press,, 2002.

PBS. "African American Lives," http://www.pbs.org/wnet/aalives/index.html (accessed August 1, 2007).

Polish Genealogical Society of America. "Dziennik Chicagoski Death Notices," http://www.pgsa.org/dzien9029.htm (accessed August 1, 2007).

Polish Genealogical Society of America. "PGSA: Databases," http://www.pgsa.org/database.htm (accessed August 1, 2007).

Reilly, James, and Ireland. *Richard Griffith and His Valuations of Ireland*. Baltimore: printed for Clearfield Co. by Genealogical Publishing Co., 2000.

"Research Guidance: Ireland: Research Outline," http://www.familysearch.org/Eng/Search/RG/guide/Ireland10.asp (accessed August 1, 2007).

Ryskamp, George, and Peggy Ryskamp. *Finding Your Mexican Ancestors: A Beginner's Guide*. Provo, UT: Ancestry, 2006.

Sack, Sallyann, and Gary Mokotoff. *Avotaynu Guide to Jewish Genealogy*. Bergenfield, NJ: Avotaynu, 2004.

Stampp, Kenneth, and Library of Congress. *Records of Ante-bellum Southern Plantations from the Revolution through the Civil War*. Frederick, MD: University Publications of America, 2000.

Streets, David. *Slave Genealogy: A Research Guide with Case Studies*. Bowie, MD: Heritage Books, 1986.

Szucs, Loretto. *The Source: A Guidebook to American Genealogy*. Provo, UT: Ancestry, 2006.

"United States Newspaper Program," http://www.neh.gov/projects/usnp.html (accessed August 1, 2007).

University of Texas Institute of Texan Cultures at San Antonio. *The Greek Texans*. San Antonio: University of Texas at San Antonio Institute of Texan Cultures, 1974.

Witcher, Curt. *African American Genealogy: A Bibliography and Guide to Sources*. Fort Wayne, IN: Round Tower Books, 2000.

Wong, Marie. *Sweet Cakes, Long Journey: The Chinatowns of Portland, Oregon*. Seattle: University of Washington Press, 2004.

"Yad Vashem The Holocaust Martyrs' and Heroes' Remembrance Authority," http://www.yadvashem.org/ (accessed August 1, 2007).

9

Using the Internet

The Internet has transformed genealogical research, making it faster, cheaper, and more efficient. Nevertheless, novice researchers who begin their research on the Internet are often frustrated. Search engines, which are the starting point for most Internet researchers, are not very effective for genealogy research. For example, when I search Google for the term "Simpson genealogy," I get many results, but none of the top results have a connection to my family. Also, many of the resulting Web pages are portals or advertisements for commercial Web sites. This search process often leads novices to conclude that there is not much genealogical information on the Internet without paying a fee, and they are uncertain whether such subscriptions are worth the price. In this chapter, I will discuss how patrons can locate useful genealogy information on the free Internet, and I will describe the content of the major subscription research services.

FREE SOURCES ON THE INTERNET

Rather than relying on a search engine such as Google, effective use of the Internet for genealogical research requires a different set of tools. Genealogists have built an impressive set of free guides for navigating the Web, from Web directories to mailing lists.

Internet Directories: Cyndi's List and Linkpedium

Cyndi's List

Genealogist Cyndi Howells created a Web directory of genealogy Web sites in 1996. Today, her Web site, http://www.cyndislist.com, contains over 250,000 links, sorted into 250 categories, and it is one of the most popular genealogy Web sites. Browsing Cyndi's List is an efficient way to discover Web sites on a particular topic, without the false results and blind alleys that sometimes plague search engine results. The site is particularly useful when confronted with an unfamiliar genealogy research topic.

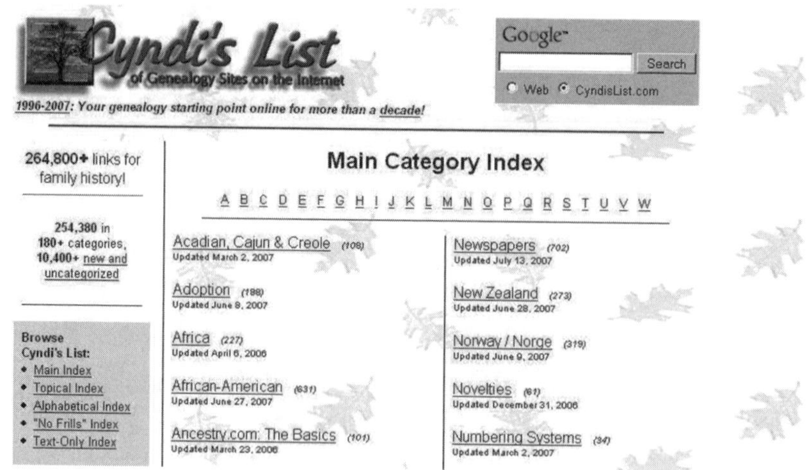

Figure 9.1. Front page of Cyndi's List.

For example, I once received a reference question about Roma people, sometimes referred to as Gypsies. Although I was familiar with this ethnic group, I had not received many questions about them, and I was not familiar with Web resources for researching Roma genealogy. Visiting Cyndi's List, I did not find a category for "Roma," so I typed this term into the site's search engine. This pointed to a set of links on "Gypsies, Romani, Romany and Travellers" under the category "Unique People and Cultures." Although a search engine such as Google might have located some of these sites, Cyndi's list eliminates many of the false results and pay portals.

Cyndi's List is also a quick way to refer patrons to Web sites about a particular topic. For example, patrons often ask for a recommendation for a company that produces wall-sized pedigree charts. I have not purchased such a chart before, so I do not have a recommendation for patrons; instead, I point patrons to the Cyndi's List category for "Supplies, Charts, Forms, etc." (fig. 9.1).

Linkpendium

Linkpendium (http://www.linkpendium.com) is an Internet directory created by two of the founders of Rootsweb. It categorizes Web pages by locality or by surname. In the category of "Simpson family," for example, there are over 500 links sorted by genre (DNA projects, family crests, family histories) and by locality. Although Linkpedium is a relatively new site, it is well organized and seems to be updated frequently.

Cooperative Genealogy Communities

Rootsweb: A Collaborative Community of Web Resources

Rootsweb grew out of several early Internet message boards and was an early place for genealogists to exchange information online. Today, Rootsweb continues to offer a number of ways for researchers to exchange information online: message

Surname	From	To	Migration	Submitter	Comment
Beaudette	1600	now	France>Canada>MN>NE>CO	bbeaudet	
Beaudette	1620	now	Poitiers,FRA>StPierrelesBecquets,PQ,CAN>ME	roldibon	
Beaudette	1800		Fra>Can>USA	bearmugs	
Beaudette	1856	now	Lotbinière,QC,CAN>MA>St-Jean-Baptiste,MB, CAN	vermal	
Beaudette	1866	----	NY>WI>Chicago,IL,USA	kfinegan	
Beaudette	1900	now	FRA>QC,CAN>ON,CAN>Detroit,MI>Massena,NY,USA	lar15	
Beaudette	c1870	now	CAN>MN,USA	matkins	

Figure 9.2. Search results from Rootsweb Surname List.

boards, mailing lists, and user-contributed databases. These include a collaborative database of pedigrees called WorldConnect, a Web site registry called Rootslink, and a set of user-contributed databases.

There are two resources on Rootsweb that I find particularly useful. The first is the Rootsweb Surname List (RSL). The RSL is a registry of researchers investigating particular names. So, for example, a search of the name "Beaudette" results in a list of researchers; clicking on the submitter name yields contact information for that researcher (fig. 9.2). For more common names, RSL is searchable by surname location, so it is possible to search for researchers studying "Simpson" in "Jackson, OH."

When I first began researching genealogy, I tended to focus on finding books and documents in libraries and overlooked the importance of networking with other researchers. As I did more family history research, I came to realize how important it is to seek out other genealogists. Unlike many other areas of inquiry, the bulk of information about any particular family is probably not in publicly accessible archives or public documents. Rather, it is kept in the attics and memories of distant cousins. Tracking down those distant connections is important. The RSL is particularly useful for locating people researching your family. In the Beaudette case study, my friend resolved a family mystery using a Rootsweb board. Her great-great grandfather Adolphus Beaudette divorced her great-great grandmother in Chicago in 1902 but seemed to disappear from records after that date. In her 1948 Social Security application, Adolphus's daughter Vera lists her father's name as "Robert Beaudette." The Chicago city directory of 1910 shows a Robert A. Beaudette. But was this the same man as Adolphus? On the RSL, she found another researcher studying the family of this Robert Beaudette. After an exchange of e-mails, they were able to determine that Adolphus and Robert were the same individual.

E-mail lists or listservs are another useful Rootsweb resource. Like the surname list, the Rootsweb mailing lists are a popular and useful way to interact with other researchers. Rootsweb has several types of lists: surnames, localities, and topical. An index of these lists is linked from the main page of Rootsweb. Researchers can subscribe to a particular list and will then receive e-mail from any other subscriber who contacts the list. Belonging to such a community of researchers can be extremely helpful. For example, I belong to the Cook County, Illinois list. Every week, researchers mail the list with difficult questions: Where can I get a coroner's report? What high schools were in the Douglas neighborhood in 1927? Where are the records of Dunning sanitarium? And every week, list subscribers respond with advice and local expertise. For librarians, the archives of these lists are a useful resource of very specific local genealogy information.

USGenWeb and WorldGenWeb: Geographical Research Networks

The USGenWeb Project began in 1996 as a way to coordinate county-based genealogy Web sites. At that early period in Internet history, many genealogists were building Web sites about particular counties. To help researchers find these sites, a group of genealogists started USGenWeb, which has a page for every state and a page for every county within those states. Because different volunteers maintain each page of the project, the content varies from page to page. The state-level pages tend to include a map of the counties in the state, a general research guide for the state, and some user-contributed data. The county-level pages usually include a research guide, links to genealogy societies and libraries in the county, and a surname registry of researchers. Whenever I research a county that is unfamiliar to me, I browse the content of the USGenWeb page.

For example, when researching the family of Coleman Young, I discovered that his parents were originally from Marengo County, Alabama, so I visited the USGenWeb page for Alabama and then navigated to the Marengo County page. The USGenWeb page for Marengo, http://www.rootsweb.com/~almareng/, contains an assortment of resources: histories of local churches, a marriage index, cemetery headstone transcriptions, a brief history of the county, and short histories of families from the area. After browsing these materials, I did not find anything immediately useful for my case study. However, the site links to a list of researchers studying particular surnames. There, I found a researcher studying the surname "Napier," the maiden name of Coleman Young's grandmother. The e-mail address for the researcher no longer worked, but after a bit of Internet sleuthing, I was able to locate her at a new address. We had a pleasant e-mail exchange, and she confirmed that she was a descendant of the same Napier family. Although our correspondence did not uncover any new information for me, it is the kind of conversation that often leads to a research breakthrough.

There is a similar geographical research network for international genealogy: WorldGenWeb (http://www.worldgenweb.org). WorldGenWeb is divided into six continental regions: North America, South America, Europe, Africa, the Middle East, and Australia. Drilling down further into the site will lead researchers to Web pages for specific countries and states. For example, for researchers studying Mexico, the NorthAmericanGenWeb page links to a page specifically about Mexico. The Mexico page has links to major research institutions, other Mexican genealogy Web sites, personal Web sites about specific families, and links to pages about every Mexican state. Some of the state pages, such as the one for the Mexican state of Sonora (http://homepages.rootsweb.com/~windmill/sonora), are quite detailed, with local histories, record indexes and research links. Other pages are simply message boards. WorldGenWeb, like USGenWeb, is volunteer-run, and the quality of any particular page is dependent upon the person maintaining it.

Ethnic Cooperatives

Beyond Rootsweb and the GenWeb networks, there are cooperative sites for specific ethnic or religious genealogy researchers. For example, there is an extensive Web site for Jewish genealogy research, JewishGen (http://www.JewishGen.org), and a great site for African-American researchers called Afrigeneas (http://www.afrigeneas.com; see the previous chapter for more information on these sites). Using Cyndi's List, the GenWeb sites, and search engines to discover such sites about a particular ethnic genealogy topic is a smart way to use the collaborative possibilities of the Internet.

Online Research Tools

There are many free Internet sources that make research easier, and I have mentioned many such resources in topical parts of this book. Here are some general tools I often consult when helping genealogists that I have not mentioned elsewhere.

Geographical Tools

There are a number of geographical tools on the Internet that help in genealogical research. Online maps such as Mapquest, Yahoo Maps, and Google Maps are basic tools for genealogy research, but beyond those basic map sites, there are other resources that provide information not found on the basic online maps.

The Geographic Names Information System (GNIS) is one such tool. GNIS is a database of geographical names in the United States, maintained by the Department of the Interior. It is freely available at http://geonames.usgs.gov/domestic/index.html. GNIS maintains place names that might appear on a map. The database includes populated places (towns and counties), schools, cemeteries, and geographical features such as lakes and woods. My most common use of GNIS is to determine what county a particular town is in, a task that genealogists often face. GNIS gives more detailed information about particular places than the major online mapping systems, and it is worth exploring when assisting genealogists.

There are a number of sources for digitized online maps. The Library of Congress's American Memory digital portal contains a variety of historical maps: Civil War maps, panoramic birds-eye views, railroad maps, and others. The railroad maps are particularly useful for genealogy, both for researchers looking for information about railroad workers and also because they show the locations of many places that do not appear on current maps. The David Rumsey map collection is another rich source of digitized

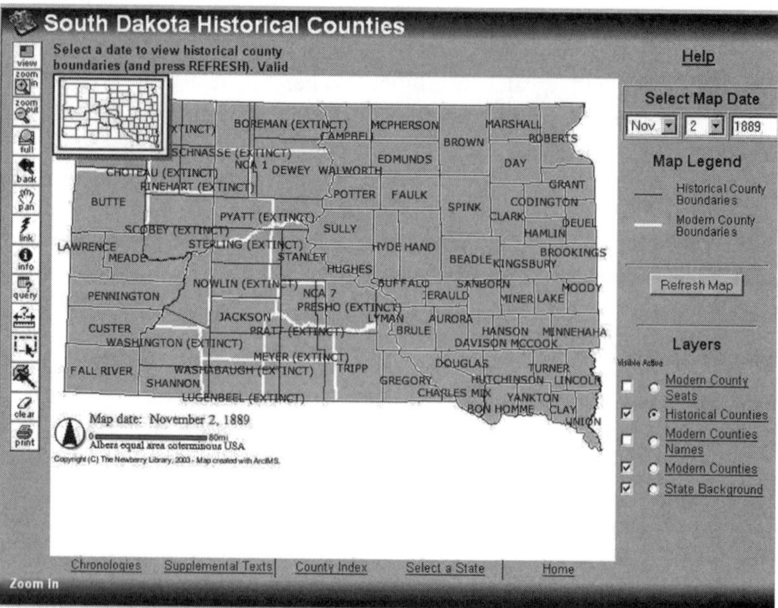

Figure 9.3. Map from the Atlas of Historical County Boundaries, courtesy of the Newberry Library.

maps (http://www.davidrumsey.com). Rumsey, a private collector, has digitized many maps from his collection and presented them online. Recently, parts of the Rumsey collection have been added to the Google Earth digital globe as an overlay, which allows researchers to toggle back and forth from a current map to a historical one. Again, this is a useful source for studying the historical geography of places an ancestor lived.

Finding the boundaries of particular counties is a difficult task, but a basic one for genealogists. Because many records are kept at the county level, researchers need to know what county covered a particular small town in a particular year. The Atlas of Historical County Boundaries is a project of the Newberry Library in Chicago that helps answer this question. The project (originally a print reference project) is creating online GIS maps of historical county boundaries; currently, the project includes maps of California, Dakota Territory, Kansas, Missouri, Montana, New Jersey, North Dakota, South Dakota, Virginia, West Virginia, and Wyoming (http://www.newberry.org/ahcbp) (fig. 9.3).

Translators

There are a number of online translators that are useful for genealogists. For example, the search engine AltaVista features a free online translator called Babelfish (http://www.babelfish.altavista.com), and Google offers another (http://www.google.com/translate). By entering a word, phrase, or block of text into the translator, a researcher can translate from one language to another. Anyone who has used such a tool to translate entire paragraphs quickly realizes some of their limitations: they make grammatical errors, and they cannot handle colloquial or antiquated phrases.

Despite these weaknesses, they are useful for common genealogy research tasks. Researchers examining foreign records sometimes need to translate a few words to understand the document's meaning. For example, a researcher who sees a column of dates entitled "Geburt" on a German church record can use Babelfish to translate that word and learn that it means "birth." Researchers studying ancestors in foreign countries can also use such translators to get the general gist of Web sites from those countries. Cyndi's List has a good set of links to specific translation engines, as well as online word lists and other translation tools, under the category of "Languages and Translations" (http://www.cyndislist.com/language.htm).

Digital Archives

In recent years, major historical libraries, state archives, and local library consortiums have been busy digitizing historical documents and placing them online. Although these digital repositories are not marketed towards genealogists, they often contain material that is very useful for family history research.

American Memory, the Library of Congress's digital archives, is one such collection with great genealogical research value. Beyond the aforementioned map collection, American Memory contains a wealth of local historical records: photographs of communities across the country, pamphlets promoting touring performers, the letters of public figures, and much more. These materials might not immediately seem useful to genealogists, but they are helpful in several ways. First, the local historical material provides context for family history research and brings obscure times and places to life. When researching my great-grandfather, for example, I found photographs from Jackson County, Ohio. Because I had never been there, these historical photographs helped me picture that area. Secondly, these digital archives sometimes have material about distant ancestors. For example, in the Alexander Graham Bell papers on American Memory, I found a letter from a patron's ancestor to Bell. I have similarly located researchers' ancestors in other collections at American Memory, such as the Variety Stage collection and the *Chicago Daily News* photographs.

Similarly, there are many valuable local digital collections. For example, the North Suburban Library System in metropolitan Chicago has digitized a wide variety of local resources as part of its Digital Past project: photographs, high school yearbooks, local histories, newspaper clippings, and more. There is no extremely effective directory of such projects, but the Repositories of Primary Research directory at the University of Idaho is worth browsing. The Idaho site is a state-by-state list of institutions that hold primary resources, but it is also a good place to browse for local history digital sites (http://www.uidaho.edu/special-collections/Other.Repositories.html).

Book Digitization Projects

Massive book digitization projects such as Google Books (http://www.books.google.com), Microsoft Live Books (http://www.live.com), and the Internet Archive (http://www.archive.org/details/texts) have transformed library research. Rare and out-of-print texts that were previously held only in large research libraries are instantly accessible to any Internet researcher. Also, it is now possible to mine the text of these books for names, which is a great development for genealogy research.

WEB 2.0 AND GENEALOGY

In recent years, the technology and culture of the Internet has promoted more interaction between Web sites and their audience. When the World Wide Web was first created, you might visit a newspaper's Web site and read about sports. Now, you might also read a Web log about your favorite team and post your own comments, or you might start your own Web log about the team. The term "Web 2.0" generally refers to this more interactive phase of Internet development.

Characteristic Web 2.0 products are the photo-sharing site Flickr, Wikipedia, and Web logging software such as Blogger. Each of these products do more than deliver information to an audience; they encourage the audience to contribute their own information. Libraries have been experimenting with adding more interactive features to their Web sites. Some libraries have allowed users to add reviews or notes to online catalog records, for example. In genealogy, both commercial Web sites and libraries have been experimenting with "Web 2.0" interactivity. The following products exemplify this trend.

Geni (http://www.geni.com)

Geni is a Web site that allows users to create, store, and share family trees online. Although other Web services such as FamilySearch and Ancestry have long offered similar capabilities, Geni focuses on online collaboration, allowing members to create profiles, Web logs, and invite other family members to collaborate in creating family trees. Geni is a for-profit company and plans to generate revenue through advertising and possibly adding some subscription services. Currently, though, all of its services are free. At the time of writing, Geni is brand new and still in a "beta" stage; some major issues, such as gracefully merging family trees, remain to be resolved. The site seems to be gaining traction, though, with major media coverage and large numbers of reported subscribers.

WeRelate.org (http://www.werelate.org)

WeRelate is a nonprofit social networking site, now affiliated with the Allen County Public Library in Fort Wayne, Indiana. Using a wiki-style interactive template, it allows users to collaborate on Web pages for particular families and places. Like Geni, it allows users to upload and share family trees. At this point, WeRelate is very new, but its wiki pages about particular places are already very useful. It will be interesting to see how it develops as more users join. It is also a promising collaboration between a social networking site and a bricks-and-mortar library.

ChicagoAncestors.org (http://www.ChicagoAncestors.org)

ChicagoAncestors.org is a project of the Newberry Library. It is a free Web site that allows users to plot genealogical and local history information on a map of Chicago. As the director of the project, I am not qualified to give an impartial assessment of the project, but it is another attempt to build an online tool that combines library resources and expertise with user content.

Encyclopedia of Genealogy (http://www.eogen.com)

The Encyclopedia of Genealogy is a growing reference wiki launched by Dick Eastman. It features user-created entries on genealogical topics such as International Genealogy Index Batch Numbers, Reading Old Handwriting, and Surety. Like other wikis, the Encyclopedia's strengths are its ease of use, detailed topical information, and ability to adapt to changes. At the time of writing, the number of entries in the Encyclopedia approached 1,000.

Web Logs and Podcasts

In the last few years, genealogy enthusiasts have created a number of popular Web logs and podcasts. Both podcasts and blogs rely on "RSS," a Web technology that creates a feed. The great advantage of these formats is that they notify subscribers when updated. Users do not need to check and recheck blogs or podcasts for new content because the RSS feed will automatically notify subscribers. As a result, blogs and podcasts are a great tool for disseminating news and fostering discussion. Here are some of the popular blogs and podcasts on genealogy.

- Eastman's Online Genealogy Newsletter (http://blog.eogn.com)
  Dick Eastman is the best known genealogy journalist. Recently, his popular newsletter has morphed into this blog. The blog is the best place for news about new genealogy resources and technology.
- The Genealogue (http://www.genealogue.com)
  The Genealogue is family history enthusiast and humorist Chris Dunham. His Web log features a mix of genealogy news, oddities, and satire, to great effect. He has also created a directory/search engine for other genealogy Web logs, the Genealogy Blog Finder.
- Dear Myrtle (http://www.dearmyrtle.com)
  Dear Myrtle is a blog and podcast created by Pat Richley. Her blog contains news and research tips, and her podcast has featured many notable genealogists as guests.
- The Genealogy Guys Podcast (http://genealogyguys.com)
  The Genealogy Guys are George C. Morgan and Drew Smith. Their podcast is a popular mix of news and analysis of genealogy topics.

SUBSCRIPTION SITES

Although there is a large amount of information freely available on the Internet, access to the major subscription databases is indispensable when building a genealogy collection. The major subscription databases provide access to a large collection of documents otherwise unavailable online: the entire U.S. census, passenger lists, and vital records indexes. There are many subscription databases vying for the attention of reference librarians and researchers; the following are the most popular and significant.

Ancestry Library Edition

Ancestry has long been the dominant product in the genealogy market, both for home subscribers and libraries. Ancestry is run by the Generations Network, a for-profit company that markets a subscription product for home users, and offers a subscription product, Ancestry Library Edition, to libraries. The library product is distributed by ProQuest.

Ancestry's market strength is due to its aggressive program of digitizing primary sources. It was the first company to completely digitize and index the population schedules of the U.S. census, which has long been the core of its content, but it continues to add more material daily. It now has a large collection of digitized military records, biographical indexes, passenger lists, and more. Overall, it includes over 4,000 databases. Because of the number and variety of these databases, I will not attempt to summarize them here because I have highlighted important Ancestry databases in topical chapters throughout this book.

One of the difficulties in using Ancestry is simply finding your way through the mass of information on the site. There are several ways to navigate. The most common way patrons navigate Ancestry is by entering an ancestor's name on the federated search on Ancestry's front page. This search will check all of the databases on the site for a specific name. This is a good way to begin research; it might find information in databases the researcher would not have checked otherwise. However, there are drawbacks to this broad search. First, it often returns too many results for common names, giving researchers too much data to sort through. Second, the broad federated search does not allow researchers advanced search options that might narrow the search effectively, so it makes sense for researchers to search some of the databases individually. The description of "advanced census searching" in Chapter Three is an example of more in-depth searching of a specific database.

Ancestry offers several other options for browsing its database holdings. First, it gives the option "see all databases" from the front page, which leads to a long alphabetical list of the databases. If you know the title of the database you are looking for, this is useful; otherwise, the list is too long for browsing purposes. Therefore, Ancestry offers a "card catalog" search of the databases on the same page. Users can search for a database by title, keyword, or category. Another useful option is to browse the databases by location. By selecting the "search" tab, users can view database holdings by location.

Currently, Ancestry Library Edition is a "must have" for libraries that want to provide their patrons with in-depth genealogy research options. Ancestry provides content that is a basic starting point for many researchers, such as the digitized U.S. census and passenger lists. Having access to these resources can make the difference between helping your patron in your library and sending them elsewhere.

HeritageQuest Online

HeritageQuest Online is a product created and distributed by Proquest. It is only available to libraries; users cannot subscribe from home. Like Ancestry, HeritageQuest has digitized the entire U.S. census. Unlike Ancestry, though, it does not offer indexes of every U.S. census schedule for every year and state, at the time of writing. Although the census database is the most popular part of HeritageQuest, the other features of the site are worth exploring.

Digitized Books

Before the Internet era, University Microfilms Incorporated (now part of Proquest) microfilmed local histories and genealogies at many libraries and sold them on microfiche. Proquest digitized those microfilm and now distributes them as part of HeritageQuest. To find them, select "Search Books" from the front page of HeritageQuest. At the time of writing, searching across the collection is not very effective, due to a clumsy search interface and algorithm. HeritageQuest has promised to improve this function, but in the meantime, users tend to overlook the rich collection of digitized books. However, if you browse the collection by title rather than search the full text, you can see the depth of the collection. I often use this resource when users are searching for a title that we do not hold, and it is remarkable how often I find the requested title.

Other Resources on HeritageQuest

Although HeritageQuest has not been as aggressive as Ancestry in adding new resources, it has added a number of significant databases in recent years. It now includes the Periodical Source Index. It features a search of pension and bounty indexes from the Revolutionary War. It also has added digitized and indexed records from the Freedman's Bank.

GenealogyBank

GenealogyBank is a product from NewsBank. Its major appeal is that it provides hard-to-locate information from newspapers. It includes a database of obituaries extracted from American newspapers published since 1977 and a database of extracts from historical newspapers. It also includes digitized primary documents and published books. Because it does not contain census and other "starting point" material for genealogy researchers, this database is not as popular as Ancestry or HeritageQuest, but it is a growing site, one that provides access to resources that were previously unavailable to most public libraries.

World Vital Records

World Vital Records is a fairly new genealogy service created by Paul Allen, one of the original founders of Ancestry.com. Like the sites mentioned above, it contains a mix of databases, digitized books, and digitized newspapers. As the name suggests, its collection is international in scope and contains a large collection of British parish records.

Footnote

Footnote is a new company that made news recently by signing an agreement to digitize documents from the National Archives. Like Ancestry or Heritagequest, Footnote hosts digitized primary documents, but places a much greater focus on social networking, allowing users to upload their own genealogical documents and tag them. So far, it has digitized some major document sets from the National Archives, including the papers of the Continental Congress and a variety of Civil War sources. It also offers some digitized printed sources, such as city directories and the *Pennsylvania Archives*. Footnote just began offering an institutional subscription, and it is also available at no charge at the regional branches of the National Archives.

Foreign Databases

A number of subscription databases featuring genealogical data from foreign countries are available. For example, the British National Archives now offers the 1901 Census of England on the site http://www.1901censusonline.com. Searching the index is free, but viewing the census images requires payment. A large collection of Swedish Church records is available on the subscription site http://genline.com>. To find similar databases for other nations, researchers should check Cyndi's List or WorldGenWeb.

REFERENCES

"1901 Census of England and Wales Online," http://www.1901censusonline.com/ (accessed August 1, 2007).

"AfriGeneas: African American & African Ancestored Genealogy," http://afrigeneas.org/ (accessed August 1, 2007).

"ALGenWeb: Marengo County," http://www.rootsweb.com/~almareng/ (accessed August 1, 2007).

"AltaVista: Babel Fish Translation," http://babelfish.altavista.com/ (accessed August 1, 2007).

"American Memory from the Library of Congress: Home Page," http://memory.loc.gov/ammem/index.html (accessed August 1, 2007).

"Blogger," https://www.blogger.com/start (accessed August 1, 2007).

"Cyndi's List of Genealogy Sites on the Internet," http://cyndislist.com/ (accessed August 1, 2007).

"David Rumsey Historical Map Collection," http://www.davidrumsey.com/ (accessed August 1, 2007).

"DearMYRTLE.com," http://www.dearmyrtle.com/ (accessed August 1, 2007).

"Eastman's Online Genealogy Newsletter," http://blog.eogn.com/ (accessed August 1, 2007).

"Eogen - Encyclopedia of Genealogy," http://www.eogen.com/ (accessed August 1, 2007).

"Flickr," http://flickr.com/ (accessed August 1, 2007).

"Footnote - The Place for Original Documents Online," http://www.footnote.com/ (accessed August 1, 2007).

"The Genealogue - Genealogy News You Can't Possibly Use," http://www.genealogue.com/ (accessed August 1, 2007).

"GenealogyBank.com," http://www.genealogybank.com/gbnk/keyword.html (accessed August 1, 2007).

"The Genealogy Guys Podcast," http://genealogyguys.com/ (accessed August 1, 2007).

"Geni," http://www.geni.com/ (accessed August 1, 2007).

"Genline: Research Swedish Genealogy Online and Discover your Swedish Ancestry and Heritage," http://genline.com/ (accessed August 1, 2007).

"Google Book Search," http://books.google.com/ (accessed August 1, 2007).

"JewishGen: The Home of Jewish Genealogy," http://www.jewishgen.org/ (accessed August 1, 2007).

"Linkpendium USA," http://www.linkpendium.com/genealogy/USA/ (accessed August 1, 2007).

Microsoft. "Live Search," http://www.live.com/ (accessed August 1, 2007).

The Newberry Library. "Atlas of Historical County Boundaries," http://www.newberry.org/ahcbp/ (accessed August 1, 2007).

The Newberry Library. "ChicagoAncestors.org," http://www.chicagoancestors.org/ (accessed August 1, 2007).

North Suburban Library System. "Digital Past," http://www.digitalpast.org/nsls.php (accessed August 1, 2007).

Ohio Genealogical Society. *Jackson County, Ohio: History and Families, 175th Anniversary, 1816–1991*. Paducah, Ky. (P.O. Box 3101, Paducah 42002-3101): Turner Pub. Co., 1991.

"Repositories of Primary Sources," http://www.uidaho.edu/special-collections/Other.Repositories.html (accessed August 1, 2007).

"RootsWeb.com Home Page," http://www.rootsweb.com/ (accessed August 1, 2007).

"The Sonoran Windmill," http://homepages.rootsweb.com/~windmill/sonora/ (accessed August 1, 2007).

The USGenWebProject. "Free Genealogy and Family History Online - The USGenWeb Project," http://www.usgenweb.com/ (accessed August 1, 2007).

U.S. Geological Survey. "Domestic Names - Main," http://geonames.usgs.gov/domestic/index.html (accessed August 1, 2007).

"WeRelate.org," http://werelate.org/wiki/Main_Page (accessed August 1, 2007).

"Wikipedia," http://www.wikipedia.org/ (accessed August 1, 2007).

"World Vital Records," http://www.worldvitalrecords.com/ (accessed August 1, 2007).

"WorldGenWeb Project," http://www.worldgenweb.org/ (accessed August 1, 2007).

10

Resources of the Family History Library

The Family History Library (FHL) in Salt Lake City is the most important genealogical institution in the world. Run by the Church of Latter Day Saints (LDS; the Mormons), it holds a massive collection of genealogical resources, mostly unpublished facsimiles of original manuscript documents. Through its network of Family History Centers, it allows church members and the general public to use its collection of research material. Its Web site offers free genealogy databases, software, and research tips. Because the resources of the FHL are so significant, helping patrons use the library is an important task for any genealogy librarian (fig. 10.1).

HISTORY OF THE LIBRARY

Family history holds an important place in Mormon theology. Mormons believe that church members can convert their deceased ancestors to the Mormon faith, and so church members compile genealogies as a religious practice. To assist members in this task, church members began the Genealogical Society of Utah in 1894. The Society started a small library that rapidly expanded in the first decades of the 20th century, collecting published family histories and other reference material.

In 1938, the library began microfilming original records held by other institutions. The library began sending out teams of microfilm operators to American county archives, village churches in Italy, and other repositories worldwide to photograph genealogical documents. This process continues today. The microfilms are sent back to the FHL in Salt Lake City, where currently the library holds over 2.4 million reels of microfilm. In 1963, the library built a mountainside vault near Salt Lake City to store master copies of the microfilm.

In 1975, the Genealogical Society of Utah was formally absorbed into the LDS church and renamed the Genealogical Department. In 1987, the library was given its current name, the FHL. The FHL is located in Salt Lake City and is open to the public.

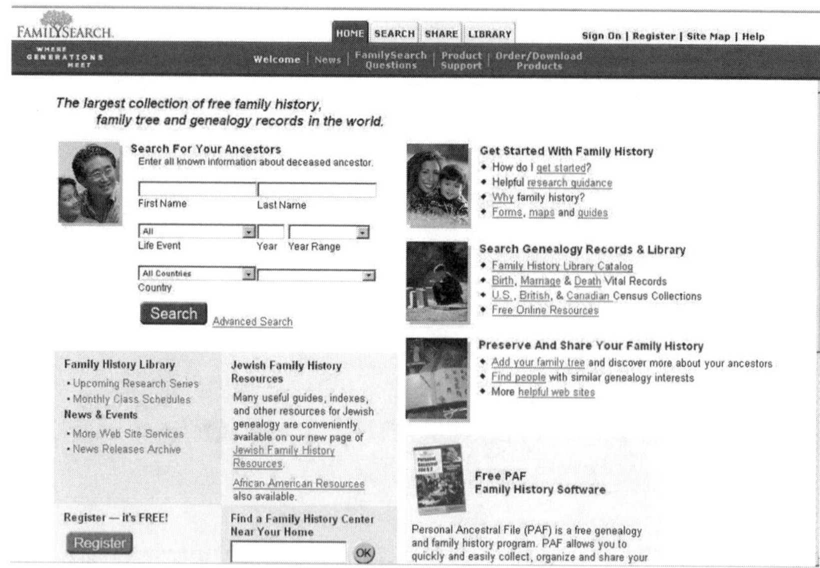

Figure 10.1. Home page of the FHL. FamilySearch.org (c) 1999–2005 by Intellectual Reserve, Inc. Used by permission.

WHAT THE LIBRARY HOLDS

The library is a massive collection of published and unpublished genealogical material. In addition to over 2.4 million reels of microfilm, the library holds over 310,000 books and 4,500 periodicals. Although all of the material is useful to genealogists, the microfilmed manuscript materials are perhaps the most significant, because they are often difficult to obtain otherwise. For instance, researchers who want to look at original Catholic church records from Chicago have two options: they can visit the Chicago Archdiocese archives, or they can obtain microfilm of the records from the FHL. For Americans searching records from other countries, the microfilm records in the FHL are particularly important. Rather than travel to Mexico or Italy and visit churches or town halls, researchers can use the collection of records from the FHL at a local Family History Center.

SEARCHING THE LIBRARY COLLECTION

The Family History catalog is available on the FHL Web site, http://www.familysearch.org/Eng/Library/FHLC/frameset_fhlc.asp, or from the home page, http://www.familysearch.org, select the "Library" tab and then the "Library Catalog" option.

The FHL catalog is not a standard library catalog, and its catalog records are not included in WorldCat. Like most catalogs, it allows searching by title, author, keyword, and Library of Congress subject. However, it has two separate search categories: "Place" and "Surname." These two searches are the most useful way to access materials in the collection.

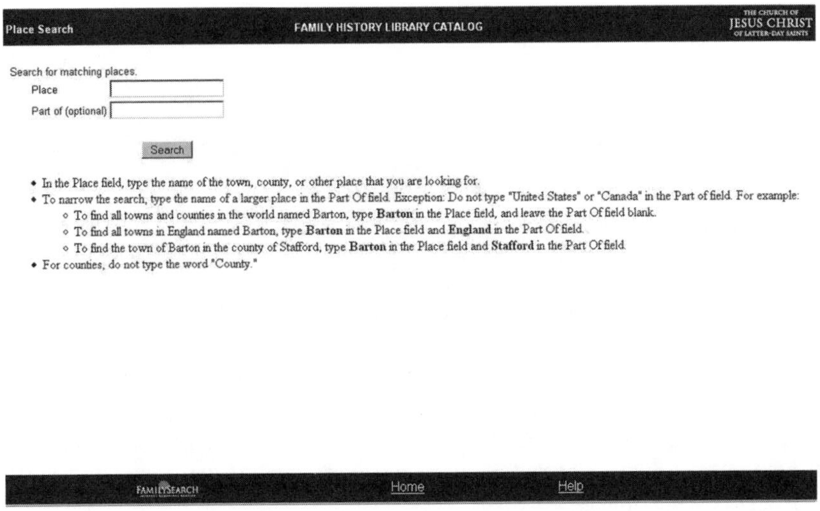

Place Search FAMILY HISTORY LIBRARY CATALOG THE CHURCH OF JESUS CHRIST OF LATTER-DAY SAINTS

Search for matching places.
Place
Part of (optional)

Search

- In the Place field, type the name of the town, county, or other place that you are looking for.
- To narrow the search, type the name of a larger place in the Part Of field. Exception: Do not type "United States" or "Canada" in the Part of field. For example:
  - To find all towns and counties in the world named Barton, type **Barton** in the Place field, and leave the Part Of field blank.
  - To find all towns in England named Barton, type **Barton** in the Place field and **England** in the Part Of field.
  - To find the town of Barton in the county of Stafford, type **Barton** in the Place field and **Stafford** in the Part Of field.
- For counties, do not type the word "County."

FAMILYSEARCH Home Help

Figure 10.2. Place search in the FHL catalog. FamilySearch.org (c) 1999–2005 by Intellectual Reserve, Inc. Used by permission.

Searching by Place

"Place" search is the most useful way to browse the FHL collection of microfilm manuscripts. Let us use Chicago as an example. Suppose I wanted to browse the church records from Chicago held by the FHL. I could start with a place search for "Chicago."

The FHL "Place" search asks for two pieces of information: a place name and what it is part of (fig. 10.2).

Generally, I fill in the first field and leave the second blank; it is best to do a broad search of all places with a certain name and then browse the results. Otherwise, if you fill in the second field incorrectly, you might miss potential matches. Entering "Chicago" in the first field and leaving the second blank gave me the following results:

Chicago
Illinois, Cook, Chicago
Chicago Heights
Illinois, Cook, Chicago Heights
Chicago Junction
Ohio, Huron, Chicago Junction

and a number of other places named Chicago. I selected the first result, which pulled up a list of subject headings:

Illinois, Cook, Chicago - Archives and libraries
Illinois, Cook, Chicago - Archives and libraries - Bibliography
Illinois, Cook, Chicago - Archives and libraries - Inventories, registers, catalogs
Illinois, Cook, Chicago - Biography
Illinois, Cook, Chicago - Biography - Civil War, 1861–1865

Illinois, Cook, Chicago - Biography - Dictionaries
Illinois, Cook, Chicago - Biography - Portraits
Illinois, Cook, Chicago - Business records and commerce
Illinois, Cook, Chicago - Cemeteries
Illinois, Cook, Chicago - Cemeteries - Directories

The list continued to include a total of 91 different subject headings for Chicago. Among them was: *Illinois, Cook, Chicago - Church Records.*

Selecting this option gave me a list of titles:

Alphabetical record of members in full connection, ca. *1846–1905 Simpson Methodist Episcopal Church (Chicago, Illinois)
Annual genealogical report, Form E, 1938–1948 Church of Jesus Christ of Latter-day Saints. West Suburban Branch (Illinois)
Annual reports, 1923–1979 Catholic Church. St. Jerome (Chicago, Illinois: Croatian)
Baptism, marriage, confirmation and communion records, 1869–1920 Catholic Church. St. Jarlath's (Chicago, Illinois)
Baptisms & marriages, 1893–1916 Catholic Church. St. Agatha (Chicago, Illinois)

Altogether, there were a total of 264 titles under this category.

Viewing the Full Record

Among these Chicago churches was one I am interested in: the Wicker Park Methodist Episcopal Church, where Adolphus Beaudette and Ella Tischer married in 1891:

Church records, 1881–1935 Wicker Park Methodist Episcopal Church (Chicago, Illinois)

By clicking on this title, I pulled up the full record of this item:

Title:	Church records, 1881–1935
Authors:	Wicker Park Methodist Episcopal Church (Chicago, Illinois) (Main Author)
Notes:	Microreproduction of original manuscripts at the Northern Illinois Conference, United Methodist Church, Evanston, Illinois
Subjects:	Illinois, Cook, Chicago - Church records Methodists - Illinois
Format:	Manuscript (On Film)
Language:	English
Publication:	Salt Lake City, Utah: Filmed by the Genealogical Society of Utah, 1994
Physical:	on 1 microfilm reel; 35 mm

I can see that this record is a microfilm facsimile of an original manuscript held at the archives of the Northern Illinois Conference of the United Methodist Church in Evanston, Illinois. By clicking on "View Film Notes," I viewed a more detailed record, including the FHL microfilm number (fig. 10.3).

The FHL film number is the call number required to request the film. In this case, the entire title is on the same film, FHL no. 1927962. The item number represents the location of the title on the microfilm: the Wicker Park Methodist Episcopal Church ledger is the fifth title on the reel. Although the item number is not necessary to request the microfilm, it is helpful to know once you have obtained the microfilm.

Statistical record Record of official members .... 1912-1913, 1923 Alphabetical record .... 1887-1903 Members in full connection .... 1891-1895 Alphabetical record of members ca. 1887-1904 full connection Record of probationers .... 1881-1904 Record of marriages .... 1887-1904 Record of baptisms .... 1887-1904 Record of official members .... 1888-1897 Pastoral and statistical record (financial data)	FHL US/CAN Film 1927962 Item 5
Record of official members (no dates) Record of probationers .... 1904- 1911 Rec. of members in alph. order ca. 1891-1912 Record of baptisms .... 1904-1912 Rec. of baptisms in alph. order ca. 1926-1934 Record of marriages .... ca. 1926-1935 Deaths 1928	FHL US/CAN Film 1927962 Item 5

Figure 10.3. FHL catalog record: film notes. FamilySearch.org © 1995–2005 by Intellectual Reserve, Inc. Used by permission.

Searching by Surname

Searching by surname allows researchers to access the library's rich collection of family histories. Searching for Beaudette, for example, returns two results:

Title: *Bodett-Bodette-Beaudette Family: Weiland, Wruck, Quigley Families, & Miscellaneous*
Author: Bodett, Thomas P.
Title: *Genealogy of the Baudet-Beaudet-Beaudette-Boudette-Bodet Family*
Author: Boudette, John E. Beaudette

Neither of these titles are found in other libraries through WorldCat. Looking at the full record of the first title indicates that it is a microfilm of an original manuscript family history. The second appears to be a self-published compilation of marriage records of Beaudette family members.

BORROWING MICROFILM

The FHL allows the general public to borrow microfilm through a network of church-affiliated research institutions (called Family History Centers) and certain nonaffiliated genealogy libraries. Otherwise, their films are not available through a standard interlibrary loan.

To find a Family History Center, researchers can search a database of locations available on the FHL Web site, http://www.familysearch.org/Eng/Library/FHC/frameset_fhc.asp. Researchers can visit one of these locations and fill out a call slip to request a microfilm. The film generally takes a minimum of two weeks to arrive and is generally kept at the borrowing institution for a month. Currently, each film costs $5.50.

The network of Family History Centers is an amazing resource for genealogy researchers. At the Newberry Library, we have FHL borrowing privileges, so patrons can visit our library to borrow microfilmed records from Italy or Poland. However, the FHL borrowing network also allows us to give remote researchers a convenient way to access our local resources. If a patron from Bozeman, Montana calls our library wanting to browse the records of St. Agatha's Catholic Church in Chicago, we can recommend that they visit the Family History Center in Bozeman and borrow the microfilm.

ONLINE DATABASES

The FHL has a set of unique databases available for free on the library's FamilySearch Web site. On the front page of the FamilySearch Web site, a cross-database search is available by entering names into the "Search for Your Ancestors" field. Alternately, researchers can explore the databases individually by selecting the "Search" tab at the top of the page. Each of the FHL databases is slightly different and provides different kinds of information for researchers.

The International Genealogical Index (IGI)

The FHL compiled the IGI by extracting names from its collection of microfilm and allowing researchers to contribute their own genealogical information. The result is a very large database of over 400 million entries, primarily birth and marriage records from 1500 to 1885. Entries submitted before the 1990s include a citation of the LDS microfilm number, whereas entries submitted more recently do not show source information or submitter number. On the pre-1990 entries, the source information is sometimes a microfilm of family information submitted by an LDS church member, and at other times, it is a microfilmed manuscript from the FHL collection.

To use an example from the John Simpson case study, I searched the IGI for the Scottish marriage record of David Simpson, the immigrant ancestor who arrived in New York in 1835. Because I knew the rough time and county, I searched for marriages of David Simpson to Ann Thompson in Fife circa 1829. One of the entries appeared promising:

DAVID SIMPSON	
Spouse:	ANN THOMSON
Marriage:	20 NOV 1829 Kirkcaldy, Fife, Scotland
Source Information:	
Batch No.:	M114429
Dates:	1820–1867
Source Call No.:	1040187
Type:	Film

By clicking on the source number, I pulled up the record of the original record from the LDS catalog:

Title:	Old parochial registers, 1614–1867
Authors:	Church of Scotland. Parish Church of Kirkcaldy

By borrowing this film, I can examine the original microfilmed church record from the church in Kirkcaldy. I have not always been so lucky in using the IGI; often, the results do not link to an original manuscript or do not give information about who submitted the record. In these cases, I advise researchers to user the entry as a possible lead but not to rely upon it as evidence.

Vital Records Index (VRI)

Like the IGI, the VRI extracts genealogical information from microfilmed manuscript records held by the FHL. The FHL has released portions of the VRI on CD-ROM, available for sale on the FHL Web site. At the time of writing, only VRI entries from Scandinavia and Mexico are available on the FHL Web site. Just as with the example from the IGI, results from the VRI will lead researchers to original source records.

Ancestral File and Pedigree Resource File

Ancestral File is a collection of electronic pedigree charts submitted to the FHL. Ancestral File differs from the IGI and the VRI in that it is made up of unverified submissions from researchers and does not directly cite primary source material. Entries were added to Ancestral File from 1989 to 2001, when the FHL stopped accepting additions to the file. Information in the Ancestral File is arranged in a pedigree chart format, so researchers can easily move from information about an individual to information about that person's parents or children. Many entries in the Ancestral File give contact information for the researcher who submitted the pedigree. For technical reasons, the FHL stopped adding information to the Ancestral File in 2001 and replaced it with the Pedigree Resource File. Like its predecessor, the Pedigree Resource File is a database of pedigrees charts. However, the full pedigrees are only available on CD-ROM at Family History Centers. The Pedigree Resource File available on the FamilySearch site is a name index to those submitted pedigree charts.

Reference Materials

In addition to the library catalog and the databases, the FamilySearch Web site contains a great deal of instructive reference material for genealogy researchers. Under the "search" tab on the Web site, there are two sets of subject guides: "research help" and "research guidance." The former category includes a large set of geographical research bibliographies, from "Alabama Historical Background" to "Yukon Territory, Canada, Vital Records." These bibliographies are a great shortcut

A Common Patron Mistake: "My Family Is Not On the Mormon Site"

When assisting patrons, I often suggest that we check the FHL catalog to see what microfilm they have on a particular place or family. Occasionally, patrons will tell me that this is a dead end because they have already been to the FamilySearch Web site and did not find anything. Usually, these patrons have visited the FHL Web site and entered a name into the databases, with no success. However, in most cases, the patron has not searched the library catalog and is unaware of the procedure for borrowing microfilm. Because the databases are more prominent on the FHL Web site, novice researchers tend to incorrectly assume they search all of the data available from the FHL. In doing so, they overlook the microfilm collection, which is a much richer source of information than the databases. Therefore, if patrons tell you they have exhausted the resources at FamilySearch, make sure they are aware of the library catalog.

when researching a new area. The "research guidance" pages similarly contain "how-to" resources for a variety of genealogy subjects.

FUTURE PROJECTS

There are several ongoing projects that will make the resources of the FHL much more accessible. The first is a major digitization program called Project Scanstone. Essentially, the FHL is planning to digitize its microfilm library and make it largely available through the Internet. Scanning is ongoing, and the first phase of the project is projected to be complete in 2011. This project is likely to revolutionize genealogical research.

Another ongoing project is a more extensive name extraction and indexing initiative using new collaborative software developed by the FHL. The software makes it much easier for volunteers to work on indexing projects through the Internet. There is a demonstration of the new software on a separate FamilySearch indexing Web site, http://www.familysearchindexing.org.

The FHL has created new software called Record Search that allows researchers to browse their newly digitized records and search the new indexes, now available at http://labs.familysearch.org/.

The Library is also working on updating its Web site with new pedigree software. Researchers can follow the progress of this project at the FamilySearch Labs Web site, http://labs.familysearch.org.

REFERENCES

Church of Scotland. Parish Church of Kirkcaldy (Fifeshire). *Old Parochial Registers for Kirkcaldy, 1614–1867* (Salt Lake City: Genealogical Society of Utah, 1951–1979), microfilm of original records in the New Register House, Edinburgh, Kirkcaldy is parish 442, FHL British film 1040187.

Family History Library. "History of the Family History Library," http://www.familysearch.org/Eng/Library/FHL/frameset_library.asp?PAGE=library_history.asp (accessed August 13, 2007).

"FamilySearch Indexing: Preserving Our Heritage," http://www.familysearchindexing.org/en/index.jsp (accessed August 13, 2007).

"FamilySearch Labs," http://labs.familysearch.org/ (accessed August 13, 2007).

Szucs, Loretto Dennis, and Sandra Hargreaves Luebking, eds. *The Source: A Guidebook of American Genealogy*. Provo, UT: Ancestry, 2006.

Wicker Park Methodist Episcopal Church (Chicago, Illinois). *Church Records* (Salt Lake City: Genealogical Society of Utah, 1994), microfilm of original manuscripts at the Northern Illinois Conference, United Methodist Church, Evanston, Illinois, FHL US/CAN film 1927962 item 5.

11

The National Archives and Other Repositories

This book is intended to guide librarians at small institutions in using resources at hand: easily available print resources or online sources. However, some patrons' research problems cannot be solved by the resources typically available at a small public library. In these cases, librarians need to refer researchers to more specialized research institutions. I have already discussed one such institution, the Family History Library. This chapter describes several other categories of institutions for further genealogy research: the National Archives and its regional branches, specialized genealogy libraries, major public library collections, and state libraries/archives.

THE NATIONAL ARCHIVES

Mission and History

The general public usually thinks of the National Archives as a building in Washington, DC that exhibits the Declaration of Independence, the Constitution, and a few other documents, but the exhibit hall of the National Archives is just the most visible part of a vital federal agency (officially, the National Archives and Records Administration [NARA]), with a vast collection of historical records. NARA stores millions of records, including the Constitution, but also Civil War pension records, ship manifests, the e-mail of recent presidential administrations, and much more. NARA includes not only the Washington, DC headquarters, but also regional branches and presidential libraries from Alaska to Atlanta. Navigating an institution of such size and complexity can be daunting for novice researchers, but librarians can help by explaining some of the basics of the NARA system.

Understanding the history of NARA helps explain how its records are organized. The National Archives is a relatively new institution; it was founded in 1934, over 150 years after the creation of the federal government. Before the creation of the Archives, federal agencies such as the Census Bureau or the Bureau of Indian Affairs kept their own historical records. Throughout the 19th and early 20th centuries, fires and floods at administrative storage facilities destroyed many important documents, including the population schedules of the 1890 census.

In the early 20th century, historical organizations such as the American Historical Association lobbied for the creation of a facility to store government documents. Meanwhile, the rapid growth of the federal government in the first decades of the 20th century made storing records a greater burden on federal agencies. Responding to these pressures, Congress passed an act creating the National Archives in 1934. The new institution was charged with the mission of preserving and making accessible government records of historical importance. It continues that mission today.

Organization of NARA Records

The organizing principle of NARA (and most archival institutions) is *provenance*. This term simply means that the records are arranged according to the agency that created them, rather than by topic. Major federal agencies are assigned "Record Group" numbers, and agency records reflect the organization of the agencies. NARA's *Guide to Federal Records* (available at http://www.archives.gov/research/guide-fed-records) gives an overview of the Record Groups. For example, the Department of Veterans Affairs is assigned Record Group 15. The *Guide*'s description of Record Group 15 shows how the records of the Department are organized (fig. 11.1).

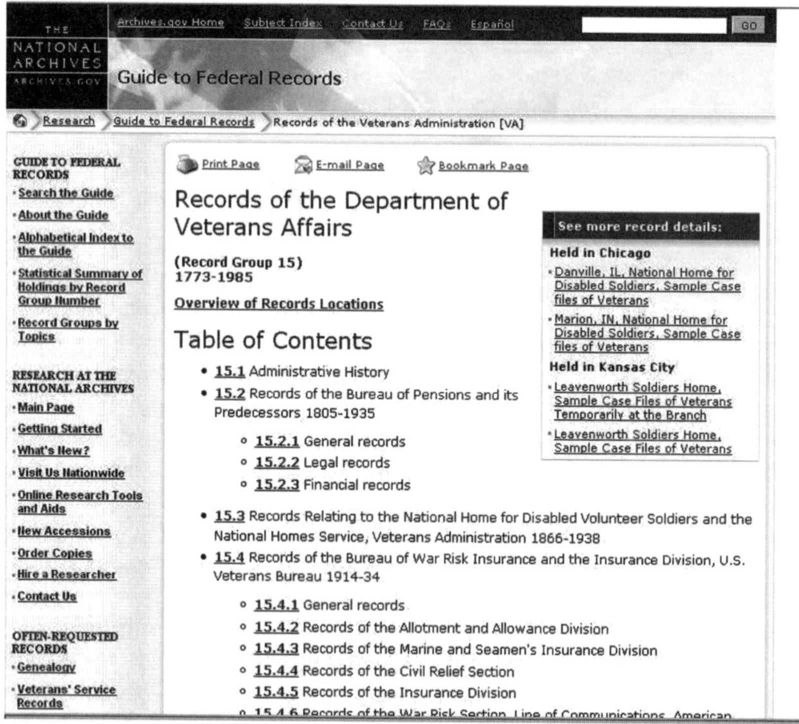

Figure 11.1. Description of Record Group 15, Department of Veterans Affairs, from the online *Guide to Federal Records*, http://www.archives.gov/research/guide-fed-records/.

For the most part, this system of organization does not mean much to the casual genealogy researcher. Because genealogists are the largest group of nonprofessional users of the National Archives, NARA has created many special finding aids and request forms for genealogists. Few genealogy researchers consult the *Guide to Federal Records* or are familiar with the concept of *provenance*. If they need to get a Civil War service record, they fill out a special form for this request, rather than navigate the Archives' organizational scheme. Nevertheless, understanding this basic organizational scheme is helpful when answering questions about federal records.

Regional Branches

The National Archives has two main facilities near the national capitol: Archives I in Washington, DC, and Archives II in College Park, Maryland. Beyond this, NARA maintains a network of regional archives. The regional branches hold original manuscript materials related to the regions they serve; they also serve as research sites where genealogists can access copies of certain federal records on microfilm. The regional branches also offer free access to Ancestry.com, HeritageQuest, and Footnote.com.

For example, the Great Lakes branch of the National Archives has original naturalization records from federal courts in the Great Lakes region (which includes Illinois, Indiana, Michigan, Minnesota, Ohio, and Wisconsin) but also holds microfilm records of the Freedmen's Bureau offices of Mississippi and other southern states (fig. 11.2).

Genealogical Holdings of the Archives

The holdings of the National Archives are vast and difficult to summarize; they consist of the variety of historical documents created by the U.S. government. Rather than attempt a survey, I will highlight some of the records genealogists find most useful.

The Archives are the official repository for many of the records discussed in earlier chapters:

- Federal census records

  NARA is the official repository of census records, although they are now primarily accessed through subscription Web sites.
- Passenger manifests

  Like the census, many passenger manifests are now available through Ancestry.com, the Ellis Island database, and other sources, but NARA is the official repository of these records.
- Naturalization records

  Naturalization records filed at federal courts are held by the Archives and are generally kept at the regional branches.
- Military records

  NARA is the official repository of U.S. military records. Indexes to some of military records have been microfilmed and are available at the regional archives or are available digitally through subscription databases. However, many of the most valuable records are still only available by visiting the capitol-area branches of the Archives or by submitting expensive copy request forms.

State	Facility
Alaska	Anchorage - NARA's Pacific Alaska Region (Anchorage)
California	Laguna Niguel - NARA's Pacific Region (Laguna Niguel) San Francisco (San Bruno) - NARA's Pacific Region (San Francisco)
Colorado	Denver - NARA's Rocky Mountain Region
Georgia	Atlanta - NARA's Southeast Region
Illinois	Chicago - NARA's Great Lakes Region (Chicago)
Massachusetts	Boston - NARA's Northeast Region (Boston) Pittsfield - NARA's Northeast Region (Pittsfield) (Microfilm Research Room only, no original records)
Missouri	Kansas City - NARA's Central Plains Region (Kansas City) St. Louis - Archival Research Room in the National Personnel Records Center
New York	New York City - NARA's Northeast Region (New York City)
Pennsylvania	Philadelphia - NARA's Mid Atlantic Region (Center City Philadelphia)
Texas	Fort Worth - NARA's Southwest Region
Washington (State)	Seattle - NARA's Pacific Alaska Region (Seattle)

Figure 11.2. Regional branches of the National Archives.

- Freedmen's records

  The Archives holds the records of the Freedmen's Bureau and Freedmen's Bank. The latter have been well indexed and are available digitally through HeritageQuest Online. Parts of the Freedmen's Bureau are now available online through Ancestry.com but are not indexed; researchers may still find the microfilm copies of the records available at regional branches of the Archives more useful.

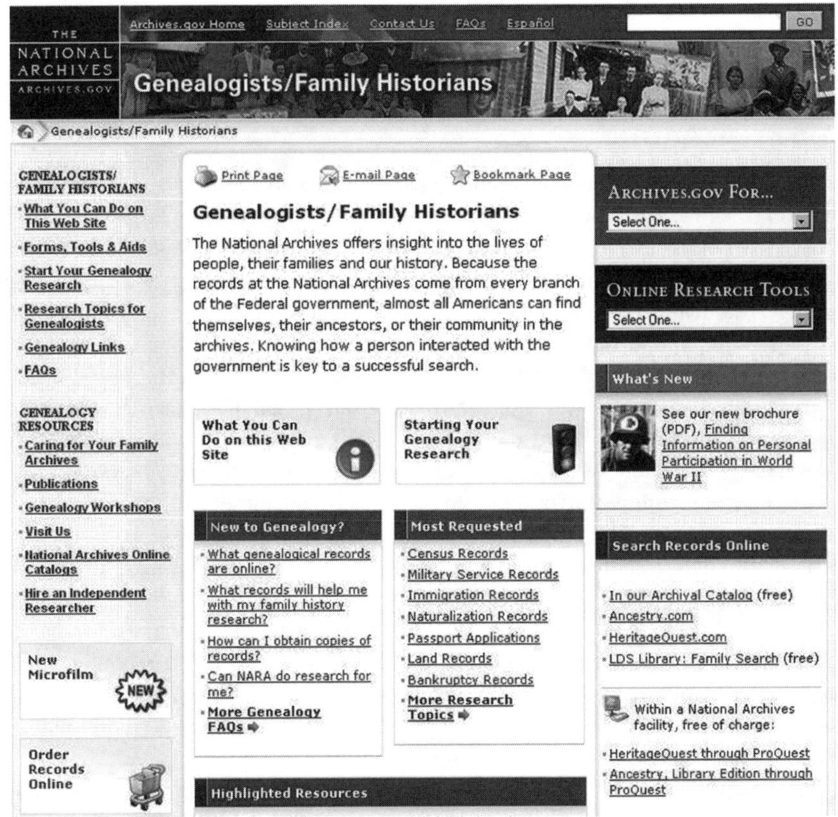

Figure 11.3. Genealogy research page from the National Archives Web site, http://archives.gov/genealogy/.

- Native American records

  The Archives holds a wide variety of records relating to Native Americans: censuses, tribal rolls, and records of the Bureau of Indian affairs.

Genealogy Guides to NARA Holdings

The archive maintains a genealogy research page on its Web site, http://archives.gov/genealogy (fig. 11.3). This page links to a number of specific guides for genealogists, such as a guide to military records (http://archives.gov/genealogy/military) and one for researching land ownership (http://archives.gov/genealogy/land).

The genealogy page also links to helpful articles in the National Archives magazine, *Prologue*. Each issue of the magazine includes an article on genealogy resources. The articles often provide an overview of a particular genealogical research topic. The genealogy articles from *Prologue* are archived online at http://archives.gov/publications/prologue/genealogy-notes.html.

The Archives also sells some printed guides to subjects including Native American records, African-American research, and Confederate records in the Archives.

These major guides are described and available to purchase on the NARA Web site at http://archives.gov/publications/lists/topic-genealogy.html.

The Archival Research Catalog (ARC) and Access to Archival Databases (AAD)

NARA maintains two searchable indexes of its holdings online: the ARC and AAD. Both tools describe a great amount of information, but neither is particularly user-friendly.

ARC is an online catalog to federal records held in NARA's Washington repositories, the regional branches, and the presidential libraries. It is currently incomplete, covering 50% of the NARA's records, and some record groups are only described at the series level, so that individual documents might not be described. In cases where NARA has digitized records, results from ARC will link to the digital copy.

I tried searching for names from the case studies, and I found a few results. A search for "Ezra Winter" (from the Renata Winter case study) returned several hits. Photographs of several of Winter's paintings are included in Record Group 66: Records of the Commission of Fine Arts. ARC found these records and linked to digitized copies of the photographs.

Coleman Young, being the mayor of a major city, naturally shows up in ARC. For example, the Jimmy Carter presidential library includes a picture of Young visiting Carter at the White House in 1977, as part of the records of the president.

Although both of these examples are of public figures, ARC does include information about individuals who were not famous. ARC includes tribal enrollment cards, Immigration and Naturalization Service documents related to individual Chinese immigrants, and court records from Fort Smith, Arkansas.

AAD is NARA's tool for searching records that were "born digital"; working databases created by federal agencies that have now been turned over to the archives. Currently, there are 475 databases in AAD, which is a small portion of the electronic records held by NARA. Most of these databases are not useful to genealogists, but AAD does include World War II enlistment records and a few other sets of data that are valuable for genealogy research.

NARA and Footnote.com

Recently, the National Archives signed a deal with Footnote.com, a new subscription database company. Footnote is allowed to digitize record sets from the National Archives, and the National Archives is given free access to the Footnote database at its regional archives. This has made more records available digitally at regional branches and has made the same records available on the Internet for a fee.

SPECIALIZED LIBRARIES AND RESEARCH INSTITUTIONS

In addition to the National Archives and the Family History Library, there are a number of other specialized genealogy research libraries that can assist your patrons.

The Allen County Public Library (ACPL) (http://www.acpl.lib.in.us/genealogy/index.html)

The ACPL in Fort Wayne, Indiana holds the second largest genealogy collection in the country, after the Family History Library in Salt Lake City. The library collects genealogies and family history source material with a national scope. The library also holds the best collection of genealogy periodicals in the country and maintains the Periodical Source Index, the major genealogy periodical source index. Recently, the ACPL underwent a major renovation, expanding and improving its physical space. It also affiliated with WeRelate.org, a genealogy social networking Web site.

The Daughters of the American Revolution (DAR) Library (http://www.dar.org/library)

The DAR is a patriotic lineage society founded in 1890. To gain membership to the organization, applicants submit lineages tracing their ancestry to an American patriot of the Revolutionary War. In 1896, the Society created a library in Washington, DC to assist genealogy researchers and maintain its members' lineages. The library holds a large collection of published family histories, printed indexes, reference material related to the Revolutionary and colonial periods, genealogical manuscript material, and more. Researchers can order DAR member applications through the DAR Library. This service answers a fairly common researcher question: "I think my great-grandmother was a DAR member; where can I find out more about this?" Librarians can refer such questions to the DAR library. There is more information about requesting copies on the DAR Library Web site.

Godfrey Memorial Library (http://www.godfrey.org)

The Godfrey Memorial Library is a small independent library in Middletown, Connecticut that specializes in genealogy. It is notable for offering library members (called "Godfrey scholars") access to a strong collection of databases through its Web portal. In recent years, the Godfrey was forced to remove some commercial databases after vendors objected to the licensing arrangement. Despite this, the Godfrey's reasonable membership rate provides researchers with access to a number of valuable electronic resources.

The Newberry Library (http://www.newberry.org)

The Newberry Library is an independent research library in the humanities located in Chicago. Founded in 1887, the Newberry is one of the oldest genealogy research institutions in the county. It holds a large collection of genealogies, local histories, maps and atlases, and other genealogy reference material. It holds some manuscript material of genealogical interest, including employment records of Pullman railroad workers. This year, it launched http://ChicagoAncestors.org, a new Web site for Chicago local history and genealogy.

The New England Historic Genealogical Society (NEHGS) (http://www.newenglandancestors.org)

The NEHGS is the oldest genealogical research institution in the United States. It was founded in 1845 and began publishing its journal, *The New England Historical and Genealogical Register*, two years later. Since its founding, the Society has assisted researchers searching for their New England ancestors or studying the history of that region. It has also undertaken major indexing and transcription projects, publishing major indexes to New England vital records, for example. In recent years, NEHGS has placed a large collection of databases on its Web site, including a full-text database of the *Register* from 1847–2000. The databases are only available to members, but the NEHGS offers a very reasonable institutional membership.

Major Public Library Collections

In addition to these specialized institutions, many large public libraries hold major genealogy collections and provide excellent reference services. For example, the Western History and Genealogy Collection at the Denver Public Library (http://history.denverlibrary.org/collections/index.html) is a major genealogy resource center. It began specializing in genealogy in 1910, and it holds extensive resources for Colorado research, Native American genealogy, Denver neighborhood research, and much more. Similarly, the Mid-Continent Public Library maintains an active genealogy branch, serving the greater Kansas City area. It holds a large circulating collection of genealogies and has a particular strength in Missouri family history.

There are many strong collections similar to the examples above: the Carnegie Library of Pittsburgh, The New York Public Library Research Center, the Clayton Library of the Houston Public Library, and the Burton Collection of the Detroit Public Library are additional examples. Public libraries are keepers of memory for local communities; therefore, many libraries hold strong collections of genealogy. If you have a patron who is having difficulty with genealogy research for a particular city or region, encourage them to explore the major public libraries in the region. This holds true for smaller communities as well as large cities; local public libraries are often the best source for genealogical material and expertise.

State Libraries and Archives

Many state governments maintain historical libraries or archives that collect genealogy material. Here in Illinois, the Abraham Lincoln Presidential Library (formerly the State Historical Library) maintains genealogy and local history reference materials and has the best newspaper collection in the state. Also, the Illinois State Archives has put a large number of genealogical databases on its Web site. In Michigan, the Library of Michigan provides genealogy reference service, creates genealogy databases, and hosts family history seminars. Many other states including Indiana, New York, Texas, Connecticut, and Ohio provide genealogy services at state libraries.

REFERENCES

"Allen County Public Library: Genealogy," http://www.acpl.lib.in.us/genealogy/index.html (accessed July 10, 2008).

"Daughters of the American Revolution Library," http://www.dar.org/library/ (accessed July 10, 2008).

"Denver Public Library: Western History and Genealogy," http://history.denverlibrary.org/ (accessed July 10, 2008).

"Footnote," http://www.footnote.com/ (accessed August 1, 2007).

"Godfrey Memorial Library," http://www.godfrey.org/ (accessed July 10, 2008).

"Mid-Continent Public Library: Genealogy and Family History Resources," http://www.mcpl.lib.mo.us/genlh/ (accessed July 10, 2008).

The National Archives. "Genealogists/Family Historians - Resources for Genealogists and Family Historians," http://archives.gov/genealogy/ (accessed August 1, 2007).

The National Archives. "Guide to Federal Records - Guide to Federal Records in the National Archives of the United States," http://www.archives.gov/research/guide-fed-records/ (accessed August 1, 2007).

The National Archives. "U.S. National Archives and Records Administration - Archives.gov Home," http://archives.gov/ (accessed August 1, 2007).

"The Newberry Library," http://www.newberry.org/ (accessed July 10, 2008).

"New England Historic Genealogical Society," http://www.newenglandancestors.org/ (accessed July 10, 2008).

Prologue: Journal of the National Archives. Washington, DC: National Archives Trust Fund Board, 1987.

Schaefer, Christina. *The Center: A Guide to Genealogical Research in the National Capital Area.* Baltimore: Genealogical Publishing Co., 1996).

12

The Genealogy Reference Interview

APPROACHES OF PATRONS TO RESEARCH

As a reference librarian, you stand between a befuddled patron and a world of genealogy information. If you have read the first part of this book and tried some of your own research, you now have a rough map of that world. The novice patron, however, has no knowledge of the research terrain and does not know where to begin. Different patrons approach this problem in different ways. Consider three typical approaches of novice genealogy patrons.

Too Much Information

Some patrons visit the reference desk and begin to recite everything they know about their family history. While simply enjoying sharing their lineage with a captive audience, most of these garrulous patrons recite what they know, hoping to provide you with a basis for helping them.

Too Little Information

Other patrons, afraid of occupying your time, will choose a short, seemingly simple question to advance their research. For example, patrons will often ask where to find birth certificates.

Complete Beginner

Some patrons will simply approach and admit they have no idea how to get started researching their family.

In each of these cases, reference librarians need to determine several things. First, what information is the researcher really looking for? Second, what is the most practical way to find it? Often, the best way to answer both questions is to walk novices through the basic starting points for genealogical research.

USING THE FOUR BASIC STEPS

In the first chapter, I discussed the four basic steps in genealogy research: getting organized, talking to relatives, using the census, and using vital records. You can use these steps to reframe researchers' questions so that they can find the information they are searching for. Although these four basic steps will not answer every question, skipping them makes research much more difficult. Consider how each of the steps can be used to help the typical patrons mentioned above.

Getting Organized

Each of the typical patrons mentioned above can benefit from organization. For the very beginner, filling out a family tree clarifies the information they are starting with. It also suggests one of the basic principles of genealogy research: work backwards in time from yourself.

For the patron who recites the saga of his or her family history, the family tree chart offers a way to narrow his or her focus to a manageable task for both patron and librarian. Helping this patron organize his or her information is a prerequisite to answering the patron's question; otherwise, the flow of details becomes overwhelming (after about a minute and two or three great-grandparents.) Rather than letting the patron speak indefinitely, a reference librarian can listen to the beginning of the patron's family history and then ask if he or she has recorded family history in a family tree. If not, the librarian can have the patron fill it out. Once the patron has a family tree, the librarian can ask the patron to pick one individual of interest and focus on helping the patron locate sources on that ancestor. This narrows the patron's focus to a manageable example. By researching that single ancestor, the patron will learn how to research the others.

In the case of an individual who gives very little information, looking at a chart can help broaden his or her focus. Instead of concentrating on finding a particular kind of document, the family tree chart helps convey the broader goal of connecting two generations. Again, a reference librarian can ask the patron to focus on one individual and to consider the many different kinds of documents that might provide information about the individual.

Using the Census

For all three kinds of researcher, the census is an extremely effective starting point for research.

For complete beginners, the census helps instill confidence. As noted in Chapter Two, the census is easily accessible and includes many individuals. With a little assistance, beginners are very likely to find their ancestors in the census. Helping a patron achieve a bit of success is important because it can change the patron's attitudes towards the research process. Many novices first approach the library with skepticism about genealogy research. They may have spent frustrating hours searching the Internet for family information and may think that their task is nearly impossible. They may also assume that because their ancestors were not rich or famous, they will not be recorded in historical documents. Helping these researchers find an ancestor in the census flips a switch in their minds. Once researchers know that success is a possibility, they are much more patient and persistent in their research.

The process of searching the census also illustrates some of the typical challenges of genealogy research: how names are often misspelled, the technique of trying different search variables, and the need to be flexible. In showing a novice how to use the census, the librarian also teaches the person about basic search techniques. This requires more than simply pointing a patron to the census; the reference librarian should also walk the patron through an example.

For patrons who ask very narrow questions, the census can help broaden their perspective. For example, consider the case of the patron who asks for a birth certificate. It is important to give the patron the answer to a direct question and to explain how to research a birth certificate, but it might be equally important to direct a patron to the census because the census might provide some of the information he or she is looking for more quickly and cheaply than a birth certificate. If the patron's grandparent was born in 1915, the 1920 census would show the child's parents (if the child was living with the birth parents at the age of 5). Therefore, the census might provide a patron with some of the information he or she is looking for: the names of the child's parents and the place of birth.

For the long-winded, disorganized patron, the census provides a document to work from. Rather than relying on a half-remembered family story told years earlier, you are working from an unchanging document. Although some of the information in the census may be inaccurate, it provides some solid data to work from. It helps disorganized researchers stick to some basic facts about the individuals they are researching.

Vital Records/Social Security Death Index

When researchers are not having success with the census, vital records are an effective starting point. Patrons who cannot find their ancestors in the 1930 census might find a more recent record in a state death index or in the Social Security death index. Like the census, such documents provide a fixed set of evidence to work from, and they also give clues that will lead to other documents. The downside of these documents is their relative inaccessibility; patrons often must pay a fee and wait several weeks before getting them. This can be discouraging for some patrons, but sometimes there is little choice.

Talking to Family Members

Generally, I do not like to send researchers away empty-handed because I want them to understand that library resources can help them. However, when patrons have difficulty getting started using the census and vital records, it sometimes helps to suggest that they talk to family members before proceeding with their research further. Perhaps other relatives can provide details that will help them break through their research problem. In these cases, I suggest they talk to other family members, fill out a pedigree chart with their help, and then return to the library and try documentary research once again.

Emphasizing the basics is the best strategy for helping novices. It will not answer every question, but it will help researchers start off on the right foot.

COMMON RESEARCHER MISTAKES

It is also important to guide researchers away from dead ends and give them realistic strategies. With that goal in mind, here are some common researcher mistakes to look out for.

Lack of Flexibility

If our case studies show us anything, it is that we need to be flexible in pursuing research. Paper documents and human memory can both be flawed, so research requires skepticism of every piece of information. Often, researchers cling to the story they have heard or treat details recorded on a legal document as the truth, thereby blinding themselves to other possibilities.

For example, I once helped a patron research a great-grandmother, who had an unusual first name and birthplace. I will fictionalize all the specific details of the case; let us call her Elspeth Tomkins, born in China. In 1910, we found her in the census, living with her husband, Robert Tompkins at 2305 West Division in Chicago. In 1923, Robert Tompkins died, and we found an obituary for him. We checked the 1930 death index, but there was no Elspeth Tompkins. So, I suggested we check all of the women named Elspeth in Chicago in the census; perhaps she remarried. "No," my patron said, "she wouldn't have remarried." However, I persuaded her to try the search anyway. In 1930, we found an Elspeth Reynolds, the same age, also born in China, also living at 2305 West Division with her husband John Reynolds. Therefore, I felt we had discovered what happened to Elspeth Tompkins; she remarried to John Reynolds following the death of her first husband. "No, I don't think so ..." said my patron. "Must be a coincidence." This is perhaps an extreme example of an inflexible researcher, but the same hesitancy to question family stories is common in many novices.

Similarly, consider all of the erroneous or confusing documents from our case studies. Perhaps the most striking example is the 1917 newspaper report of the death of Ezra and Vera Beaudette. They were reported as dying on a torpedoed ocean liner, but they were never actually on the ship. Sources are no more trustworthy than family stories. They usually record some truth but may contain serious errors. Part of genealogy reference is gently teaching novices that flexibility and skepticism will help them find information.

Confused Chronology

I have a background in history; I was a history major and attended history graduate school. As a result, I have a fairly good grasp on the chronology of American history. I have learned, however, that this is not always the case for beginning genealogy researchers. Novices are often confused about the dates of events such as the U.S. Civil War or the Great Depression. I do not point this out to be smug or superior; I would have the same problems if I tried to research physics, chemistry, or basic home repair. I highlight this problem because it can make research difficult for novices. For example, when a researcher seeks help finding information about an American male born around the 1840s, I always wonder if they were in the Civil War, but many researchers do not consider looking for Civil War records because they do not have the date of the Civil War in the back of their minds. Therefore, I sometimes notice that researchers are looking in the wrong time period for a particular kind of records and need to suggest that they try a different time period.

Database Difficulties

Genealogy research means spending time scouring databases for information. Running and rerunning database queries is second nature to many reference librarians, but that is not the case for many genealogy novices. For example, some novices instinctively fill in every field on a database search form. In most genealogy databases, this eliminates most results because database entries rarely match every field exactly. Novices who do not understand database searching often erroneously conclude that their ancestors are not in the database when they do not return results on the first query. Simply pointing researchers towards a database is not always adequate. Many researchers need to be taught how to broaden and narrow database queries.

Focus on Famous Ancestors

Often, researchers visit the reference desk looking to find their connection to a distant ancestor, often a famous person. In the case of my Simpson family, I had heard that we were distantly related to Ulysses Simpson Grant. In these cases, it is best to advise that researchers begin by carefully researching their own family, starting with themselves and moving backwards. Starting with the famous ancestor and researching forward is an ineffective strategy for two reasons. First, it is much harder to trace forward in time than backwards: a death certificate will tell you where an individual was born, but a birth certificate will not tell you where they are going to die. Secondly, it may be the case that the "famous ancestor" is merely famous and not an ancestor. This seems to be the case with myself and Ulysses S. Grant: having researched my own ancestry and read genealogy information about General Grant, I cannot find any connection. If I had started with the family of Ulysses Grant, I would have had to research each of his children, then their children, and so on, which would have been very difficult and ultimately fruitless.

Unrealistic Assumptions

Some patrons assume that their research is recorded in a book, and they simply need to find that book and their research is done. This is rarely the case. Although genealogy research is not as hard as some might assume, it is still an involved research process. It requires a considerable commitment of time and effort. Educating researchers about the complexity of the research is part of the job of reference librarians. In cases where patrons want genealogy information but do not want to expend any effort, you might point them to professional researchers, who will research for a fee. There are several ways to contact professional researchers. The Association of Professional Genealogists maintains an online directory of researchers, searchable by geographic location or field of expertise (http://www.apgen.org/directory/index.html). Professional researchers are also sometimes listed on USGenWeb (http://www.usgenweb.com) pages for particular counties.

DIFFICULT CASES

Adoption

Adoption is a common genealogy research subject, for adoptees looking for their birth parents and for genealogists searching for information about their parent's or grandparent's adoption. Unfortunately, there is very little public information about recent or historical adoptions. The availability of recent adoption information varies from state to state, but adoption records are generally closed to researchers. Some states have established registries to help reunite birth parents and adoptees. Other states have a research surrogate system that allows adoptees to hire a surrogate empowered to look at closed records. To help adoption researchers, it is important to have information about the research process in your state available.

Historical adoptions are also difficult to research. Even very old records of adoption are often closed by state law, and other records have been lost. Orphans in institutions are enumerated in the U.S. Census, so that sometimes can allow researchers to identify the institution where an ancestor resided prior to adoption. Recently, a number of books and Web sites on orphans of the late 19th and early 20th centuries have been published. Cyndi's List has good lists of resources on orphans (http://www.cyndislist.com/orphans.htm) and adoption (http://www.cyndislist/adoption.htm).

Very Limited Information about Recent Ancestors

Some patrons may not have even the most basic information about their family members. For example, a woman who was born in the mid-1970s is looking for her father. The father left her mother when she was two years old, and her mother never talked about him. The patron's birth certificate lists her father's name but no other identifying information. Her parents were not married. His name does not appear in the Social Security Death Index. Many of the standard strategies and resources do not apply to such a case. There are other strategies that might help, but they are more familiar to private investigators than genealogists, such as searches of public records. Often, there are not many sources available in the library to help in such a case, so you might suggest they consider hiring an investigator. *Locating Lost Family Members and Friends* by Kathleen W. Hinckley (1999) outlines some strategies for such research.

REFERENCES

"Association of Professional Genealogists." http://www.apgen.org/.

"Cyndi's List - Adoption." *Cyndi's List*. http://www.cyndislist.com/adoption.htm.

"Cyndi's List - Orphans." *Cyndi's List*. http://www.cyndislist.com/orphans.htm.

"Free Genealogy and Family History Online - The USGenWeb Project." *USGen Web*. http://usgenweb.org/.

Hinckley, Kathleen W. *Locating Lost Family Members & Friends: Modern Genealogical Research Techniques for Locating the People of Your Past and Present*. Cincinnati: Betterway Books, 1999.

13

Professional Toolkit

RESOURCES FOR PROFESSIONAL DEVELOPMENT

I hope that this book has given its readers an introduction to genealogical reference. However, genealogy resources and strategies are constantly evolving, so professionals need to keep up with the latest developments. The following resources help genealogy librarians stay abreast of research developments and keep in touch with a community of research professionals.

Librarians Serving Genealogists

Librarians Serving Genealogists (http://www.cas.usf.edu/lis/genealib/index.html) is a Web site with a variety of professional resources for librarians. Maintained by Drew Smith, an instructor at the University of South Florida, it includes bibliographies, collection development policies, and links to other professional development resources. The site also hosts a popular listserv, GENEALIB (http://www.cas.usf.edu/lis/genealib/list.html). The listserv is an extremely useful tool for keeping up with news in the genealogy library community and is also a great place to get help with unusual reference questions. Users can also search the archives of the mailing list to search through previous discussions.

Conferences

There are two major annual genealogy conferences: the National Genealogical Society's Conference in the United States (usually held in the spring) and the Federation of Genealogical Societies Conference (usually held in late August or September). Both conferences are large, with several tracks of lectures and many exhibitors. The sessions both conferences are very practical and focused on research methods, so they provide a great continuing education opportunity for librarians. In the past, both conferences have offered a special "librarians' day," with seminars specifically designed for librarians. These conferences are also the favored venue for major announcements by information companies and genealogical institutions. Beyond these two major conferences, there are smaller, more specialized conferences throughout the year. These range from topical conferences, such as Brigham Young University's Computerized Family History and Genealogy conference, to regional conferences, such as the Indiana Genealogical Society's annual conference. Cyndi's List has a good list of annual conferences in the "Education" category.

Seminars

There are a number of seminars in genealogy research methods, both online classes and classroom programs. For researchers willing to commit some time and travel money, there are several in-person immersion programs. For example, the National Institute on Genealogical Research offers a week-long course on genealogy research in Washington, DC every summer. The Institute offers scholarships to the seminar. (http://www.rootsweb.com/~natgenin/). Similarly, the Samford University Library in Birmingham, Alabama hosts the Institute of Genealogy and Historical Research every summer (http://www.samford.edu/schools/ighr/).

There are also many online options for librarians. The National Institute for Genealogical Studies in Toronto, Canada, offers an in-depth curriculum of genealogy seminars at http://www.genealogicalstudies.com. Among other topics, the Institute offers a course in genealogical librarianship. Online seminars are also available through the National Genealogical Society and Ancestry.com. I teach an online seminar through the American Library Association (ALA; http://www.ala.org/ala/rusa/rusaevents/professionaldevelopmentonline/prodevonline.cfm). Again, Cyndi's List provides a good rundown of available online classes in the "Education" category.

Web Logs and Podcasts

In the Internet age, the research environment is in constant flux, and keeping up with new developments is an important part of serving your patrons. Web logs and podcasts are great tools for keeping track of new resources and trends in research. The web logs and podcasts mentioned in Chapter Nine provide are the best tools for keeping research professionals in the know. In addition, there are several web logs of special interest to reference librarians. Research Buzz (http://www.Researchbuzz.org) is a great web log/newsletter written by Tara Calishain about new research tools. Calishain's site is not focused on genealogy but often covers major new genealogical or historical databases. Several commercial genealogy services also offer web logs, such as Ancestry's 24/7 Family History Circle blog (http://blogs.ancestry.com/circle).

Journals

In Chapter Five, I gave a broad outline of genealogy periodicals; here, I would like to highlight a few of particular interest to librarians. The National Genealogical Society publishes the *National Genealogical Society Quarterly* and the *NGS News Magazine*; both are great sources for news and book reviews. *Prologue*, the National Archives journal, provides detailed articles explaining genealogical methods in federal records.

Genealogy and the ALA

The ALA has an active genealogy committee, which is part of the history section of the Reference and User Services Association (RUSA). The Genealogy Committee of ALA-RUSA meets twice a year and plans programs, educational preconference seminars, and guidelines for collection development. For more information about these activities or to volunteer for the committee, visit the RUSA History section Web site at http://www.ala.org/HISTORYmainTemplate.cfm?Section=historysection.

MORE THAN TWENTY GREAT REFERENCE BOOKS

Although much of this book talks about online sources, print reference sources are an extremely user-friendly, dependable source for beginners. If I did not believe this, I would not have written a book! In this section, I describe some of the reference sources that I often use. I have excluded large, expensive reference sets such as *Germans to America* and focused on affordable works no longer than a few volumes. I have also emphasized works that have been written or revised fairly recently because there has been so much change in the research environment in the last decade. My list is subjective and idiosyncratic, but it is based upon my personal experience assisting beginners.

1. **Szucs, Loretto Dennis, and Sandra Hargreaves Luebking, eds. *The Source: A Guidebook of American Genealogy*. Provo, UT: Ancestry, 2006.**

   First published in 1984, *The Source* is now in its third edition. It remains the most important reference work for American genealogy. It is an encyclopedic guidebook, with lengthy chapters written by subject specialists, such as Tony Burroughs on African-American research, Lloyd deWitt Bockstruck on military records, and Stephen C. Young on the Family History Library. *The Source* is a work that both novice researchers and reference librarians will return to for its detailed examination of all of the major topics and sources in American genealogy.
2. **Greenwood, Val D. *The Researcher's Guide to American Genealogy*. Baltimore, MD: Genealogical Publishing Co., 2000.**

   Like *The Source*, Greenwood's *Guide* is a cornerstone work of American genealogy reference. In contrast to the encyclopedic format of *The Source*, the *Researcher's Guide* is an overview of sources and strategy in a single engaging voice. Now in its third edition, this work is an excellent overview of the genealogy research process.
3. **Everton, George B. *The Handybook for Genealogists: United States of America*. Logan, UT: Everton Publishers, 2006.**

   Eicholz, Alice, ed. *Ancestry's Red Book: American State, County & Town Sources*. Salt Lake City, UT: Ancestry, 1992.

   The *Handybook* is the basic print resource for finding local genealogical records in the United States. It contains a chapter for each state and an entry for each county. The state chapters include a short history of the state, an overview of vital records procedures for the state, addresses of genealogy societies and libraries, and a bibliography of genealogical works on the state. Each county entry describes which vital records and court records exist for that jurisdiction and where to locate them. The latest edition also contains appendices with state-by-state county maps and an atlas of migration trails. *Ancestry's Red Book* is a similar state-by-state genealogical guide.

4. **Mills, Elizabeth S. *Evidence!: Citation & Analysis for the Family Historian.* Baltimore, MD: Genealogical Publishing Co., 1997.**

   Carmack, Sharon DeBartolo. *You Can Write Your Family History.* Cincinnati: Betterway Books, 2003.

   The book you are reading is primarily about helping beginners start their research. Once your patrons begin compiling information, they will want to know how to record their family history. The two books listed above are guides to this process. Elizabeth Shown Mills' work is a slim but authoritative guide to analyzing and citing evidence in genealogical research. It advises researchers on how to judge the accuracy of evidence in family history research and how to share evidence with other researchers through proper citation of sources. Sharon DeBartolo Carmack's book is a broader look at the process of writing a family history. It discusses research project management, the process of writing a family narrative, and the use of social history in genealogy and includes tips on publishing and distributing family histories.

5. **Evans, Barbara Jean. *The New A to Zax: A Comprehensive Genealogical Dictionary for Genealogists and Historians.* Champaign, IL: B.J. Evans, 1990.**

   What was your ancestor referring to when she criticized a *dog-leech* in a letter? When your great-great-grandfather was arrested and charged with *hamesucken*, what was his crime? The New A to Zax is a dictionary of such archaic terms genealogists encounter in old records. It is particularly useful for identifying legal terms, medical references, and household and agricultural tools. It also includes a useful glossary of nicknames. For the record, *hamesucken* is a term for home invasion, and a *dog-leech* is a disparaging term for a veterinarian or quack doctor.

6. **Kemp, Thomas Jay. *International Vital Records Handbook.* Baltimore, MD: Genealogical Publishing Co., 2000.**

   This handbook collects contact information and vital records request forms from the United States and foreign countries. For example, for Columbia, it provides the address of the Superintedente de Notarido y Registro Civil, the dates vital records have been kept in the country, information about obtaining adoption records, the address of the Columbian Embassy in the United States, a list of published works on vital records in Columbia, and a photocopy of the vital records request form. Even in the Internet era, locating this information can be difficult, especially for foreign countries; therefore, this work remains relevant.

7. **Hone, E. Wade. *Land & Property Research in the United States.* Salt Lake City, UT: Ancestry, 1997.**

   Hatcher, Patricia Law. *Locating Your Roots: Discover Your Ancestors Using Land Records.* Cincinnati: Betterway Books, 2003.

   Researching land and property is an important task for genealogy researchers, but a complicated one. Records describing land ownership and geography vary greatly depending on location and time period. E. Wade Hone's book offers a historical look at land ownership records from the colonial period to the present. Patricia Law Hatcher's book offers a user-friendly guide to researching deeds and other land records.

8. **Kashuba, Melinda. *Walking with Your Ancestors: A Genealogist's Guide to Using Maps and Geography.* Cincinnati: Family Tree Books, 2005.**

   Geographical research is a somewhat overlooked element of family history methodology, but perhaps Melinda Kashuba's book will help remedy that. Kashuba, a genealogist and geographer, describes a variety of geographical resources for genealogical use: historical maps, gazetteers, county atlases, and more. *Walking With Your Ancestors* demystifies the world of geographical research for novice genealogists.

9. **Schaefer, Christina K.** ***Guide to Naturalization Records of the United States.*** **Baltimore, MD: Genealogical Publishing Co., 1997.**

   As I observed in Chapter Seven, naturalization records are complicated and vary greatly over time and location. Researching naturalization is further complicated by the variety of repositories that hold these records, including local court archives, county record offices, and the National Archives. Christina Schaefer's book does a great job of demystifying the search process. The book includes an historical overview of naturalization in the United States and a state-by-state, county-by-county guide to the records that are available.

10. **Smolenyak, Megan.** ***Trace Your Roots with DNA: Using Genetic Tests to Explore Your Family Tree.*** **Emmaus, PA: Rodale, 2004.**

    DNA analysis is having a revolutionary effect on genealogical research. Name studies have allowed researchers to confirm or disprove family connections where the historical record is sketchy or incomplete. As a librarian, I do not assist researchers with DNA projects because this kind of research occurs outside of the library, but it is important for librarians to help researchers learn the basics of DNA research. Megan Smolenyak's book is a user-friendly guide to a complicated subject. Beyond explaining the basic DNA tests and what they can prove, Smolenyak's book provides tips on starting or joining a collaborative DNA project and a helpful glossary.

11. **Askin, Jayne.** ***Search: A Handbook for Adoptees and Birthparents.*** **Phoenix, AZ: Oryx Press, 1998.**

    Strauss, Jean A.S. ***Birthright: The Guide to Search and Reunion for Adoptees, Birthparents, and Adoptive Parents.*** **New York: Penguin Books, 1994.**

    Adoption is a common research topic, but a very difficult one. Because of privacy restrictions, there are not many public sources for adoption resources. Beginning adoption research requires that the researcher get an overview of adoption disclosure laws and a specific understanding of the law where the adoption occurred. Jean Strauss's book gives a good overview of the adoption search process, with a particular focus on the emotional impact of the search process. Jane Askin's book is a more recent in-depth guide to the search process. Because adoption laws vary by state, it is also worth collecting informational pamphlets or guides from local adoption advocacy groups.

12. **Sperry, Kip.** ***Reading Early American Handwriting.*** **Baltimore, MD: Genealogical Publishing Co., 1998.**

    Interpreting archaic scripts (also called paleography) is a challenge for researchers using handwritten church records, court documents, and personal letters. Kip Sperry's book is a useful tool for researchers puzzling over old American documents. It provides general guidelines for interpreting handwriting, sample alphabets, a list of archaic terms, and a guide to common abbreviations and contractions. It also contains a wealth of sample transcriptions.

13. **Schaefer, Christina K.** ***The Hidden Half of the Family: A Sourcebook for Women's Genealogy.*** **Baltimore: Genealogical Publishing Co., 1999.**

    Carmack, Sharon DeBartolo. ***A Genealogist's Guide to Discovering Your Female Ancestors: Special Strategies for Uncovering Hard-to-find Information About Your Female Lineage.*** **Cincinnati: Betterway Books, 1998.**

    In many of the documents used for genealogy research such as wills, city directories, and naturalization records, our female ancestors go unrecorded. Women's rights of property, suffrage, and citizenship were unequal to men for most of American history, and this disparity is reflected in historical documents. As a result, illuminating the lives of female ancestors requires special search strategies. Both Carmack's and Schaefer's books provide researchers with ideas for researching female ancestors. Carmack's book provides suggestions for sources, strategies for finding married women's maiden names, and helpful case studies. Schaefer's book provides state-by-state information on legal history, record repositories, and reference works on women's history.

14. **Hanks, Patrick, ed. *Dictionary of American Family Names.* Oxford: Oxford University Press, 2003.**

    Researchers are often curious about the origins and meaning of surnames. Generally, I discourage too much focus on the surname because names can be changed or spelled in variant ways, as we see in the case of Kubrike/ Kubrick and Tischer/Thischer/Fischer. Despite this, the study of names is of great interest to genealogists, and the Oxford Dictionary is a helpful overview of name origins. Entries describe the country of origin, etymology, and early records of the name in North America.

15. **Fox-Davies, Arthur Charles. *A Complete Guide to Heraldry.* Skyhorse Publishing, 2007.**

    Von Volborth, Carl Alexander. *Heraldry: Customs, Rules and Styles.* Poole, United Kingdom: Blandford Press, 1981.

    Rietstap, Johannes Baptist. *General Illustrated Armorial.* Lyon, France: Sauvegarde Historique, 1954.

    In addition to names, novice genealogists are often curious about family crests. Again, I generally try to discourage a strong focus on crests because most families are not associated with crests. In other words, there may be a Simpson family that used a crest, but that does not mean that that family is related to my own Simpsons. Nevertheless, it is important to provide researchers with resources on this topic. Fox-Davies and Von Volborth's books provide a good overview of the history and iconography of family crests. Reitstap's Illustrated Armorial is somewhat difficult to purchase, but it provides what many researchers are searching for: an illustrated index of crests, arranged by family name.

16. **Ritchie, Donald A. *Doing Oral History: A Practical Guide.* New York: Oxford University Press, 2003.**

    Recording family history from relatives is a basic part of family history research. There is an art to gathering such information, and researchers benefit from a book such as Ritchie's with advice on recording technology and eliciting information from interview subjects.

17. **American Medical Association. *Directory of Deceased American Physicians, 1804–1929: A Genealogical Guide to Over 149,000 Medical Practitioners.* Chicago: American Medical Association, 1993.**

    This book abstracts and indexes obituaries in the *Journal of the American Medical Association.* Because questions about ancestors who worked as doctors are fairly common, this index gets considerable use in our genealogy reference room. Entries describe the education, practice, and death date of physicians who died in the period 1804–1929.

18. **Sagraves, Barbara. *A Preservation Guide: Saving the Past and the Present for the Future.* Salt Lake City, UT: Ancestry, 1995.**

    Taylor, Maureen Alice. *Preserving Your Family Photographs.* Cincinnati: Betterway Books, 2001.

    Genealogy requires gathering and preserving materials such as old letters, photographs, and scrapbooks. Researchers are often curious about saving these resources, and these works help explain the basics of archival preservation.

19. ***Lippincott's Gazetteer of the World: A Complete Pronouncing Gazetteer.* Philadelphia: J.B. Lippincott, 1893.**

    This gazetteer, published in 1893, helps locate many small towns that no longer appear on modern atlases. Although it is available digitally through the *Making of America* Web site from the University of Michigan (http://quod.lib.umich.edu/m/moagrp/), this is the kind of reference book that is worth having in print. Luckily, reprints can be purchased through the *Making of America*.

20. **DuMelle, Grace. *Finding Your Chicago Ancestors: A Beginner's Guide to Family History in the City and Cook County.* Chicago: Lake Claremont Press, 2005.**

    Guzik, Estelle. (New York). *Genealogical Resources in New York.* New York: Jewish Genealogical Society, 2003.

    Genealogical research requires learning about the particular resources available about the places where ancestors lived; researching Cleveland, Ohio requires different sources and methods than researching the New Hampshire seacoast. As a result, local guides to genealogical research are important. The two titles above are both good examples of the genre (disclaimer: I wrote a few chapters in *Finding Your Chicago Ancestors*).

REFERENCES

"24/7 Family History Circle." *Ancestry.com.* http://blogs.ancestry.com/circle/.

"ALA : Genealogy 101." *American Library Association - RUSA.* http://www.ala.org/ala/rusa/rusaevents/professionaldevelopmentonline/genealogy101/genealogy101.cfm.

"ALA | History Section." *American Library Association - RUSA.* http://www.ala.org/ala/rusa/rusaourassoc/rusasections/historysection/historysection.cfm.

Ancestry's Red Book: American State, County & Town Sources. Rev. ed. Salt Lake City, UT: Ancestry Publ, 1992.

Askin, Jayne. *Search: A Handbook for Adoptees and Birthparents.* 3rd ed. Phoenix, AZ: Oryx Press, 1998.

Carmack, Sharon DeBartolo. *A Genealogist's Guide to Discovering Your Female Ancestors: Special Strategies for Uncovering Hard-to-Find Information About Your Female Lineage.* 1st ed. Cincinnati, Ohio: Betterway Books, 1998.

"Cyndi's List - Education." *Cyndi's List.* http://www.cyndislist.com/educate.htm.

Dictionary of American Family Names. Oxford, UK: Oxford University Press, 2003.

Dumelle, Grace. *Finding Your Chicago Ancestors : a beginner's guide to family history in the city and Cook County.* Chicago: Lake Claremont Press, 2005.

Evans, Barbara Jean. *The New A to Zax: A Comprehensive Genealogical Dictionary for Genealogists and Historians.* 2nd ed. Champaign, IL: B.J.Evans, 1990.

"Federation of Genealogical Societies - Conferences." http://www.fgs.org/conferences/index.php.

Fox-Davies, Arthur Charles. *A Complete Gide to Haldry.* New York: Skyhorse Publishing, 2007.

Greenwood, Val D. *The Researcher's Guide to American Genealogy.* 3rd ed. Baltimore, Md: Genealogical Pub. Co, 2000.

Guzik, Estelle M. *Genealogical Resources in New York.* NY: Jewish Genealogical Society, 2003.

Hafher, Arthur Wayne, Fred W. Hunter, E. Michael. Tarpey, and American Medical Association. *Directory of Deceased American Physicians, 1804–1929...* Chicago: American Medical Association, 1993.

The Handybook for Genealogists: United States of America. 11th ed. Logan, UT: Everton Publishers, 2006.

Hatcher, Patricia Law. *Locating Your Roots: Discover Your Ancestors Using Land Records.* 1st ed. Cincinnati: Betterway Books, 2003.

Hone, E. Wade. *Land & Property Research in the United States.* Salt Lake City: Ancestry, 1997.

"Institute of Genealogy & Historical Research - Samford University Library." http://www.samford.edu/schools/ighr/.

Kashuba, Melinda. *Walking with Your Ancestors: A Genealogist's Guide to Using Maps and Geography.* 1st ed. Cincinnati: Family Tree Books, 2005.

Kemp, Thomas Jay. *International Vital Records Handbook.* 4th ed. Baltimore: Genealogical Pub. Co, 2000.

"Librarians Serving Genealogists (LSG): GENEALIB mailing list." http://www.cas.usf.edu/lis/genealib/list.html.

"Librarians Serving Genealogists (LSG): Home Page." http://www.cas.usf.edu/lis/genealib/.

Mills, Elizabeth S. *Evidence!: Citation & Analysis for the Family Historian.* Baltimore: Genealogical Publishing Co, 1997.

National Archives (U.S.), United States, National Archives Trust Fund Board, United States, and United States. *Prologue: The Journal of the National Archives.* Washington, DC: National Archives and Records Service, General Services Administration.

National Genealogical Society. *National Genealogical Society Quarterly.* Washington, DC: National Genealogical Society, 1912.

"NGS I NGS Conferences and Activities." *National Genealogical Society.* http://www.ngsgenealogy.org/conf.cfm.

"NIGR Home Page." *National Institute on Genealogical Research.* http://www.rootsweb.ancestry.com/~natgenin/.

"ResearchBuzz." http://www.researchbuzz.org/wp/.

Rietstap, J. B, and Societe de Sauvegarde Historique. *General Illustrated Armorial.* Lyon: Sauvegarde Historique, 1953.

Sagraves, Barbara. *A Preservation Guide...* Salt Lake City: Ancestry, 1995.

Schaefer, Christina K. *Guide to Naturalization Records of the United States.* Baltimore: Genealogical Pub. Co, 1997.

Schaefer, Christina K. *The Hidden Half of the Family: A Sourcebookfor Women's Genealogy.* Baltimore: Genealogical Pub. Co, 1999.

Smolenyak, Megan. *Trace Your Roots with DNA: Using Genetic Tests to Explore Your Family Tree.* Emmaus, PA: Rodale, 2004.

The Source: A Guidebook of American Genealogy. 3rd ed. Provo, UT: Ancestry, 2006.

Sperry, Kip. *Reading Early American Handwriting.* Baltimore: Genealogical Pub. Co, 1998.

Strauss, Jean A. S. *Birthright: The Guide to Search and Reunion for Adoptees, Birthparents, and Adoptive Parents.* New York: Penguin Books, 1994.

Taylor, Maureen Alice. *Preserving Your Family Photographs: How to Organize, Present, and Restore your Precious Family Images.* Cincinnati: Betterway Books, 2001.

Thomas, Joseph. *Lippincott's Gazetteer of the World...* Philadelphia: J.B. Lippincott, 1893.

Von Volborth, Carl Alexander. *Heraldry: Customs, Rules and Styles.* Poole, UK: Blandford Press, 1981.

Appendix A: Simpson Case Study

When I started researching my family, I did not know a great deal about the ancestors of my paternal grandfather (fig. A.1). I knew my grandfather grew up in Uniontown, Pennsylvania, where his father was a mine manager. I remembered hearing that his father died when he was fairly young, before he went to college. I also knew that my father, my grandfather, my great-grandfather, and I all went by the name John William Simpson. My grandfather had a sister, my great-aunt Blanche. I knew that my grandfather's father was originally from Ohio.

My grandfather died while I was in high school. After his death, my parents found an old letter addressed to him from his father, shortly before his father died. In the letter, my ailing great-grandfather expressed regret about the circumstances of his own death, but nobody in my family knows the exact circumstances he was lamenting. Unfortunately, in disposing of my grandfather's things, my parents also lost the letter. When I began researching my family, the story of my grandfather Simpson's background was particularly interesting to me, perhaps because of this mystery. As a genealogy reference librarian, I have noticed that a curiosity about family secrets is a common motivating factor for researchers.

JOHN W. SIMPSON AND CLARA GILLESPIE

Although I remembered my grandfather's death, I did not remember exactly when it occurred, nor did I recall his age at the time of death. One of the first sources I checked was the Social Security Death Index, which indicated that he was born on September 9, 1906, and he died on December 2, 1987. Because I knew he grew up in Uniontown and stayed through at least some of his adolescence, I could expect to find him there in the 1920 census, when he would be around thirteen years old, so I checked the 1920 census for Fayette County, Pennsylvania, and found a John

David SIMPSON
John William SIMPSON (b.1835-New York,New York;m.10 Mar 1875;d.1917-Jackson County,Ohio)
Ann Kathryn THOMPSON (b.Scotland)
John William SIMPSON (b.1876-Ohio;d.1926-Connellsville,Pennsylvania)
Martha Ellen LEACH
John William SIMPSON (b. 1906;d.1987-Ypsilanti,Michigan)
Clara GILLESPIE
John William SIMPSON Jr. (b.1934)
John William SIMPSON III (b.1970-Detroit)

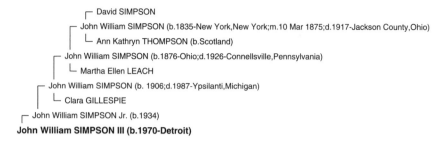

Figure A.1. Ancestors of the author.

W. Simpson with a son named John W. and a daughter named Blanche living in Connellsville, which is just outside of Uniontown (fig. A.2).

This provided me with the first name of my great-grandmother, Clara. It also indicated that around nine years earlier, when my great-aunt Blanche was born, the family was in West Virginia. Around thirteen years earlier, when my grandfather was born, the family was in Ohio. The census also indicated that my great-grandfather and both of his parents were born in Ohio.

At the Newberry, we have a city directory for Uniontown from 1923. It records both my great-grandfather, *Simpson John W (Clara B.) mgr h 61 Cleveland Av*, and my grandfather, *Simpson Wm J student res 61 Cleveland Av*.

My grandfather went by the nickname Bill, so the fact that he is listed as William did not surprise me. This directory entry indicated that my great-grandfather was alive at that time, when my grandfather was around 16. Therefore, I estimated that he died between 1923 and 1927, if he really did pass away when my grandfather was a teenager. I checked the Web site of the Uniontown public library and found that they kept an obituary index that covered the period up to 1930. I sent them a request for an obituary look-up and soon received John W. Simpson's obituary, published in the *Uniontown Morning Herald* on March 10, 1924. It read:

John W. Simpson, aged 48 years, superintendent of the Evans Coal and Coke company, died at the Uniontown hospital, Saturday evening, March 8, 1924, following an illness of heart trouble, the primary cause of death being acute cardiac failure. Deceased had been ill at his home, 61 Cleveland Avenue for some time before being removed to the hospital. He is survived by his wife, one son, William, and one daughter.

The remains were removed to the Minerd mortuary to be prepared for burial and this morning the funeral party will leave on the 11 o'clock Pennsylvania train for Wheeling, W. Va., where interment will take place on Tuesday.

221	184	196	Simpson John W	Head	1	R	M	W	44	M
			— Clara B	Wife			F	W	45	M
			— John W	Son			M	W	13	S
			— Blanche G	Daughter			F	W	9 8/12	S

Figure A.2. U.S. Federal Census, 1920; census place, Connellsville Ward 4, Fayette, Pennsylvania; roll, T625_1568; page, 8B; enumeration district, 12; image, 387.

Because I now had his exact date of death, I wrote to the Pennsylvania Department of Health and requested a copy of the death certificate (fig. A.3).

The death certificate confirmed most of the information I had already gathered and provided some new clues. It gave the name of his father (John W. Simpson) and the maiden name of his mother (Martha Thompson). It gave a more specific location for his birth: Jackson, Ohio. The cause of death was listed as a duodenal ulcer with an acute cardiac failure given as a contributory cause. In the box for "Place of Burial or Removal," it appears that Wheeling, West Virginia was written in and then crossed out, and (illegible) Ohio appears to be written in above.

I tried looking for the family in the 1910 census. Based on the information in the 1920 census, it seemed that they might be West Virginia at that time. I had a difficult time finding them, and I gave up for several years. Recently, while working on the final draft of this book, I took another look. I searched for women named Clara Simpson born in Ohio and living in West Virginia and found the family living in Brooke County, West Virginia, in a town called Buffalo. Several aspects of the census record made it difficult to locate. Clara's age is illegible and is incorrectly recorded in the Ancestry.com index as 65. Both my grandfather and great-grandfather are listed as

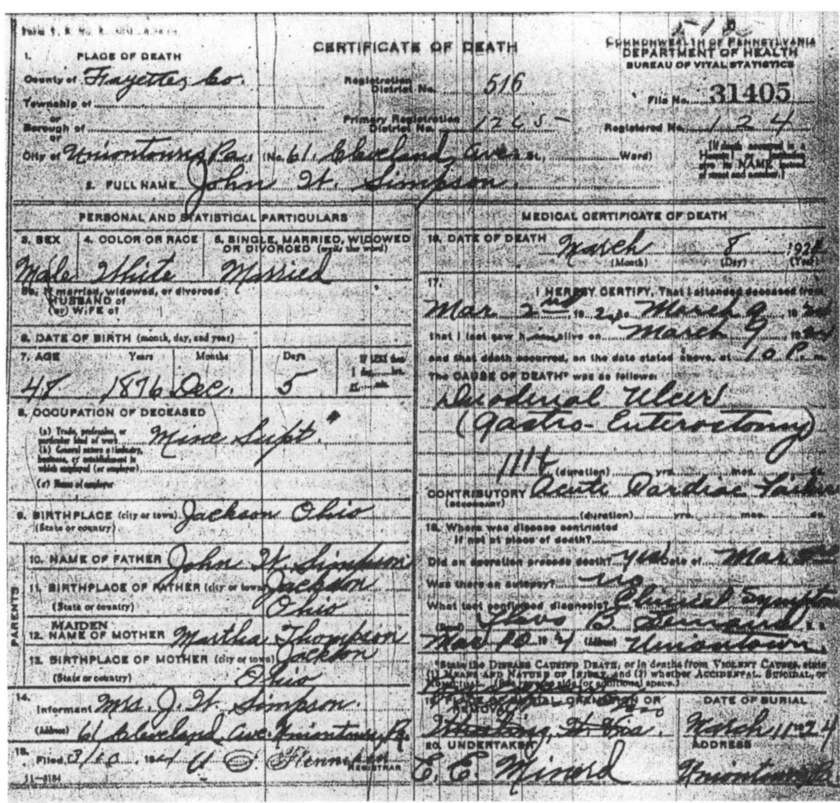

CERTIFICATE OF DEATH

COMMONWEALTH OF PENNSYLVANIA
DEPARTMENT OF HEALTH
BUREAU OF VITAL STATISTICS

1\. PLACE OF DEATH
County of Fayette Co.
Registration District No. 516
Township of
or Borough of
Primary Registration District No. 1265
File No. 31405
Registered No. 124
or City of Uniontown Pa. (No. 61 Cleveland Ave. St., Ward)

2\. FULL NAME John W. Simpson

PERSONAL AND STATISTICAL PARTICULARS

3\. SEX Male
4\. COLOR OR RACE White
5\. SINGLE, MARRIED, WIDOWED OR DIVORCED (write the word) Married
5a. If married, widowed, or divorced HUSBAND of (or) WIFE of
6\. DATE OF BIRTH (month, day, and year) 1876 Dec. 5
7\. AGE Years 47 Months Days
8\. OCCUPATION OF DECEASED
(a) Trade, profession, or particular kind of work Mine Supt.
(b) General nature of industry, business, or establishment in which employed (or employer)
(c) Name of employer
9\. BIRTHPLACE (city or town) (State or country) Jackson Ohio
10\. NAME OF FATHER John W. Simpson
11\. BIRTHPLACE OF FATHER (city or town) (State or country) Jackson Ohio
12\. MAIDEN NAME OF MOTHER Martha Thompson
13\. BIRTHPLACE OF MOTHER (city or town) (State or country) Jackson Ohio
14\. Informant Mrs. J. W. Simpson
(Address) 61 Cleveland Ave. Uniontown Pa.
15\. Filed 3/10 1924 U. S. Flenniken REGISTRAR

MEDICAL CERTIFICATE OF DEATH

16\. DATE OF DEATH March (Month) 8 (Day) 1924 (Year)
17\. I HEREBY CERTIFY, That I attended deceased from Mar. 2nd 1924 to March 8 1924
that I last saw him alive on March 8 1924
and that death occurred, on the date stated above, at 10 P. m.
The CAUSE OF DEATH* was as follows:
Duodenal Ulcer
(Gastro-Enterostomy)
(duration) yrs. mos. ds.
CONTRIBUTORY (secondary) Acute Cardiac Failure
(duration) yrs. mos. ds.
18\. Where was disease contracted if not at place of death?
Did an operation precede death? yes Date of Mar.
Was there an autopsy? no
What test confirmed diagnosis? Clinical Symptoms
(Signed) M.D.
Mar 10 1924 (Address) Uniontown
*State the DISEASE CAUSING DEATH, or in deaths from VIOLENT CAUSES, state (1) MEANS AND NATURE OF INJURY, and (2) whether ACCIDENTAL, SUICIDAL, or HOMICIDAL. (See reverse side for additional space.)
19\. PLACE OF BURIAL, CREMATION OR REMOVAL Wheeling, W. Va.
DATE OF BURIAL March 11 1924
20\. UNDERTAKER E. C. Minard
ADDRESS Uniontown Pa.

Figure A.3. John Simpson, death certificate no. 31405 (1924), Commonwealth of Pennsylvania, Bureau of Vital Statistics, Harrisburg.

"J.W." rather than John. They had a one-year-old daughter, listed as "Martha"; presumably, this is my great-aunt Blanche (U.S. Federal Census, 1910; census place, Buffalo, Brooke, West Virginia; roll, T624_1677; page, 4B; enumeration district, 2; image, 543).

JOHN W. SIMPSON AND MARTHA LEACH

I moved on to 1900, and I searched for my great-great-grandfather. According to his son's death certificate, he was named John W. Simpson, and his wife was named Martha. I searched and found a John Simpson with a wife named Martha and a son named John. The family was living in Jackson County, in a village called Coalton. The son was listed as being born in December of 1875 (fig. A.4).

The father's occupation was listed as farmer, and the son was working as a coal miner. The son listed his birthplace as Ohio, but the father listed his own as New York and recorded that both of his parents were born in Scotland (fig. A.5).

I searched for the same family in 1880; if John Simpson was born in Jackson in 1876, presumably, the family was there four years later. Searching the 1880 census, I did not find a matching family in Jackson County, but a John and Martha Simpson lived in the neighboring county of Lawrence, with a four-year-old son named John. The senior John again listed his birthplace as New York and his parents' birthplace as Scotland. John's neighbors were James Simpson and William Simpson (fig. A.6).

There is no regular 1890 census because it was destroyed by fire. However, parts of the special veteran's schedule survived, including the Ohio section. I searched Jackson County in 1890 and found John Simpson.

Because I now had a sense that the family spent some time in Jackson County, Ohio, I searched for histories of the county. At the Newberry Library, we have a history of the county published in 1991: *Jackson County, Ohio: History and Families, 175th Anniversary, 1816–1991*. Searching the history, I found a short history of the Simpson family. It gave a fairly detailed narrative of the life of John W. Simpson, who we see married Martha in 1880. According to the history, he was born in New York City in 1835. His parents were Scottish immigrants, David Simpson and Ann Kathryn Simpson, whose maiden name was Thompson. They had arrived in New York that same year. Shortly after the birth of John William, the family moved to

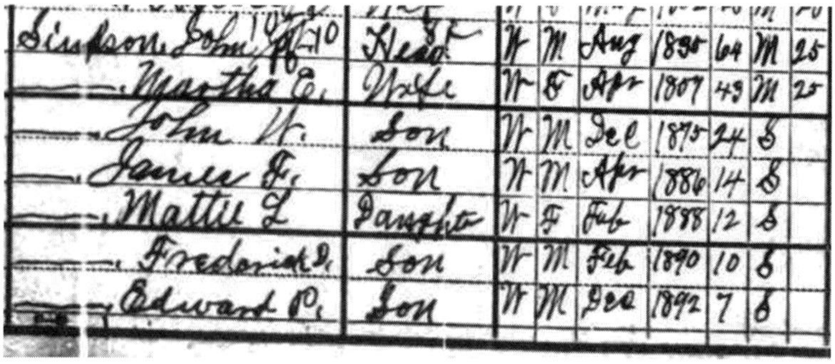

Simpson, John W.	Head	W	M	Aug	1835	64	M	25
—— Martha E.	Wife	W	F	Apr	1857	43	M	25
—— John W.	Son	W	M	Dec	1875	24	S	
—— James F.	Son	W	M	Apr	1886	14	S	
—— Mattie L.	Daughter	W	F	Feb	1888	12	S	
—— Frederick D.	Son	W	M	Feb	1890	10	S	
—— Edward P.	Son	W	M	Dec	1892	7	S	

Figure A.4. U.S. Federal Census, 1900; census place, Coal, Jackson, Ohio; roll, T623 1289; page, 9A; enumeration district, 44.

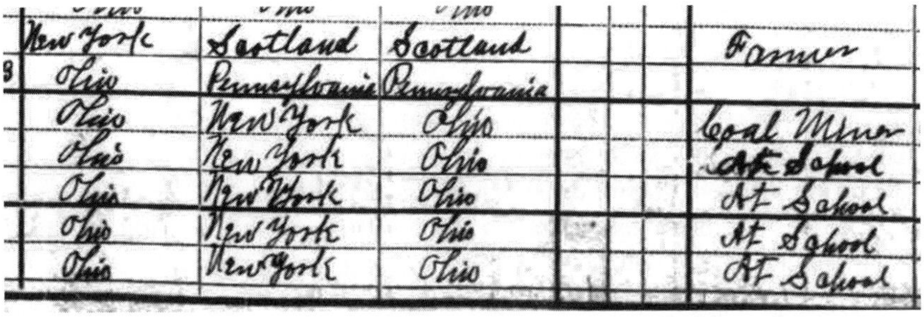

New York	Scotland	Scotland	Farmer
Ohio	Pennsylvania	Pennsylvania	
Ohio	New York	Ohio	Coal Miner
Ohio	New York	Ohio	At School
Ohio	New York	Ohio	At School
Ohio	New York	Ohio	At School
Ohio	New York	Ohio	At School

Figure A.5. U.S. Federal Census, 1900; census place, Coal, Jackson, Ohio; roll, T623 1289; page, 9A; enumeration district, 44.

the Shenandoah Valley, where David worked in an iron furnace. David died there during the Civil War. The history confirmed John's Civil War service in Company F of the Potomac Home Brigade.

After the war, he moved to Lawrence County, Ohio, where he married Martha Ellen Leach. On this fact, the history contradicts the 1924 death certificate of John W. Simpson, which listed his mother's maiden name as Martha Thompson. Further research seems to confirm the accuracy of the history.

In 1875, John and Martha moved to Jackson County, Ohio, where they purchased land and raised a family. They had a farm and small coal mines on the property. One mine ran below their house, and miners could be heard digging below. The history records that their oldest son, John William, moved to Connellsville, Pennsylvania. This fact clearly tied my great-grandfather to this family.

After reading this history, I searched the Jackson County USGenWeb page for other researchers studying this family. I found an e-mail address for the same person who wrote the narrative in the 1991 history. I sent her an e-mail, and she confirmed that we were indeed distant cousins. She also sent me a pedigree chart and other family information.

Despite all I had discovered about this family, I still did not know where they came from in Scotland. Several years later, I saw another researcher post information

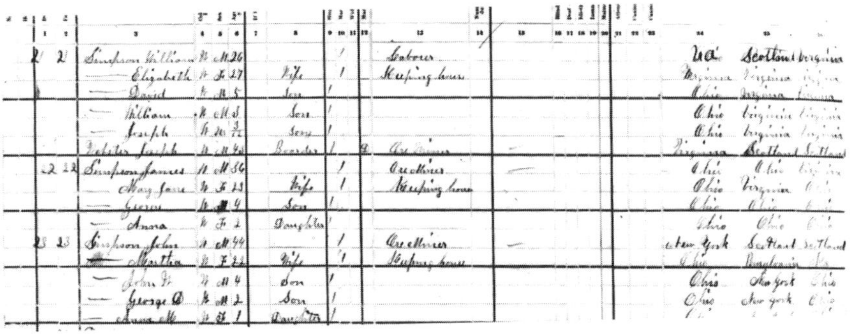

21	21	Simpson William	W	M	26		Laborer	[illegible]	Scotland	Virginia
		Elizabeth	W	F	27	Wife	Keeping house	Virginia	Virginia	Virginia
		David	W	M	5	Son		Ohio	Virginia	Virginia
		William	W	M	3	Son		Ohio	Virginia	Virginia
		Joseph	W	M	[illegible]	Son		Ohio	Virginia	Virginia
		Webster Joseph	W	M	[illegible]	Boarder	Ore Miner	Virginia	Scotland	Scotland
22	22	Simpson James	W	M	36		Ore Miner	Ohio	Ohio	Virginia
		Mary Jane	W	F	23	Wife	Keeping house	Ohio	Virginia	Ohio
		George	W	M	4	Son		Ohio	Ohio	Ohio
		Anna	W	F	2	Daughter		Ohio	Ohio	Ohio
23	23	Simpson John	W	M	44		Ore Miner	New York	Scotland	Scotland
		Martha	W	F	24	Wife	Keeping house	Ohio	Pennsylvania	[illegible]
		John W.	W	M	4	Son		Ohio	New York	Ohio
		George D	W	M	2	Son		Ohio	New York	Ohio
		Anna M	W	F	1	Daughter		[illegible]	[illegible]	[illegible]

Figure A.6. U.S. Federal Census, 1880; census place, Washington, Lawrence, Ohio; roll, T9_1039; family history film, 1255039; page, 377.4000; enumeration district, 99; image, 0746.

about the family on a Simpson family message board. It indicated that there was a marriage record for a David Simpson and an Ann Thomson in Kircaldy, Fife, Scotland from 1829. I obtained that marriage record from the Family History Library (fig. 6.2). This seems to be a close match with the couple who gave birth to John William Simpson in 1835. However, we do not have conclusive proof of that. After all, both Simpson and Thompson/Thomson are common names, as are David and Ann. Nevertheless, this record suggests that further research in Kirkcaldy or Fife might turn up additional evidence.

Recently, I looked up John W. Simpson's Civil War pension record, which provided more details about him. It included an affidavit affirming that John Simpson and Martha Leach were married in Lawrence County, Ohio on March 10, 1875. It also included his 1917 death certificate, which confirmed his birth date, birthplace, and the names of his parents.

Despite all of this research, I still have not found any significant information about the mysterious circumstances of my great-grandfather's death. However, as I mentioned in the introduction to these case studies, I have really just begun my research. A research trip to Uniontown, for example, might turn up more evidence.

Appendix B: Winter Case Study

My friend Megan asked me to help her research the Chicago background of her family (fig. B.1). Her grandmother was born Jeanette Winter, the daughter of a muralist named Ezra Winter and his wife, Vera, whose maiden name was Beaudette. Vera was born in Chicago, and I focused on that branch.

VERA BEAUDETTE AND EZRA WINTER

Megan had heard a considerable amount about Vera and Ezra from her family. The couple had met in Chicago, where Ezra was an art student, and Vera was modeling. They were married in Chicago. Ezra then won the Prix de Rome, an art prize that funded study in Italy, and the couple moved to Rome. The couple had three daughters before divorcing. The older daughters were born in Rome, but Jeanette was born after the couple's return to the United States.

Census research confirmed this outline. In 1930, Vera Winter was living in Chappaqua, New York, with her three daughters (fig. B.2).

Her oldest daughter, Renata, was seventeen years old and was born in Italy. Thirteen-year-old Sarah was also born in Italy. Megan's grandmother was ten and was born in New York. Therefore, if the record is correct, Vera was in Italy roughly between 1913 and 1917 but was in New York by 1920. Vera describes herself as 38 and born in Illinois. She recorded that she was widowed, but we know that is not the case: newspaper articles indicate that the couple was divorced in 1925. Other evidence shows that Ezra lived until 1949. I was not able to find Ezra in the 1930 census.

In the census of 1920, Vera is listed as married and living in Westchester County, New York (U.S. Federal Census, 1920; census place, New Castle, Westchester, New York; roll, T625_1281; page, 9A; enumeration district, 107; image, 594).

Ezra is not enumerated with her, but he is recorded on a separate page in Manhattan. He described himself as married and listed his occupation as "artist" (U.S.

Ancestors of Jeanette WINTER

Page 1

┌ Ezra WINTER (b.1886-Manistee,Michigan;m.1911;d.1949-Connecticut)
Jeanette WINTER (b.c. 1920-New York State)
│ ┌ Adolphus BEAUDETTE
└ Vera BEAUDETTE (b.30 Mar 1892-Chicago,Illinois;d.May 1980-Connecticut)
  │ ┌ Otto TISCHER (b.10 Mar 1842-Leutenberg Thuringen,Germany;d.7 Jul 1931-Hines,Illinois)
  └ Ella Palma TISCHER (b.21 Mar 1869)
    └ Clara VON OBSTFELDER

Figure B.1. Ancestors of Jeanette Winter.

Federal Census, 1920; census place, Manhattan Assembly District 10, New York, New York; roll, T625_1202; page, 6A; enumeration district, 708; image, 823).

In 1910, Vera is enumerated in Oak Park, Illinois. Her age is not legible; it looks like she is listed as eleven years old, and that is how the index on Ancestry.com records her. In reality, she was probably seventeen years old. Her occupation is listed as "dressmaker"; oddly, she is also listed as the head of the household. She was living with a thirty-five-year-old woman named Palma E. Lovgren, who was unemployed and listed as a "roomer." Later, I realized this was almost certainly her mother (fig. B.3).

The same year, the twenty-one-year-old Ezra Winter is enumerated in a rooming house in Chicago. He listed his marital status as single and listed his occupation as landscape artist (U.S. Federal Census; year, 1910; census place, Chicago Ward 7, Cook, Illinois; roll, T624_247; page, 16A; enumeration district, 395; image, 590).

Unlike most of the people in these case studies, Ezra was mildly famous, and so he appears in the newspaper fairly often. The *New York Times* reported on the marriage of Ezra and Vera on September 9, 1911. It described the Bingham, Michigan marriage of the twenty-four-year-old "farmer-artist" who had recently won a prize of ten thousand dollars. The article recorded his bride as "Miss Vera J. Burnett (sic) of Chicago, known as one of the most beautiful artists' models in that city." The *Chicago Tribune* reported on Vera and Ezra's divorce on April 22, 1925. Ezra's suicide was reported in the *New York Times* on April 8, 1949.

DEPARTMENT OF COMMERC[E]
FIFTEENTH CENSUS OF T[HE UNITED STATES]
POPULATIO[N]

State: New York
County: Westchester
Township or other division of county: New Castle Town (part)
Unincorporated place: Chappaqua Village (part)

Line	Dwelling	Family	Name	Relation	Home	Value	Radio	Farm	Sex	Race	Age	Marital	Age at marriage	School	Read/write	Person	Father	Mother
51	41	45	Winter, Vera B	Head-H	O	$8000	R	No	F	W	38	Wd	19	No	Yes	Illinois	New York	Illinois
52			—, Renata	Daughter				V	F	W	17	S		Yes	Yes	Italy	Michigan	Illinois
53			—, Sarah A.	Daughter				V	F	W	13	S		Yes	Yes	Italy	Michigan	Illinois
54			—, Jeannette	Daughter				V	F	W	10	S		Yes	Yes	New York	Michigan	Illinois

Figure B.2. U.S. Federal Census, 1930; census place, New Castle, Westchester, New York; roll, 1663; page, 3B; enumeration district, 283; image, 40.0.

Figure B.3. U.S. Federal Census 1910; census place, Oak Park, Cook, Illinois; roll, T624_239; page, 9A; enumeration district, 70; image, 716.

Perhaps the most peculiar newspaper article about the couple dates from 1915, during the First World War. Trolling for any information I could find about Vera, I searched the newspaper archive of Ancestry.com for "Vera Beaudette." Among the results, I found an article about Ezra Winter and Vera Beaudette Winter's death in the bombardment of the ship *Ancona* from the *Fort Wayne News* of November 13, 1915 (fig. B.4).

Once I found this report, I searched the Chicago newspaper for follow-up articles. I knew that this was a mistaken report, so I expected to find a retraction. On November 11, 1915 (oddly, several days before the *Fort Wayne News* article), the *Chicago Daily News* reported that Ezra and Vera did not sail on the ship, and they were alive and well (fig. B.5).

SATURDAY EVENING, NOVEMBER 13, 1915.

FEAR AMERICAN ARTISTS WERE LOST ON THE STEAMER ANCONA

Left to right: Eugene Savage, Ezra Winter and Mrs. Winter.

Ezra Winter of the Chicago Academy of Fine Arts, and winner of the Prix de Rome in 1911, is feared to have been lost on the Italian liner Ancona, with his wife, Mrs. Vera Beaudette Winter, and their three-year-old daughter, Renata. A similar fate, it is feared, has overtaken Eugene Savage, of Bloomington, Ill., winner of the Prix de Rome in 1912, who planned to return to America on the Ancona.

Figure B.4. *Fort Wayne News* article on death of Vera and Ezra Winter. Courtesy of http://Ancestry.com.

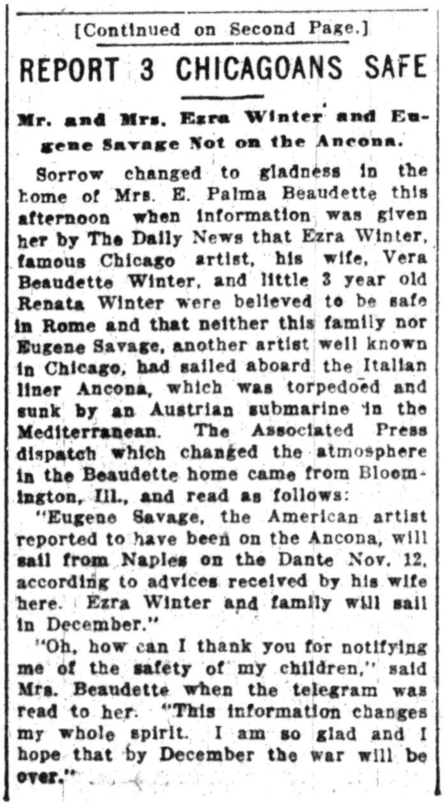

[Continued on Second Page.]

REPORT 3 CHICAGOANS SAFE

Mr. and Mrs. Ezra Winter and Eugene Savage Not on the Ancona.

Sorrow changed to gladness in the home of Mrs. E. Palma Beaudette this afternoon when information was given her by The Daily News that Ezra Winter, famous Chicago artist, his wife, Vera Beaudette Winter, and little 3 year old Renata Winter were believed to be safe in Rome and that neither this family nor Eugene Savage, another artist well known in Chicago, had sailed aboard the Italian liner Ancona, which was torpedoed and sunk by an Austrian submarine in the Mediterranean. The Associated Press dispatch which changed the atmosphere in the Beaudette home came from Bloomington, Ill., and read as follows:

"Eugene Savage, the American artist reported to have been on the Ancona, will sail from Naples on the Dante Nov. 12, according to advices received by his wife here. Ezra Winter and family will sail in December."

"Oh, how can I thank you for notifying me of the safety of my children," said Mrs. Beaudette when the telegram was read to her. "This information changes my whole spirit. I am so glad and I hope that by December the war will be over."

Figure B.5. *Chicago Daily News* reports Ezra and Vera alive. Newberry Library.

Later, I found a record of Ezra, Vera, the four-year-old Renata, and the baby Sarah Ann arriving in New York on board the ship *Giuseppi Verdi*. The ship sailed from Naples and arrived on December 16, 1916.

ADOLPHUS BEAUDETTE AND ELLA PALMA TISCHER

Megan was particularly curious about Vera's parents, Ella Palma Tischer and Adolphus Beaudette. Family stories described Ella as a character, and Adolphus Beaudette was somewhat mysterious. He was generally called Adolphus in most family information, but Vera's Social Security application (fig. 4.5) recorded him as "Robert Beaudette." The 1900 census shows Vera and her parents (fig. B.6). Her father is described as a salesman. He and Ella recorded that they had been married for nine years.

Megan told me she believed that Adolphus and Ella were divorced, so I went to the Cook County Circuit Archives to look for a divorce record. After checking an index, I found a divorce case from March, 1902. Ella P. Beaudette filed for divorce against Adophus Beaudette on the grounds of cruelty. The divorce case contained some lurid testimony from Ella:

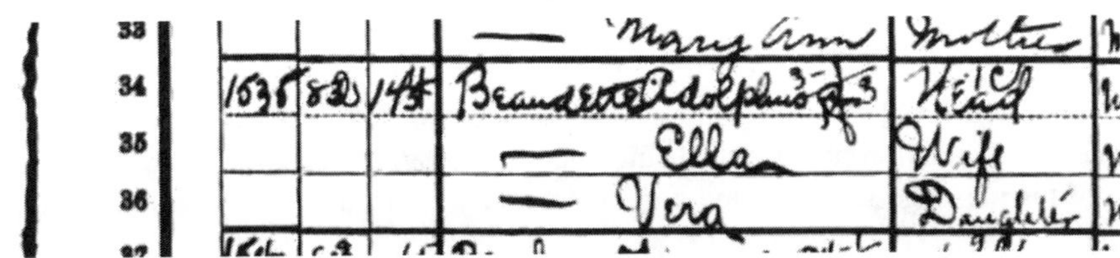

Figure B.6. U.S. Federal Census 1900; Census place: Chicago Ward 15, Cook, Illinois; Roll T623 265; Page: 8A; Enumeration District: 449.

Question: *Do you remember the time he assaulted you at Kokoma (sic) Indiana?*
Answer: *He took and held me against the wall and held a revolver against my head and told me he was going to blow out my brains.*
Question: *Do you remember in 1896 at your home, did he ever threaten you with a knife or a gun?*
Answer: *Yes he picked up a carving knife and threatened to cut my heart out.*

(*Ella P. Beaudette vs. Adolphus Beaudette*, Cook County, Illinois Circuit Court Case; Gen No. 225, 865 Term No. 11, 224; March 22, 1892).

Beyond the description of Adophus's cruelties, the divorce file contained some important genealogical information. For example, it recorded that Ella and Aldophus were married in Milwaukee, Wisconsin on May 23rd, 1891. I used this information to search for a marriage record from Milwaukee; later, I also found a second marriage for Adolphus and Ella in Chicago (see Chapter Four).

At first, I had difficulty finding more information about Ella Palma Beaudette. Then, by a stroke of luck, I found a book she had authored. One day at the Newberry Library, I was giving a talk on genealogy research and using the Beaudettes as an example. One of my fellow librarians was sitting in on the talk. Several days later, she was looking at a history of Chicago Heights, Illinois, and noticed the name of the author: Mrs. E. Palma Beaudette. This find did not lead to more sources, but it did provide a photograph of Ella (Beaudette, E. Palma, 1914, Chicago Heights, Illinois, 1914, and Steger, Glenwood, Thornton, and Homewood). When the *Chicago Tribune* was digitized, I also found several articles about her involvement in suburban politics and the shady side of the publishing business, which I describe in Chapter Five.

OTTO TISCHER AND CLARA VON OBSTFELTER

Ella's parents, Otto and Clara Tischer, were mentioned in her divorce record, when they were listed as witnesses. I was able to use this information to find Otto Tischer in the Illinois State Death index, which led me to his obituary.

His obituary, transcribed in Chapter Five, gives considerable detail about his life. It records his status as a veteran of the Civil War and the name of the unit he served in. It lists his date and place of birth (March 10, 1842 in Leydenburg, Schwartzburg, Germany). It also records his wife's maiden name as Von Obstfelter.

The census records of confirm the outline of Otto's life as described in his obituary. In 1900, he and Clara lived alone in Chicago. In 1880, they are enumerated in

Chicago with their three daughters. Finding the 1880 record was difficult due to the misspelling of the last name as Thischer, as explained in Chapter Four.

In Chapter Six, I describe Otto's Civil War pension file, which was a very rich source of information about him. It included a photograph of Otto, details about the date of his marriage to Clara, and a more accurate description of his birthplace.

Appendix C: Coleman Young Case Study

When I was growing up in the suburbs of Detroit in the 1970s, Mayor Coleman Young was a dominant political figure in the region (fig. C.1). He was a controversial character, known for his political toughness and his salty wit. I selected him partially because I find him to be an interesting historical figure but also because his background fit certain criteria I was looking for. I wanted to use an African-American case study to contrast with the others. I also wanted to use someone born in the 1910s or 1920s, so that they would show up in the 1930 census with their parents. Coleman Young's World War II participation also made him a good candidate.

I began my research by checking Wikipedia. Many librarians have understandable reservations about using Wikipedia; because it is not fixed, it is somewhat unreliable. In this case, though, that makes Wikipedia a good stand-in for family stories, which are also often unreliable. Besides, we will be using other data to confirm or reject the information from Wikipedia.

At the time of writing, Young's Wikipedia entry gave the following information about his early life:

Young was born in Tuscaloosa, Alabama to Coleman Young, a dry cleaner, and Ida Reese Jones. His family moved to Detroit in 1923, where he graduated from Eastern High School. He worked for Ford Motor Company, which soon blacklisted him for involvement in labor and civil rights activism. He later worked for the United States Postal Service. During the second World War, Young served in the 477th Medium-Bomber Group (Tuskegee Airmen) of the United States Army Air Forces as a bombardier and navigator.

I located the Young family in the censuses of Michigan in 1930 and Tuscaloosa in 1920. For the most part, they confirmed the basic information in the Wikipedia entry, as is explained in Chapter Three. In these censuses, however, Coleman Young's father is listed as William C., rather than Coleman.

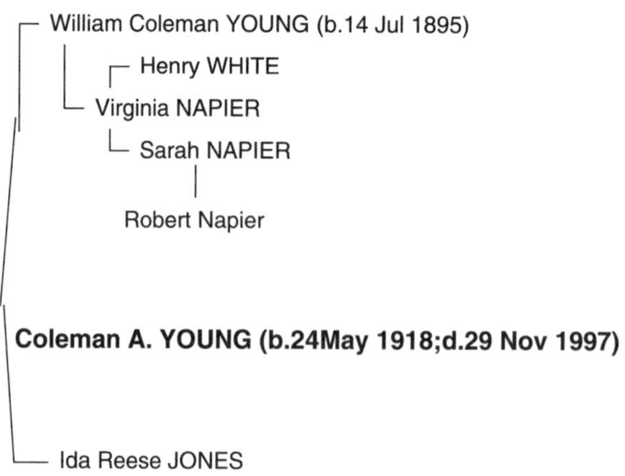

Figure C.1. Ancestors of Coleman A. Young.

Using microfilm from the Family History Library, I was able to find a 1918 record of Coleman Young's birth in Tuscaloosa, described in Chapter Four. In the 1920 census, twenty-four-year-old William Young is listed as living with his wife and nineteen-month-old son, Coleman, in Tuscaloosa, Alabama (fig. 2.10). He worked as a barber.

Searching the census of 1910, I was unable to find a matching William Young in Alabama. However, I did find a fourteen-year-old Coleman Young, living with his parents Alex Young and Virginia Young in Demopolis, Marengo County, Alabama (fig. C.2).

Alex Young's occupation is listed as "dray man." Coleman had several brothers, one who worked as a hostler, or stableman, and another who worked as a barber. The fourteen-year-old Coleman worked as a bootblack. This record is promising for several reasons. First, Demopolis is not far from Tuscaloosa. Second, the family was

Young Alex	Head	M	Mu	56	M1	23			
— Virginia	Wife	F	Mu	44	M1	23	7	7
— Robert	Son	M	Mu	21	M1	1		
— Rufus	Son	M	Mu	20	S			
— Coleman	Son	M	Mu	14	S			
— Walter	Son	M	Mu	10	S			
— Gladie	Daughter	F	Mu	9	S			
Elmore George	Head	M	Mu	37	M			
Gary Lizzie	Cook	F	B	39	S			

Figure C.2. U.S Federal Census 1910; census place, Demopolis, Marengo, Alabama; roll, T624_24; page, 2A; enumeration district, 40; image, 689.

made up of urban trade workers, including a barber. It would make sense that Coleman/William might learn the barber trade from his brother and move to the bigger town of Tuscaloosa to practice. However, these are just conjectures; I would need to find more evidence.

I noticed that William Young is listed as a veteran of the First World War in his 1930 census record, so I checked the database of World War I draft cards on Ancestry.com. I found a 1917 draft card for a twenty-one-year-old Coleman Young of Tuscaloosa, Alabama. He listed his occupation as "barber and (illegible)." Because this record is very close to his the 1920 census record for William Young, I can guess that they are the same person. The draft card gives a birthplace for Coleman Young, which I originally read as Farnsdale, Alabama. I did not find a Farnsdale, Alabama, but there is a Faunsdale in Marengo County. This seemed to confirm that the Coleman Young in the 1910 census in Demopolis is the same person recorded as William in Tuscaloosa ten years later (Coleman Young Draft Registration Card; Tuscaloosa County Roll, 1509472; http://Ancestry.com; World War I Draft Registration Cards, 1917–1918, database online, Provo, UT; The Generations Network, Inc., 2005; original data. United States, Selective Service System; World War I Selective Service System Draft Registration Cards, 1917–1918; Washington, DC: National Archives and Records Administration, M1509).

I interlibrary loaned Mayor Coleman Young's autobiography, *Hard Stuff* (1994). Young's memoir contains a short summary of his family history. He records that he was born in Tuscaloosa in 1918. Before that time, his parents lived in Marengo County. His father was trained as a tailor but also worked at barbering and other work at times. He father's father was a drayman and barber in Demopolis, Marengo County, Alabama. His grandmother was named Virginia, nee Napier. Virginia was the child of a former slave named Sarah Napier. According to Young, Sarah unlawfully married the owner of the plantation where she labored as a slave, Robert "Cap" Napier. He recounts the relationship:

Although it was anything but unusual in those days for white planters to father children with the black women who lived on their land, for the two to live together

Young Alex [illegible]	Head	B	M	Jun	1856	43	M	14
— Virginia	Wife	B	F	Feby	1868	32	M	14
— Rob J	Son	B	M	May	1888	12	S	
— [illegible] C	Son	B	M	Feby	1890	10	S	
— Geo W	Son	B	M	July	1891	8	S	
— [illegible] H	Son	B	M	Oct	1892	6	S	
— Coleman	Son	B	M	Dec	[illegible]	4	S	
— Walter	Son	B	M	Aug	1896	3	S	
— [illegible]	Daughter	B	F	Jun	1898	1	S	

Figure C.3. U.S. Federal Census, 1900; Census place, Faunsdale, Marengo, Alabama; roll, T623 29; page, 7A; enumeration district, 65.

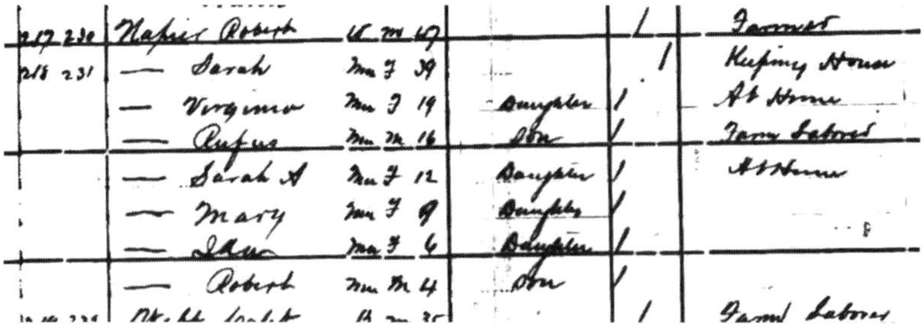

Figure C.4. U.S. Census, 1880; Census place, Macon, Marengo, Alabama; roll, T9_23; family history film, 1254023; page, 666.4000; enumeration district, 101; image, 0247.

without pretense or shame was openly defiant … (T)hey did it without compromise, moving not only Sarah into Caps big cedar log house but her children, too. Napier gave his last name even to the kids whom Sarah had previously borne to a black or mulatto man from Virginia named Henry White, including a daughter named Virginia, my paternal grandmother. (Young, p. 10–14)

Clearly, Young's memoir ties the Young family on the 1910 census schedule to Mayor Coleman Young. I looked for the same family in 1900. In the 1900 census, the family is recorded in Faunsdale, where Alex was farming. Alex and Virginia recorded that they had been married for fourteen years (fig. C3).

I looked for Virginia under her maiden name of Napier in the 1880 census. I found her enumerated in Marengo County. The representation of her family is interesting. She is listed below her mother, Sarah. Above Sarah is Robert Napier. Sarah and her children are classified as "mulatto," whereas Robert is listed as white. Robert is given a separate dwelling and family number, which would seem to indicate that he is not part of Sarah's family. Yet, Sarah's last name is represented as a dash, which is how a married woman is usually listed below her husband (fig. C.4). The 1870 census records a similar family configuration, also in Marengo county (fig. C.5).

In 1860, a twenty-four-year-old Robert Napier is listed in the household of sixty-five-year-old Richard Napier in Marengo County. Richard Napier is also counted as

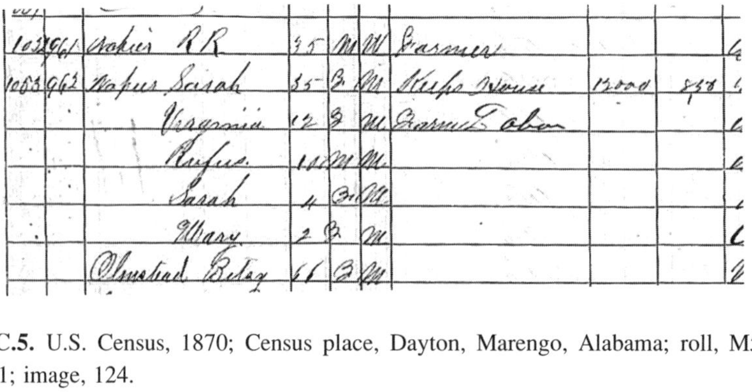

Figure C.5. U.S. Census, 1870; Census place, Dayton, Marengo, Alabama; roll, M593_28; page, 271; image, 124.

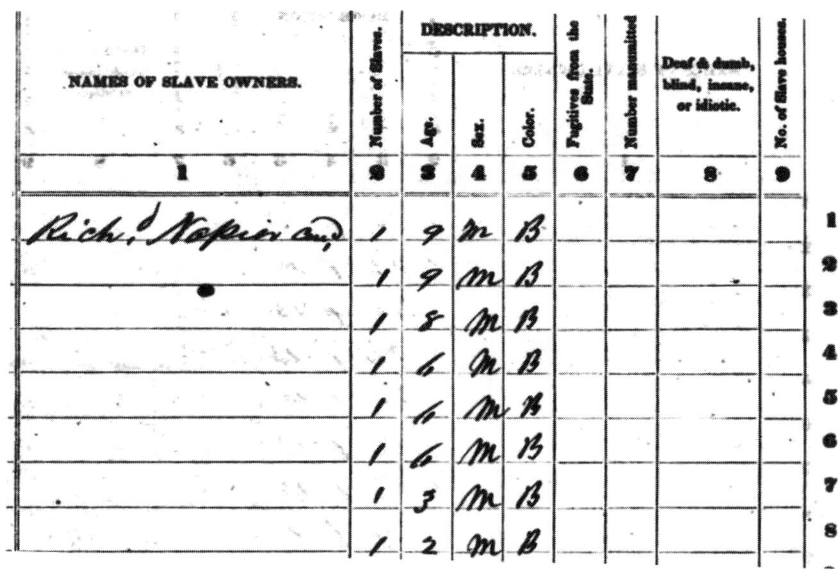

NAMES OF SLAVE OWNERS.	Number of Slaves.	DESCRIPTION. Age.	Sex.	Color.	Fugitives from the State.	Number manumitted.	Deaf & dumb, blind, insane, or idiotic.	No. of Slave houses.	
1	2	3	4	5	6	7	8	9	
Richd Napier [illegible]	1	9	m	B					1
	1	9	m	B					2
	1	8	m	B					3
	1	6	m	B					4
	1	6	m	B					5
	1	6	m	B					6
	1	3	m	B					7
	1	2	m	B					8

Figure C.6. U.S. Federal Census, Slave Schedule, 1860. Western Division, Marengo, Alabama; page, 110; image, 31.

a slave owner on the separate slave schedule that year. His is listed as owning 75 slaves. Given the ages of the slaves, it is plausible that Sarah and her children are among those listed, although it would be difficult to prove (fig. C.6).

To a great degree, the census research confirmed the family history in Coleman Young's memoir. I searched for more information on the history of Marengo County and the Napier family, but without much luck. I was able to contact a researcher connected to the Napier family using the USGenWeb page for Marengo county, but at the time of writing, I had not been able to follow up on the leads she provided.

Some directions for further research would be death and probate records for Richard and Robert Napier and Freedmen's Bureau records for the region around Marengo County.

REFERENCES

Wikipedia. "Coleman Young." http://en.wikipedia.org/wiki/Coleman_Young (accessed August 10, 2007).

Young, Coleman A. *Hard Stuff: The Autobiography of Coleman Young* (New York: Viking, 1994).

Appendix D: Kubrick Case Study

I chose Stanley Kubrick's family as a case study because it promised to illuminate some of the strategies and challenges of researching ancestors who immigrated from Europe in the late 19th and early 20th centuries (fig. D.1). Many Americans have ancestors who arrived in the United States during this period of heavy immigration, and I wanted to draw upon one such example.

As with Coleman Young, I began with Wikipedia as a substitute for family information. At the time of writing, it provided the following information about Kubrick's family background:

(Stanley) Kubrick was born on July 26, 1928 at the Lying-In Hospital in Manhattan, New York City, United States, the first child of Jacques Kubrick and his wife Gertrude (born as Perveler). His sister, Barbara, was born in 1934. Jacques, whose parents had been Jewish immigrants of Austro-Romanian and Polish origin, was a successful doctor. At the time of Stanley's birth, the Kubricks lived in an apartment on 2160 Clinton Avenue in The Bronx.

The 1930 census largely confirmed the information in this entry, figure D.2.

Using a Soundex search in Ancestry.com, I was able to locate Jack Kubrick ten years earlier, in the 1920 census. The seventeen-year-old Jack is listed with the last name Kubrik. He is recorded with his father and mother, Alias and Rose Kubrik. "Alias" recorded that he arrived in the United States in 1902 and was naturalized in 1911. The family was living in the Bronx (fig. D3).

In the 1910 census, I searched for Rose Kubrick, and I eventually found her using the Soundex option. In this census, the parents of the family are listed as Elias and Rose Kabrick. Jack is listed as Jacob (fig. D.4).

Ancestors of Stanley KUBRICK

```
        ┌─ Elias KUBRICK (b.27 Nov 1877)
   ┌─ Jacob KUBRICK (b.21 May 1902)
   │    └─ Rosa SPIEGELBLATT
Stanley KUBRICK (b.28 Jul 1928;d.7 Mar 1999)
   └─ Gertrude PERVELER
```

Figure D.1. Ancestors of Stanley Kubrick.

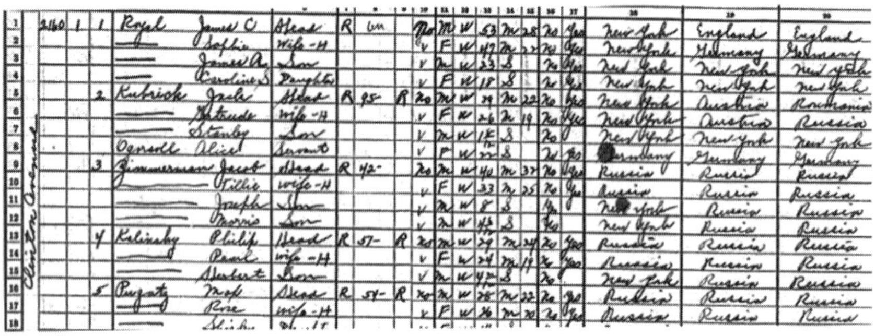

Figure D.2. U.S. Federal Census, 1930; Census place, Bronx, New York; roll, 1484; page, 1A; enumeration district, 541; image, 69.0.

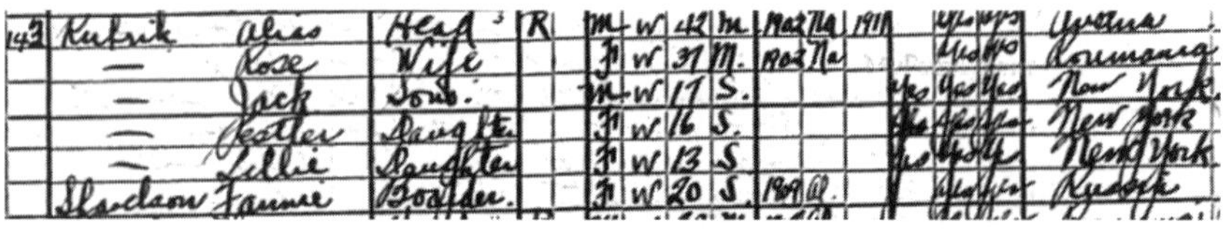

Figure D.3. U.S. Census 1920; census place, Bronx Assembly District 2, Bronx, New York; roll, T625_1133; page, 7A; enumeration district, 149; image, 367.

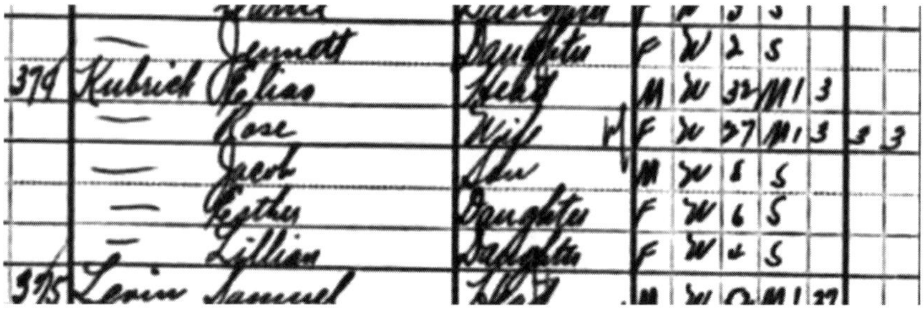

Figure D.4. U.S. Census 1910; Census place, Manhattan Ward 12, New York; roll, T624_1017; page, 18A; enumeration district, 396; image, 496.

The information in these census reports helped me locate a passenger list and a naturalization record for Elias and Rose Kubrik, as described in Chapters Seven and Eight.

REFERENCES

Wikipedia. "Stanley Kubrick." http://en.wikipedia.org/wiki/Stanley-Kubrick (accessed January 29, 2007).

Index

ABOUT THE AUTHOR

JACK SIMPSON is the Curator of Local and Family History at the Newberry Library in Chicago. He is a graduate of Grinnell College and also attended Wayne State University and the University of Michigan School of Information. He is the co-creator of ChicagoAncestors.org (with Ginger Frere). He grew up in the Detroit area, and he now lives in the Chicago neighborhood of Humboldt Park with his wife and daughter.